MIGRATION NATI🍁N

A Practical Guide To Doing Business In Globalized Canada

Robin Brown & Kathy Cheng

Foreword by Michael Adams
Introduction by Dr. Doug Norris

Environics Research Group

4.
Products and Services Through the Cultural Lens

5.
Connecting With Migration Nation

6.
Toward a Borderless Future

Preface:
Why Read This Book?

by Robin Brown & Kathy Cheng

For most businesses and organizations in Canada, growth is a top priority. Achieving that growth, however, isn't as easy as it used to be. Following the global financial crisis, pundits have described a "new normal" of cautious, value-focused consumers and stagnant markets. The baby boomers are aging; this large generation that has been responsible for so much growth over the past several decades cannot be relied upon to keep up their high levels of consumption and economic activity as they move into retirement. Their demanding and discriminating offspring, the millennials, are also a large generation but they currently lack the financial clout and confidence to fill the boomers' shoes.

The challenge facing the leaders of Canadian organizations and businesses is to find the people—the customers, donors, voters, volunteers, fans—who will enable them to grow in the years ahead. So, where is the growth? One thing is certain: growth in Canada is new Canadians and their children—a more ethnoculturally diverse group than ever before.

If you're holding this book in your hands, you're probably familiar with the broad numbers. In one widely cited 2006 estimate (from Statistics Canada's blandly titled "Projections of the Diversity of the Canadian Population"), by 2031 between 25% and 28% of the Canadian population will be foreign-born and the proportion of Canadians who belong to a visible minority group will be between 29% and 32%. But most leaders of most organizations aren't thinking about 2031. They are looking for growth opportunities now and over the next five years. Providing a road map to those opportunities is what this book is about.

Right now, according to Environics Analytics' HouseholdSpend data, for every $100 spent in Canada, $21 comes from someone who was not born here.

FIG. 0.1

Multicultural Canada: Where the growth is

Consumer spending growth in Canada, 2008–2013
All ethnic groups shown include both Canadian-born and foreign-born

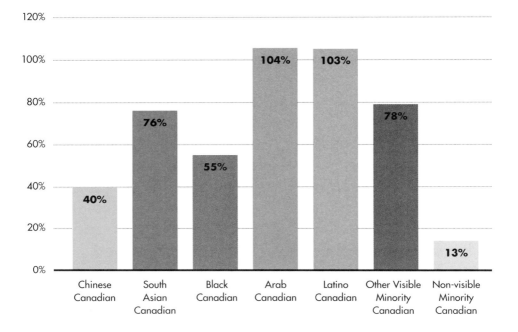

Strategies designed exclusively to meet the needs of the Canadian-born are appropriate only if you are willing to give up that $21. In cities, ignoring diversity means giving up even more of the spending pie.

And if you want to talk about growth, migrants and diverse ethnocultural communities are where the action is. According to Environics Analytics' HouseholdSpend data, total consumer spending in Canada has grown by 21% overall in the last five years (2008 to 2013)—from $976 billion to $1.177 trillion. But among some ethnic groups the rate of growth over the same period has been dramatically higher. Among South Asian Canadians the rate of growth has been 76%. Among Chinese Canadians, it's been 40%. Spending among Latino Canadians has grown at an eye-popping 103%. These spending rates are unlikely to decline, since population growth and spending growth go hand in hand.

Environics Analytics' DemoStats 2013 projects that by 2018 the Canadian population will have grown to 36,708,145. But some ethnic groups are growing at a much faster rate than others. The population that once comprised Canada's "bicultural" majority (white people of French or British heritage) is projected to grow by only 2.7%. Other groups—the rest of the multi in multicultural Canada—will grow by 18%, and will account for the majority of the country's population growth (62%). In fact, overall growth in Canada looks distinctly Asian. Almost a third of the population growth in the next five years will come from Chinese, South Asian, and Filipino Canadians.

Anyone looking for growth in this country simply cannot afford to ignore migrants, their children, and the diverse ethnocultural groups that are growing rapidly, in both numbers and influence, in cities across Canada.

Foreword:
Multiculturalism is Canada

by Michael Adams

Canadian multiculturalism was an afterthought. The idea first emerged from debates surrounding Canada's Royal Commission on Bilingualism and Biculturalism. Convened in 1963, the "Bi and Bi Commission" was an effort by the federal government to reckon with the emerging social, economic, and linguistic dynamics in Canada in the wake of Quebec's Quiet Revolution. But a funny thing happened as the Commission set about addressing the concerns of a newly confident Quebec: the over one-quarter of Canadians whose heritage was neither British nor French expressed the conviction that they were also part of Canada's heritage.

Even in the mid-1960s, Canada was obviously much more than two founding peoples descended from those who had migrated from France and the British Isles. John Diefenbaker, of German ancestry, had just served as prime minister, and Ukrainians (one of whom, Jaroslav Rudnyckyj, sat on the Royal Commission) and others used the platform of the Bi and Bi Commission to insist on their place in the Canadian mosaic. Not only did they live here, they argued, but many of their forebears had made significant contributions to the creation of Canada—by settling and farming the vast western prairies, for instance. Within a decade of launching its historic Royal Commission, Canada remained bilingual (and remains so today), but it had also adopted an official policy of multiculturalism.

Multiculturalism has been called both a sociological fact and an ideological statement. The sociological fact was the one asserted by Ukrainian Canadians, Polish Canadians, and others: we are here, and we are citizens too. The ideological orientation was an affirmation—even a celebration—of cultural diversity, accompanied by a conviction that positive identification with an ethnocultural group was not at odds with loyalty to and pride in Canada.

Over time, multiculturalism took hold in the Canadian imagination. By the 1990s, Canadians of all backgrounds—including the Canadian-born, and

people of British and French origin—began to see multiculturalism as describing their own society. "Multiculturalism" didn't mean "them"; it now meant "us." Canada had evolved from having explicitly racist immigration policies to policies that not only prohibited discrimination but encouraged people of all backgrounds to sustain and take pride in their heritage cultures. We had evolved from xenophobia to a kind of xenophilia—from fearing the other to tolerating differences to actually savouring diversity.

Multiculturalism became part of the national identity, taking its place as a symbol of Canada alongside bilingualism, the flag, the national anthem, medicare, and even hockey. Although official multiculturalism is only a few decades old, some scholars, including American historian David Hackett Fischer and Canadian public intellectual John Ralston Saul, have dared to map this sensibility—the respectful and even fruitful coexistence of identity groups—back through Canadian history, even as far as Champlain's collaboration with indigenous peoples in the early 1600s. (Needless to say, many moments in Canadian history, including the frequently brutal treatment of Aboriginal peoples, have not lived up to the multicultural ideal.)

Today, social diversity is the air Canadians breathe. It has even evolved beyond diversity of language, ethnicity, and religion to encompass diversity of sexuality, family, and ability. Several years ago, I reflected on the effects of multiculturalism on Canadian civic culture in my book *Unlikely Utopia*. Today, my two colleagues Robin Brown and Kathy Cheng have done a remarkable job of explaining how multicultural diversity in Canada and globalization around the world are changing the way Canadians live, work, communicate, consume, and have fun. This research-based, down-to-earth book will be of immense value to Canadian marketers, communications professionals, fundraisers, and businesspeople.

Migration Nation makes a compelling case that understanding and connecting with Canadian diversity is an important part of achieving success, not in narrow "ethnic markets" but in the Canadian marketplace at large. It is no longer simply true (if it ever was) that migrants come to Canada and are changed by it. Rather, foreign-born and Canadian-born change each other. Together, we are defining and building the new Canada.

Introduction:
Current Demographic Trends

by Doug Norris

Canada is often called a nation of immigrants. That's true now, and it's been true for as long as an entity called Canada has existed. But a nation of immigrants can be many things. The 400,000 people who arrived in this country in 1912 might not be surprised to learn that mass migration would be happening in Canada a hundred years later—but they might be surprised to learn that Islam is now Canada's fastest-growing religion, or that as of 2011 there are more people in Canada who were born in China or India than were born in the United Kingdom.

Migration Nation is a guide for organizations pursuing relevance and success in the famously diverse place called Canada. This Introduction sets the context for the book by drawing on Statistics Canada data to offer a brief primer on the demographic trends at work in this nation of immigrants as we find it today.

The size of the migrant population

Over 6.7 million people in Canada—one in five (20.6%)—were born in another country, and two in five (39%) are either immigrants or the children of immigrants. Canada has the largest foreign-born population in the G8, and among its close comparator countries, only Australia (where 26.8% of the population were born elsewhere) has a proportionally larger immigrant population. Both countries have proportionally far more migrants than the second-place G8 country, Germany (13%). The United States, heavily mythologized as a destination for migrants, has proportionally about half the foreign-born population of Australia and two-thirds that of Canada: 12.9%.

Historically, it's not unprecedented for such a large proportion of Canada's population to be made up of people born elsewhere. In the first decades of the 20th century, as European migrants fled strife and sought economic opportunity in the New World, the proportion of the Canadian population composed of migrants hovered around 22%.

FIG. 0.2
Mass migration is not new to Canada

Immigrants as a percentage of population, Canada (millions) and total # of immigrants

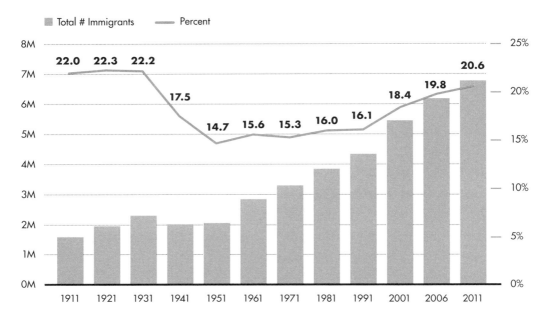

FIG. 0.3
The foreign-born are more urban than other Canadians

Proportions of foreign-born and Canadian-born living in CMAs

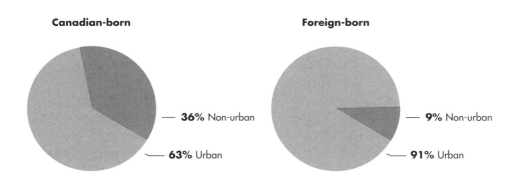

Still, the proportion of immigrants in the Canadian population is higher today than it's been at any time since World War II. Canada's population has also increased overall, so in absolute terms there are many more foreign-born people living in Canada today than at any other time in the country's history.

The presence of migrants is especially strongly felt in Canada's largest cities. In Toronto, almost half the population (46%) has arrived from outside the country. In Vancouver the proportion is 40%, and in Calgary, whose abundance of economic opportunity has drawn an increasing proportion of migrants, a quarter (26%) are first generation.

And the strong presence of migrants extends beyond Canada's few largest cities: mid-sized cities like Windsor, Hamilton, and Abbotsford have migrant populations that, as a proportion of their total populations, exceed the national average. Other cities—including Edmonton, Guelph, Winnipeg, and Ottawa-Gatineau—are within a point or so of the national average. Overall, whereas six in ten of the Canadian-born live in one of Canada's Census Metropolitan Areas, the same is true of nine in ten migrants (91%).

Not all foreign-born Canadians are recent arrivals, of course; some have been in Canada for several decades. About one in five (19%) arrived before 1971. And even as newcomers, many of these people would have had a vast ocean but a fairly narrow cultural distance to cross, arriving from English-speaking countries such as England and Ireland.

By contrast, about a third of the foreign-born population (32%) have arrived since 2001. These more recent immigrants come from a wider range of countries, and regions whose religious, linguistic, and socio-cultural norms differ more sharply from the ones that originally predominated in Canada (British and French, Protestant and Catholic).

Where have migrants come from?

Prior to 1971, over three-quarters of immigrants to Canada arrived from Europe. Many of these arrived from the British Isles, their presence complementing the legal and political structures of the new colony with the norms and habits of the "mother country." Other Europeans—notably Italians, Ukrainians, Poles, and Hungarians—also arrived in large numbers as the 20th century progressed.

Before 1971, just 15% of migrants arrived from Asia, Africa, and the Caribbean and South and Central America. Although many families with origins outside Europe have histories in Canada that stretch back well over a century, people from these regions were very much in the minority across most of the country.

FIG. 0.4
One third of immigrants have been in Canada less than 10 years

Immigrants by period of immigration, Canada, 2011

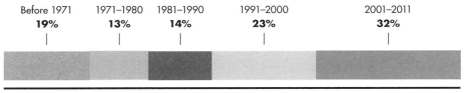

Before 1971	1971–1980	1981–1990	1991–2000	2001–2011
19%	**13%**	**14%**	**23%**	**32%**

0%   100%

FIG. 0.5
Source countries once mainly European, now mainly Asian

Immigrants by region, Canada, 2011

■ Asia   ▨ Africa   ■ South/Central America/Carribbean   ▨ U.S/Oceana   ■ Europe

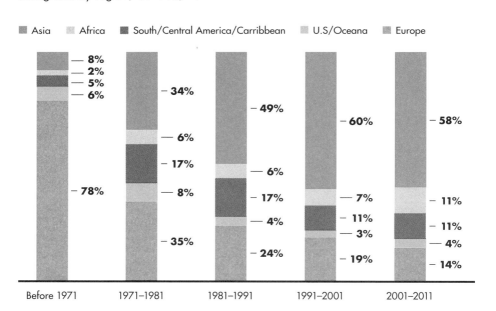

By the decade from 2001 to 2011, however, the proportion of migrants arriving from Europe and the proportion arriving from elsewhere had reversed almost exactly—with eight in ten (80%) arriving from Asia (58%), Africa (11%), and the Caribbean and the Americas (11%), and just 14% coming from Europe.

Today, the number of Canadians who were born in the United Kingdom (537,000) is similar to the number of Canadians born in India (548,000) or China (546,000). But while just 10% of migrants from the U.K. arrived in the last decade, that's true of almost half of Indian- (45%) and Chinese-born (49%) Canadians.

Who gets in?

What brought about this major change in Canada's immigration inflows? To a great extent, reform of the immigration system is responsible. Until the 1960s, Canada's immigration rules were either explicitly discriminatory (recall the Chinese head tax and the exclusion of Jewish refugees fleeing the Nazis) or at least allowed for discrimination based on nationality and other such factors.

In 1962, however, regulations were changed to eliminate overt racism, and in 1967 the Points System was introduced, awarding points to would-be migrants based on qualities that were seen as likely to promote successful social and economic integration into Canada, such as educational attainment and proficiency in official languages.

With official discrimination out of the way, the number of successful applicants for immigration from outside Europe increased steadily and the seeds for Canada's exceptional levels of socio-cultural diversity were planted. According to Citizenship and Immigration Canada, the change didn't take long: "In 1966, 87 percent of Canada's immigrants had been of European origin, while only four years later 50 percent came from quite different regions of the world: the West Indies, Guyana, Haiti, Hong Kong, India, the Philippines, and Indochina."

Canadian immigration policy allows for a number of different "classes" of immigrants. The origins of these classes lie in the Immigration Act of 1976, which established the fundamental principles of Canadian immigration as it exists today. The Act directed the federal government to actively plan and manage its immigration program, not just by keeping an orderly queue, but by setting targets designed to achieve particular demographic, social, and economic objectives. Here are the immigration classes as they stand today:

FIG. 0.6
Large populations from many countries: Hyperdiversity

Top countries for total migrants, 100,000 or more in 2011

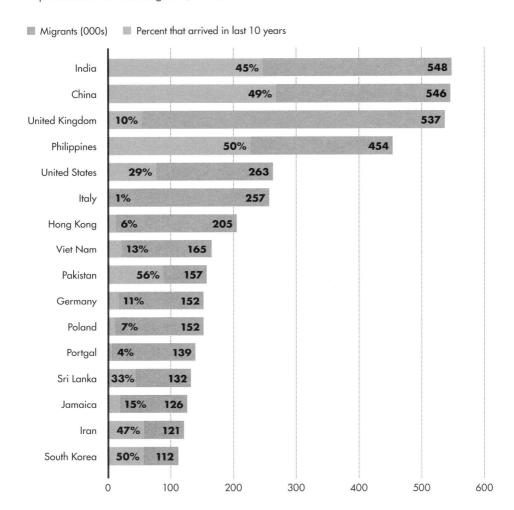

Migrants (000s)   Percent that arrived in last 10 years

Country	Percent	Migrants
India	45%	548
China	49%	546
United Kingdom	10%	537
Philippines	50%	454
United States	29%	263
Italy	1%	257
Hong Kong	6%	205
Viet Nam	13%	165
Pakistan	56%	157
Germany	11%	152
Poland	7%	152
Portgal	4%	139
Sri Lanka	33%	132
Jamaica	15%	126
Iran	47%	121
South Korea	50%	112

Economic. Economic Class immigrants can be admitted to Canada under a range of programs. Some of these (such as the Federal Skilled Worker Program) pertain to the would-be migrant's job credentials. Others fall under the rubric of the Business Class program (a subset of the Economic Class). Self-employed people who meet specific criteria may successfully apply as Business Class migrants. Canada's immigration program also often includes one or more immigration categories aimed at attracting migrants who are willing and able to invest substantial amounts of money in Canada.

Family. Family reunification has been a longstanding priority of the Canadian immigration system. Immediate family members (spouses and dependent children) can migrate automatically with a successful Economic Class immigrant. Other family members (including parents of Economic Class immigrants) must be admitted through a separate process, sponsored by their relatives who have already settled in Canada.

Refugee and other humanitarian. People who are escaping persecution, torture, or other such threats in their home countries.

In 2012, Canada accepted 160,819 Economic Class immigrants, 65,008 Family Class immigrants, 23,094 refugees, and 8,961 "other" (people accepted for humanitarian reasons but not strictly refugees).

In addition to the categories just named, another large group of people are admitted to Canada each year through the **Temporary Foreign Worker Program.** Strictly speaking, this isn't an immigration class, since, as the name suggests, it's designed to move people into Canada only temporarily. Promoted by the federal government as a means of filling short-term gaps in the labour market, the Temporary Foreign Worker Program enables employers to bring in non-Canadians for up to four years, provided the employers are unable to find Canadian workers to fill the necessary roles. There is some potential for temporary foreign workers to achieve citizenship, although caps — overall limits as well as specific caps on the admittance of people who do particular jobs — mean that only a small proportion of these workers are able to gain permanent legal status.

Some have expressed concern about the Temporary Foreign Worker Program, saying that the traditional strength of Canada's immigration program has been its commitment to encouraging migrants' permanent settlement and full citizenship (as well as labour market participation). Canada stands out internationally in the extent to which its migrants naturalize: 89% of the foreign-born have become citizens.

FIG. 0.7
Number of temporary residents growing markedly

Stocks of temporary residents (workers, students, humanitarian) living in Canada (000s)

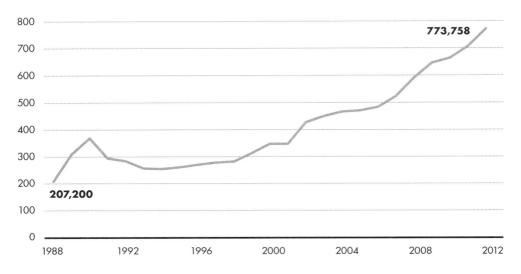

FIG. 0.8
Western cities increasingly attracting migrants

Percentage change in migrant inflows, selected Canadian CMAs, 2006–2011 versus 2001–2006

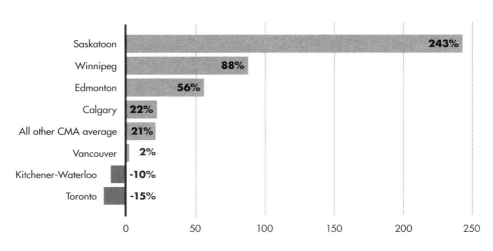

Where do migrants settle?

Just as the source countries of migrants to Canada have changed a great deal over time, so too have the destinations in which migrants have settled. Early 20th century Canada was a predominantly rural society, and migrant settlement patterns reflected that: migrants acquired land and joined their fellow Canadians in agricultural work, or participated in resource extraction, logging, fishing, and other rural labour.

During the 20th century, Canada became an increasingly urban society, and migrants' settlement patterns reflected this shift as well. Growing proportions landed in cities—especially Toronto, Montreal, and Vancouver—and partici-pated in urban economies, for instance as shopkeepers, builders, and profes-sionals. Toronto's Kensington Market exists in many Canadians' imaginations as the quintessential immigrant settlement area, peopled by successive waves of migrants—especially Europeans building lives in Canada after the devastation of the Second World War.

Over the last decade or so, two shifts have happened that are at odds with this decades-old image of immigrants bootstrapping it in downtown Toronto. First, migrant settlement patterns have become increasingly suburban, with many newcomers bypassing the downtown cores of Canadian cities and moving directly to adjacent areas where housing is more affordable and where members of their ethnic and linguistic groups have (in many cases) already put down roots. In the Greater Toronto Area, for instance, between the 2001–2006 and 2006–2011 periods, the proportion of migrants settling downtown declined by a fifth (19%). Meanwhile, settlement in nearby areas like Halton (about 50 km west of downtown), Vaughan, and Richmond Hill (each about 40 km north) has increased. Today, the municipalities with the highest proportions of foreign-born residents tend to be suburbs, including B.C.'s Richmond (60%) and Burnaby (50%) and Ontario's Markham (58%).

Second, although in absolute terms Toronto, Montreal, and Vancouver remain the biggest hubs for settlement, in recent years proportionally more newcomers have been settling in western cities, where booming economies have offered better odds of economic success. The roughly 45,000 migrants who landed in Winnipeg between 2006 and 2011 are a small group relative to the 382,000 who landed in Toronto, but the Winnipeg figure represents an 88% increase over migrant inflows between 2001 and 2006, whereas Toronto's number represents a 15% decline.

Amid these changes—more suburban settlement and more settlement in western and prairie provinces—one traditional settlement pattern has held steady:

FIG. 0.9
Most migrants' mother tongues are neither English nor French

% of migrants with mother tongues other than English or French

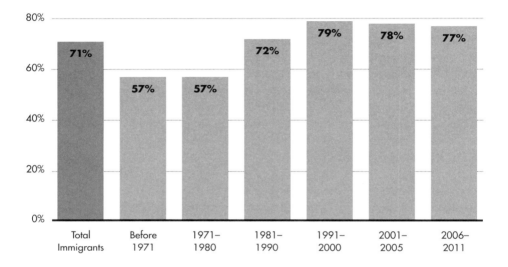

newcomers tend to gravitate to places where others from their ethnic and linguistic groups have already established a community. The rising number of "ethnic enclaves" has provoked concern from some commentators who have worried about the formation of segregated neighbourhoods or even ghettos. Generally speaking, however, ethnic concentration is not in itself a cause for concern; many neighbourhoods that fit the definition of "ethnic enclave" are communities of choice that function well—not ghettos formed by poverty and discrimination. Ethnic enclaves can help ease the transition of migration, allowing for large enough populations to support specialty shops and letting more tenured migrants provide support to newer arrivals. And in any case, in most Canadian neighbourhoods where particular ethnic groups are concentrated, they tend to form a slim majority or a large plurality—not a majority so large as to be homogeneous.

Language and ethnicity

Canada's large cities are some of the most ethnoculturally diverse on earth, which is no surprise, given the range of countries and regions from which migrants have arrived. In the Canadian population, eighty-nine countries are represented by ten thousand people or more, and in the 2011 National Household Survey, more than two hundred ethnic origins were reported. Thirteen of these were claimed by more than a million people: Canadian, English, French, Scottish, Irish, German, Italian, Chinese, First Nations (North American Indian), Ukrainian, East Indian, Dutch, and Polish.

It's worth noting that the National Household Survey accepts (as the Census did) multiple ethnic origins, and many respondents offer more than one, often in combination with "Canadian." Indeed, four in ten Canadians (42%) claim multiple ethnicities. Some of these people may see themselves as having a single ethnic origin (Chinese or Irish, for instance) but claim "Canadian" as a way of registering their sense of belonging to Canadian society. Others may have multiple ethnocultural threads in their families—something that's true of more and more Canadians.

As of 2006, only about 4% of Canadian couples (3.9%, representing 289,400 couples) were mixed unions. The 2011 numbers (not yet released as of this writing) are likely to show significant growth in this area. While mixed unions make up only a small proportion of all couples across the country, past Census waves have found them to be growing quickly. Between 2001 and 2006, mixed unions grew at more than five times the rate of unions overall.

The proportion of mixed couples is higher in Canada's largest cities, where migrants (and ethnic diversity) are concentrated: in Vancouver 8.5% of couples

were mixed in 2006, while in Toronto the proportion was 7.1% and in Calgary 6.1%. Canadians with higher levels of education are also more likely to be in mixed unions: 6.4% of couples in which at least one person had a university degree were mixed, while the same was true of just 3.2% of those who had completed only high school.

In short, mixed unions are a phenomenon associated with urbanization, education, and high concentrations of diversity—all trends that are on the rise in Canada. In the future we should expect to see more such unions, whose children will mean more Canadians claiming multiple ethnic identities on their census forms.

As the ethnocultural diversity of migrants to Canada has increased over time, so too has the extent to which diverse languages have been heard in Canadian towns and cities. Even during much of the 20th century, when migration to Canada was predominantly European, the presence of non-official languages was strong. The majority (57%) of migrants who arrived prior to 1971 (recall that 78% of these came from Europe) had a mother tongue other than English or French. In more recent decades, the proportion of migrants who are allophones (having a non-official language as a mother tongue) has been closer to eight in ten.

The 2011 National Household Survey found over two hundred languages being spoken most often in Canadian homes. Of these, twenty-two languages are spoken by a hundred thousand people or more.

What now?

Mass migration has made Canada one of the most diverse societies that have ever existed. This diversity, along with an official multiculturalism policy that encourages migrants to maintain and celebrate their heritage cultures, has created a unique and complex socio-cultural landscape. Governments, businesses, nonprofits, and organizations of all kinds must continually adapt to this reality if they're to remain relevant to the Canadian public. Although it's impossible for every project or message to resonate perfectly with every group, the data and insights in *Migration Nation* aim to help organizations chart an informed course.

1.

Migration Nation:
We All Live There

Multicultural Marketing: Not Just for Migrants

In 2012, a Toronto journalist named David Sax travelled to the suburb of Mississauga to ask a seventy-one-year-old woman a question. He showed Lilian Ow some photographs of a few dishes at a new Singaporean restaurant in a cool and gentrifying downtown Toronto neighbourhood. Then he asked her what she thought. "Hmmm," she considered. The food looked tasty—but the preparation did not appear strictly traditional. Her food, available at her restaurant, Lion City, located in a strip mall in Mississauga, was traditional.

David Sax is the author of People Place Food, a regular feature in Toronto's popular free weekly newspaper, *The Grid*. The paper was only a year old when Sax visited Lion City, but had it already earned a devoted readership and been recognized by the Society for Newspaper Design for its "engaged writing, smart editing and heavy research … done in a young, sophisticated voice."

So what does this young, sophisticated Toronto paper like? Khinkalis from Georgia, churrasco from Chile, accras from Martinique, ajvar from the Balkans, kashke bademjan from Iran, and—of course—Lilian Ow's brisket curry. People Place Food has drooled over those dishes and many more. Its writer visits a restaurant, deli, bakery, or other family-owned food spot roughly once a month. He tastes the goods and writes up the experience. But this is no ordinary restaurant review. In addition to describing the fare, People Place Food profiles the people who make it. Invariably, these are migrants who have interesting relationships with the foods of their homelands—and generally a strong desire to share these flavours with their fellow Torontonians.

In the 1990s, the economic shifts loosely called "globalization" combined with the rise of the internet to create a sense that the world was shrinking rapidly. As giant American brands—Nike, McDonald's, and the rest—spread across borders, some foresaw the erosion of all local flavour and cultural difference. Would every noodle stand and sidewalk café on the planet be steamrolled by these multinational titans? Would every shop on every street corner ultimately answer to a head office in Chicago or Bentonville or Atlanta?

Two decades later, the world has indeed gotten smaller and in some ways more homogeneous. But cultural influence has moved in many directions— not just from America outward. Yes, Starbucks devotees can get a latte from Helsinki to Jakarta and young people in almost any city can be found tapping on iPhones in Nike sneakers. But in any large Canadian city you can pick up a bubble tea, take in a Bollywood movie at a mainstream cinema, or slip into a karaoke booth. You can grab a pupusa or some dim sum, and pick up some Pokémon cards for your addicted kids on the way home. If American pop music is on the radio in every shop you visit, it might come as a relief: at least you get a break from the Korean mega-hit "Gangnam Style."

Diverse cultural and consumer offerings haven't been trampled by the trends associated with globalization. Instead, diversity has flourished—and Canada is a place where this flourishing is especially palpable. Migrants don't simply arrive here and get absorbed into an overpowering, vaguely Anglo-European mainstream. They arrive in a socio-cultural environment churning with influences from around the world, creating unlikely collisions and synergies every day.

Importantly, it's not only newcomers who are affected by this stew of influences. Canadians whose families have been here for multiple generations are touched by the global mix as well. Indeed, although many countries have high rates of immigration, Canada is unique in the extent to which diversity and cultural sharing have become part of the national identity—hence *The Grid*'s People Place Food feature and the City of Toronto's official motto: "Diversity Our Strength." In short, "multicultural marketing" doesn't just mean understanding and reaching out to immigrants and their children. It means understanding and reaching out to a whole society that has diversity and cultural cross-pollination in its DNA. It means recognizing that Canada is not just a country that's home to a lot of immigrants—Canada is Migration Nation.

UNDERSTANDING MIGRATION NATION

Many of our clients tell us they've known for a while that they needed to find ways of responding to Canada's growing socio-cultural diversity, but that they simply didn't know where to start. Fair enough. The topic is daunting. About a quarter-million immigrants and an even greater number of migrant workers arrive in Canada each year. They come from dozens of countries, speak dozens of languages, and have a wide range of histories and aspirations. The result is a churning global society where cultural influences move in complex ways.

But despite all this complexity, we know from our research and our work with clients that some fairly simple frameworks can give organizations a solid foundation for understanding where they stand in Migration Nation. Part of our goal in this book is to distill a complex set of issues into some manageable questions that organizations can answer and act on.

First, it's useful to begin with some background on where the field of multicultural marketing has been in the past and where it stands today.

THE EVOLUTION OF MULTICULTURAL MARKETING

The term "multicultural marketing" first emerged in the United States; it referred to the practice of targeting specific ethnic segments using communications designed with their culture or identity in mind. This approach has existed in Canada for over a century, taking shape long before the term "multiculturalism" began to circulate.

But the practice we now think of as multicultural marketing is relatively new. In Canada, one can argue that governments actually led the way, being leaders in providing services and information in a range of languages other than English and French. In the 1990s, parts of the private sector began to grasp the potential of Canada's large and growing migrant communities. The nonprofit sector, civil society organizations, and political parties have also gradually had their eyes opened over the past couple of decades. Today, the field is reaching maturity: the first multicultural marketing conference was held in Toronto in 2008, and the first multicultural marketing award was presented by *Marketing* magazine in 2010.

From its beginnings in the late 1980s and early 1990s, the practice of multi-cultural marketing has changed in some significant ways. It has:

Moved beyond translation. Companies were once pleased with themselves if they took the trouble to translate a brochure or poster into a non-official language, or to place an ad in an ethnic newspaper. Although mere translation can still work for some applications, most organizations aiming to thrive in Migration Nation go deeper.

Shifted from representation to understanding. Just as translation was once seen as cutting-edge outreach, picturing diverse people in advertising material was thought to signify engagement with diversity. Today, it's no longer enough to show smiling faces from around the world; marketers must show a more sophisticated understanding of their multi-ethnic, multicultural audiences.

Gone from ethnic to multi. In its early days, multicultural marketing wasn't very multi. It would have been more accurate to call it ethnic marketing: the practice of targeting specific ethnic groups. Such targeting is by no means obsolete as an approach, but the field is moving increasingly toward truly multi-cultural outreach. No group (including multi-generational Canadians of British or French origin) is an island. Cultural influences move through Canadian society in many directions; in this context, multicultural marketing strategies that engage a larger swath of society—not just one group—are gaining traction. We're starting to see organizations that are communicating to a multicultural society rather than thinking about "mainstream" communication alongside "ethnic" targeting.

Moved from the margins to the centre of the strategy. Multicultural marketing was once an add-on at the end of the process of developing a strategy or campaign. The thinking was "The creative is complete. Time to have it translated." Today the best practitioners consider the multicultural elements of a strategy or campaign early; an awareness of Migration Nation is woven into the fabric of the overall approach.

Gotten deeper—focusing on consumer motivations, not cultural recognition. For many years, multicultural marketing could be summed up in one word: recognition. Marketers sought to build relationships with minority ethnic groups by simply nodding to their presence in society: showing a Chinese family starting a Registered Education Savings Plan for their child,

---

"The reality of Migration Nation is that the old boundaries between mainstream and minority no longer hold and the targets are constantly moving."

or showing a happy South Asian family driving their new sedan. Recognition itself isn't outdated; people of all backgrounds and ages respond to seeing themselves in advertising. But today, strong multicultural marketers use research and analysis to understand consumer motivations more deeply. It's no longer safe to assume (if it ever was) that the most important thing to know about a Chinese newcomer family is that they're Chinese newcomers.

The old approach to multicultural marketing tended to include a few basic steps. First, identify a population segment with considerable size and consumer potential. Second, figure out how "ethnic" they are: how much they differ from the mainstream in their habits, tastes, and thinking. Third, reach out to the segment in ways that focus on their differences from the mainstream.

The problem with this old approach is that it assumes boundaries and a stability that no longer exist. What's the Canadian mainstream? Do the 39% of the population made up of migrants and their children really exist outside that mainstream? What does it mean to target the "niche" markets of 1.77 million Canadians of South Asian origin or the 1.56 million Canadians of Chinese origin—groups that have migrated over multiple decades and that could each form a city larger than Calgary or Ottawa? The reality of Migration Nation is that the old boundaries between mainstream and minority no longer hold and the targets are constantly moving.

Given these realities, effective multicultural marketing means more than targeting ethnic segments. It means developing an awareness of the key factors that shape people's perceptions of the offerings in the Canadian landscape (products, services, messages, and so on). It means understanding how people's perceptions may change over time, especially as they move through their Settlement Journey. It means considering how your own offerings might look when seen through a migrant's *Cultural Lens*.

UNDERSTANDING THE CULTURAL LENS
From ethnic culture to Canadian culture?
Migration Nation isn't so simple

The old way of thinking about how migrants integrate into their new society is linear. This thinking says that on the day they arrive, their ethnic culture places them outside the mainstream. With time in Canada, they draw closer to the mainstream and become part of it: increasingly, they eat the same foods as everyone else, seek the same consumer goods, and consume the same media. In this linear model, connecting with migrants meant figuring out where they were in that linear acculturation process—and therefore how much special targeting it would take to reach them.

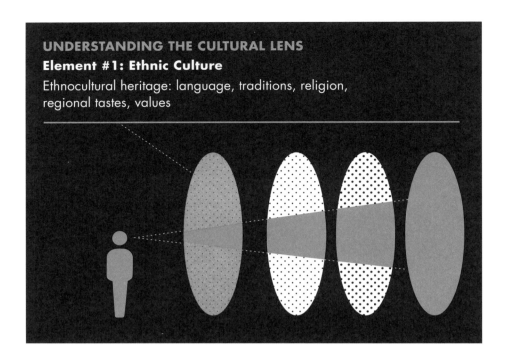

UNDERSTANDING THE CULTURAL LENS
Element #1: Ethnic Culture
Ethnocultural heritage: language, traditions, religion, regional tastes, values

If this model ever was sufficient, it no longer is today. People's movements around the globe, the speed of communication, the globalization of many aspects of culture and commerce, and the hyperdiversity of Canadian society make the model unworkable. In the past, when people spoke of acculturation they tended to assume that there was one fixed "Canadian" lifestyle to which newcomers adapted. A quick look around, however, tells us that what is Canadian is being constantly shaped by immigration. On arrival in Canada, migrants are immersed in a dynamic environment. Newcomers to Canada do acculturate—but they also do a great deal to shape the society around them. Acculturation is a two-way street in Migration Nation.

So the Canadian "norm" is a slippery concept—not only is it always changing, but it also encompasses many variations. A migrant from India who lives in the Toronto suburb of Brampton and associates almost entirely with other Indian families is living in one version of Canada. A migrant from Hong Kong who lives in a condo tower of diverse young professionals in Vancouver is living in another. A migrant from Russia who settles in Alberta or Saskatchewan in pursuit of a resource job is living a third social and economic reality. All will have different levels of exposure to their own ethnic communities, all will be exposed to Canadian diversity in different ways, and all will have different networks of retail and media outlets, community organizations, and so on.

All these factors—as well as employment experiences, neighbourhoods, and personal inclinations—will affect acculturation.

It's not that ethnic cultures and Canadian culture don't exist, it's just that you can't draw a line from one to the other and call that the acculturation process. Moreover, ethnic culture—and its strength or weakness as an influence in people's lives—is just one of the three elements we need to think about in order to understand someone's Cultural Lens.

The three elements of the Cultural Lens, through which people view products, services, and brands in the Canadian landscape, are as follows:

1. Ethnic Culture
2. Pre-Migration Inputs
3. Post-Migration Inputs (including the Settlement Journey)

1. Ethnic culture. We all have an ethnic culture that we absorb from our society and especially from our families. It's made up of our language, religion, and our deeply held values on such serious matters as health, fairness, and community. Although everyone has an ethnic culture—not just migrants—those who spend their whole lives in one society (especially as members of the dominant culture) are typically less conscious of it; when an ethnic culture is widely shared, it becomes almost invisible.

In addition to informing our deepest values, ethnic culture can shape our more superficial tastes and preferences. Many Chinese Canadians like orange juice but tend not to drink it first thing in the morning as many other Canadians do; they find it too cold and acidic to be part of breakfast. This is a preference that correlates strongly with ethnic culture, but few Chinese would say that avoiding OJ at breakfast is central to their cultural identity.

The importance of ethnic culture in consumer choices may be strong or weak depending on the product category. Food is heavily cultural, a mobile phone plan not so much. The importance of ethnic culture can also change—and generally does—as migrants settle in a new society. Still, no matter how much people's lives change, the culture in which they were raised continues to affect them in ways both conscious and unconscious. Our ethnic culture doesn't define us entirely, but as influences go, it's pretty stubborn.

Ethnic culture is often overemphasized
Most new Canadians come from fast-developing economies. As a result, a migrant arriving in Canada from China today may share the same ethnicity— even the same home town—as a Chinese migrant who arrived twenty years

ago. But the two migrants are in fact setting out from two different societies of origin (1993 China and 2013 China). Each has travelled the same geographic distance, but the more recent migrant has traversed a much smaller cultural and economic gap. The same is true of people from India and a number of other societies that send large numbers of immigrants to Canada.

The migrant arriving today is likely to be a "globalized person": someone who's been exposed to a wide range of cultural influences and consumer offerings. This migrant is likely to be much more knowledgeable and savvy about her adoptive society than were previous waves of immigrants. So not only will her acculturation likely happen more quickly once she lands, but she might *already* be better acculturated than a compatriot who migrated earlier and has been living in Canada for some time.

The various ethnic cultures of migrants to Canada are an important part of the Cultural Lens through which they view products, services, and messages. But ethnic culture is often overemphasized in the way people think about migrants. Too often, people trying to connect with migrants think only of ethnicity and not of the other important factors in their outlooks: their pre-migration consumer experiences, and the post-migration inputs they are encountering, including the stage they've reached in the Settlement Journey.

2. Pre-migration inputs. In 1854, an English-born settler in Canada, Catharine Parr Traill, published a manual to help other women in her situation. Leafing through *The Female Emigrant's Guide, and Hints on Canadian Housekeeping*, a young woman preparing to sail across the Atlantic would have found much practical advice about the life that awaited her. The section ominously titled "Coffee and tea, substitutes for" wastes no time on sympathy. It gets straight to the point. "Necessity … has taught the old settlers, in both the States and Canada, to adopt certain leaves, roots, and berries, as a substitute for the genuine article; and habit has reconciled them to the flavour." Goodbye English Breakfast, hello steeped roots.

The challenge of approximating one's life back home is as old as migration. The young Englishwoman of the 1850s, transplanted to a farm in Upper Canada, longed for a hot cup of tea. Today, despite the globalization of many aspects of consumer culture, different markets continue to have distinct qualities—not only in their products and services, but in the rhythms and conventions of the customer experience.

We have so many experiences as consumers—from the brands we can spot on the grocery shelf from thirty feet away to the format of our mobile phone bills—that many of us aren't aware of our accumulated expectations until they go unmet.

BRAND LOYALTY: ON THE WANE IN CANADA, BUT STRONG IN IMMIGRANT SOURCE COUNTRIES

One sign that consumers in affluent countries are growing less attached to brands is the growing popularity of store brands or private labels as opposed to manufacturers' brands. According to a 2011 Nielsen report, the dollar share of private-label products is now 24% in Canada. Europeans are even more indifferent to brands in some categories; in the U.K., private labels enjoy a 43% market share.

Brands once offered guarantees of quality and consistency that were otherwise difficult to find. Today, consumers in brand-saturated markets feel that, in some categories, big-name brands guarantee little more than a higher price. Four in ten Canadians agree, for instance, that "The quality of most private-label brands is as good as name brands." In short, brand loyalty in places like Canada is declining.

"I come from a land far away, where brands still matter"

Enter migrants. Although migrants' levels of brand loyalty can vary for a number of reasons, on average they're likely to be more loyal than the Canadian-born. This is because a large proportion of newcomers are arriving from emerging markets, where brands still have some of the same salience they once enjoyed in North America and Western Europe. Their pre-migration market experiences have been in contexts where name brands continue to deliver some important differences in quality and consistency. Evidence of greater brand loyalty in emerging markets can be found both in survey results and in private labels' much smaller market share. The Nielsen report that showed private labels occupying a quarter of the Canadian market found private labels commanding much smaller shares in major source countries of migrants to Canada, such as Brazil (5%), Hong Kong (5%), China (1%), and the Philippines (1%).

Consumer attitudes also register stronger brand loyalty outside of Europe and North America. The Nielsen report indicates that 30% of consumers in the Asia-Pacific region agree that "Name-brand products are worth the extra price." In North America, only 10% agree. Consumers in Asia-Pacific are also more likely to see private-label products as things one buys only under duress: 40% of Asia-Pacific consumers agree that "Private-label brands are meant for those on tight budgets or those that can't afford the best brand." Agreement with this statement in North America is about half that: 18%.

> **"Although migrants' levels of brand loyalty can vary for a number of reasons, on average they're likely to be more loyal than the Canadian-born."**

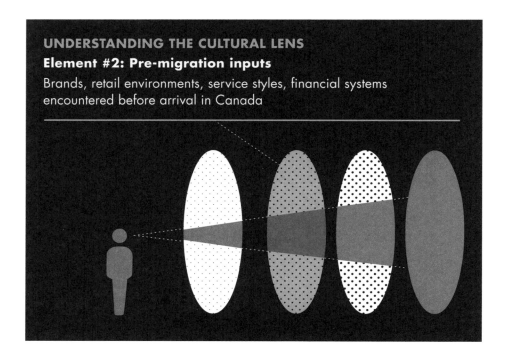

UNDERSTANDING THE CULTURAL LENS
Element #2: Pre-migration inputs
Brands, retail environments, service styles, financial systems encountered before arrival in Canada

A telling vignette appeared in the *New Yorker* a couple of years ago in which a diplomatic Chinese tour bus operator explained to his passengers the need for patience when they visited Parisian shops:

> "We have to get used to the fact that Europeans sometimes move slowly," he said. When shopping in China, he went on, "we're accustomed to three of us putting our items on the counter at the same time, and then the old lady gives change to three people without making a mistake. Europeans don't do that." He continued, "I'm not saying that they're stupid…. They just deal with math in a different way."

It's unlikely that any of the tourists on that bus had ever given much thought to the "old lady" who doled out their change so efficiently. She was part of their Cultural Lens and they didn't even know it.

People's pre-migration experiences are composed of many elements:

Brands. In many major source countries of migrants to Canada, big global brands are not only available, they're more important to consumer decision-making than they are in Canada. Of course many multinational corporations have moved into "emerging markets" in recent years to capitalize on burgeoning middle classes there. But some brands have been global for much longer, in part due to colonial ties. British-based Cadbury, for instance, first began marketing products in newly independent India in 1948.

Retailing. Although some giant multinationals pop up in similar forms in most major cities, there's generally a lot of diversity in retail experiences around the world. Stores and chains vary, as do the styles of the retail experiences — from supermarkets to street carts, from strip malls to luxury malls, from mom-and-pop shops to big box stores. Online shopping and related services, including mobile wallets, add further variations in how people access goods and services.

Service style and conventions. If you read an online forum where expats talk about cross-cultural customer service experiences, you'll find many anecdotes about minor discomforts and confusion. Sometimes these result from different cultural styles (whether shop assistants' smiles are seen as friendly or fake, for instance). But sometimes differences are more substantial. In some regions haggling over price is normal, whereas in others it's unheard of or reserved for such big-ticket items as cars and homes.

Other cultural factors. Of course, ethnic culture and consumer environments are linked in some ways. In predominantly Muslim countries, the last few decades have seen a growing number of Sharia-compliant banks seeking to cater to those who want their financial lives to adhere to Islamic law. Culture also shapes gender norms around shopping and consumption. Do both men and women shop? Are they equally likely to access leisure spaces such as restaurants? Who makes decisions about household spending? The list goes on.

As consumers shaped by particular commercial environments, we all have our assumptions and expectations. Migrants face the task of shifting their expectations as they settle in Canada. In some cases, adaptations are easy or even pleasurable. Some Indian newcomers have told us in focus groups, for instance, that they prefer Canadian-style supermarkets to grocery retail experiences in India. Other adaptations are more difficult.

One task for businesses operating in Canada is to understand migrants' pre-migration experiences, and how these experiences have shaped their habits and preferences. Not every difference in habits or expectations should be attributed to ethnic culture.

3. Post-migration inputs. So far we've discussed two of the three elements in the Cultural Lens: ethnic culture and pre-migration consumer experiences. Migrants arrive in Canada with each of these established, and then they add the third element: immersion in Canada. As they spend time in Canada,

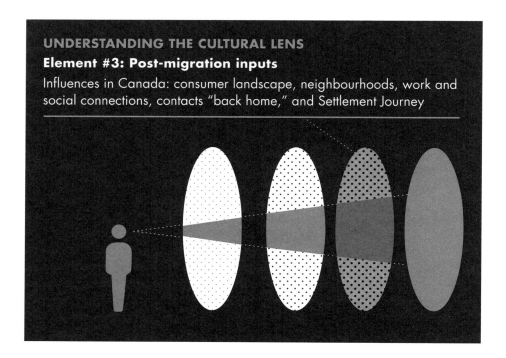

UNDERSTANDING THE CULTURAL LENS
Element #3: Post-migration inputs
Influences in Canada: consumer landscape, neighbourhoods, work and social connections, contacts "back home," and Settlement Journey

migrants are exposed to new cultural mores and new consumer offerings, and, typically, to the lifestyles and adaptations of their fellow migrants.

As they navigate this new environment, they also proceed through the stages of something we call the Settlement Journey.

The journey of migration and settlement is far bigger than a flight across an ocean. It tends to unfold over a decade or so as individuals and families negotiate a new landscape and make choices about how they want to live in their new society.

The influence of one's original ethnic culture evolves during this period, but not uniformly. It doesn't decline in a linear fashion, gradually replaced by "Canadian" culture; rather, it ebbs and flows depending on the phase of settlement. (And for migrants' children, it continues to ebb and flow in new ways.) We explore the Settlement Journey in greater detail in Chapter 3, but its basic stages, in brief, are as follows:

Disorientation. Upon arrival, individuality and ethnic culture are suppressed as newcomers scramble with the basics: finding groceries (any groceries!), getting phones connected, setting up a bank account, and so on. This is a stressful time during which convenience and simplicity are top priorities.

THE CULTURAL LENS: NOT JUST FOR MIGRANTS

Everyone has some version of a Cultural Lens—not just migrants. Consider those who are Canadian-born and whose family background is British. Their Cultural Window is informed by their British ethnic culture, and although they don't have either a Settlement Journey or a Pre-Migration Consumer Experience element, they'll certainly have international influences that might play a somewhat similar role.

An extended trip abroad or even repeated business travel to the United States will add a layer to their attitudes as consumers—making them more likely to notice, for instance, the inconvenience of going to a separate store for a bottle of wine, when in an American grocery store they could get ingredients for dinner and a bottle of Chianti in the next aisle. Moreover, their consumer experiences in Canada are continually evolving in response to immigration and globalized culture. Even if they've never set foot outside the country, they're finding sriracha and basmati rice in their grocery aisles and Korean pop music on their kids' phones.

"Even if they've never set foot outside the country, they're finding sriracha and basmati rice in their grocery aisles and Korean pop music on their kids' phones."

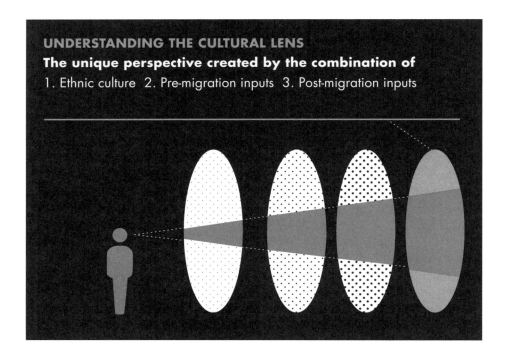

UNDERSTANDING THE CULTURAL LENS
The unique perspective created by the combination of
1. Ethnic culture 2. Pre-migration inputs 3. Post-migration inputs

Orientation. After a few months, the basics are taken care of and the stress of landing subsides. The Orientation phase is often a fun period, when newcomers feel proud of the progress they've made. At this time, many take pleasure in exploring their new context in a more relaxed way—and seeing whether they can track down those favourite foods from home they've been missing.

Belonging. A year or two into their Canadian experience, the novelty of their new life has subsided and things begin to feel normal—usually for better *and* for worse. On the upside, people feel more established and empowered. On the downside, the fantasy of a new life in Canada has given way to reality. This is always a difficult transition, even if the reality is pretty good. It's a time of refining arrangements (Did I get suckered on this mobile plan when I first arrived? Is this really the right neighbourhood for me?) and making more deliberate choices.

Independence. Migration is a profound experience that echoes throughout one's life. In practical terms, however, the Independence phase is the end of the Settlement Journey. At this point, migrants are likely to relate to both their ethnic culture and Canadian culture in a way that's more or less permanent. Depending on the individual, this may mean identifying strongly as Canadian and deliberately mixing with a diverse social group, or it may mean living in an ethnic enclave and associating almost exclusively with members of one's own group. Not everyone arrives at the same destination, but when migrants reach the Independence phase, they're at the final destination that feels right to them.

To summarize, then, at left is a diagram of the Cultural Lens through which migrants—based on their ethnic culture, their pre-migration inputs, and their post-migration inputs (including their Settlement Journey)—view products, services, and messages in Canada.

Each of these three influences changes over time—but all three will persist. People's relationship with their ethnic culture will evolve as they spend time in Canada. Their recollections of the consumer environment back home may fade, or may remain vivid as they continue to visit and communicate with friends and family there. Their consumer experiences in Canada will change as Canadian offerings become more familiar, and as they find the balance of mainstream retailers and specialty shops that meets their needs. But although the effect that each element has on people's Cultural Lenses may change, all three will remain in play.

What's Ahead in This Book

Over the course of this book, we return continually to the ideas we've sketched here: how ethnic culture, pre-migration experiences, and post-migration experiences (including the Settlement Journey) combine to create the Cultural Lens through which migrants see products and services in Canada.

In Chapter 2, we discuss what's new about Canadian diversity today. Canada has always been a destination for immigrants–but it hasn't always warranted the name Migration Nation. What's changed?

In Chapter 3, we describe the stages of the Settlement Journey in greater detail, and consider when migrants may be most receptive to particular products and services.

In Chapter 4, we look at specific categories, fields, and industries through the Cultural Lens.

In Chapter 5, we discuss marketing and communications strategies for reaching Migration Nation.

In Chapter 6, we sketch some leading-edge trends—such as global Asian youth culture and the rise of diasporas—that will shape the future.

2.

Today's Diversity In Context: What's Really Changed?

From the time of its first non-Aboriginal inhabitants, Canada has been populated by immigrants. Although, as discussed in the Introduction, the sheer scale of immigration to Canada may not be unprecedented, the mix of voices and influences that Canadians of all backgrounds encounter in their daily lives right now is radically new. And it's unique in the world.

WHAT'S NEW ABOUT CANADIAN DIVERSITY TODAY?
Hyperdiversity: Beyond "minority" groups

Although immigrants have always been an important part of the Canadian population, most have belonged to a small number of groups. Canada has never been a monoculture, but for most of its history it's had a clear mainstream— anglophone and Protestant in much of the country, francophone and Catholic in Quebec—with a few substantial subgroups. Depending on the region, significant minorities of Scots, Irish, Ukrainians, Italians, or others might have constituted the local "diversity."

Today, especially in Canadian cities, substantial subgroups have come from all over the planet. Doug Norris noted in the Preface that as of 2011, Canada had ten thousand or more immigrants from each of eighty-nine countries. It also has a thousand immigrants or more from over 150 countries, with over two hundred languages and dialects spoken in Canadian homes.

This level of diversity—what some call *hyperdiversity*—is a recent development in Canada, and it puts Canadian cities at the leading edge of a phenomenon that's shaping cities around the world. As Michael Adams has written in *Unlikely Utopia*, there are cities that have higher foreign-born populations than Toronto and Vancouver, but migrants in these cities tend to be drawn overwhelmingly from one or two countries. Miami has a large proportion of Cuban migrants, Dubai has a large number of Indians, and Singapore has a large proportion of Malaysians, to name a few examples. But Greater Toronto, for instance, not only has over 2.5 million foreign-born residents (46% of the population of the Census Metropolitan Area), they come from nearly every country on earth. As of 2011, the twenty most represented countries accounted for only two-thirds of the foreign-born population.

Such diversity is significant because it means that those of all backgrounds are running up against different people, languages, food, shops, music, and media—a milieu where there is no single dominant group, and no single

FIG. 2.1
Hyperdiversity in Canada's largest city

Countries of origin of Toronto CMA residents

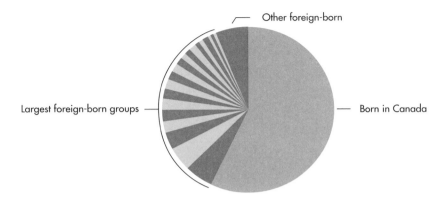

downtrodden "other." Economic characteristics cut across ethnic and linguistic categories. This isn't to say that discrimination doesn't exist, or that it's easy to be an immigrant. It *is* to say that social and economic gulfs aren't so great that people don't encounter one another in restaurants, movie theatres, schools, shopping malls, parks, and other public places. Especially in cities, people of diverse backgrounds encounter each other every day. And these encounters shape business, consumption, cultural tastes, and personal life.

Difference is good

There's something different about difference these days. Consider the success of the hit television series *Glee*, in which each member of the high school chorus draws strength and artistic brilliance from his or her different-ness. Kurt and Santana are gay; Rachel is contorted by her own perfectionism and has two dads; Quinn got pregnant in high school; Mercedes is a full-figured African-American powerhouse who senses that either her size or her race (or both) keeps her out of some leading roles; Mike longs for a life on the stage but has a high-pressure Chinese-American dad who wants him to go into business; Artie rocks out from his wheelchair. The music kids are ostensibly pariahs in their high school, but of course they're the heroes of the show and are cheered by auditoriums full of their peers at least once per episode. Indeed, one character even fakes a speech impediment to fit in with the other charmingly diverse glee club members. *Glee* without social difference would be like *Cats* without cats.

CANADA–U.S. DIFFERENCES IN MULTICULTURAL MARKETING

Multicultural marketing tends to be more advanced in the U.S. than it is in Canada. After all, the U.S. has large Latino and African-American populations, and some firms have been working on marketing to them for a long time—African-American-targeted print and radio ads go back to the 1940s. As well, the geographic concentration of Latinos and African-Americans means that in some areas failing to connect with these populations would simply mean failing: a firm in New Mexico that isn't thinking about Latinos probably isn't thinking. So in America, not only is the multicultural imperative more established in some markets, but with often just one large minority group to address, the nature of the task is also more obvious.

In Canada, the field is younger and the project more complex. First, Canada has proportionally more immigrants than the U.S. (20.6% of the Canadian population is foreign-born, as compared with 12.9% south of the border). And multicultural marketing in Canada is heavily focused on these immigrants and their children, whereas in the U.S., most African Americans and Hispanics are American-born, meaning that many of the complexities of the Settlement Journey (described in Chapter 3) don't apply. Second, Canada has more multi in its multiculturalism than America does. Both societies are diverse, but a greater number of ethnic groups are present in larger proportions in the Canadian population. Third, although this difference is more difficult to measure, there is evidence to suggest that diversity and multiculturalism have been more widely embraced as defining features of Canadian society, meaning that even multigenerational Canadians of, say, British origin are more likely to see themselves as participants in a society defined by cultural exchange and experimentation. As we've argued elsewhere, multicultural marketing in Canada isn't ethnic marketing—it's mainstream marketing.

In sum, multicultural marketers in Canada must connect with a more diverse set of people than in the U.S., take the settlement process more heavily into account, and recognize that most Canadians—not just immigrants and their children—see themselves as citizens of Migration Nation.

"Both societies are diverse, but a greater number of ethnic groups are present in larger proportions in the Canadian population."

Whether it's ethnicity, religion, sexuality, or gender identity, being different is a matter of huge preoccupation and interest these days. The candy-coated boosterism of *Glee* might be a fad, but the show wouldn't have been made in decades past. As the trends we describe throughout this book unfold—as migrants move across borders in increasing numbers and with increasing speed—people are becoming more interested in each other's socio-cultural particularities, as well as their own.

It has not always been thus in North America. In the mid-20th century, being "normal" was celebrated, and marketing reflected this. The advertising of the 1950s typically depicted nuclear families living in similar homes, driving similar cars, consuming similar products, and having similar lifestyles and aspirations. Advertising may not be a reliable portrait of the lives of real people, but it does offer a view of the ambitions and expectations of the time and place in which it's produced. Advertising in the post-war years reflected a homogenizing *zeitgeist* given life by a large and growing middle class; suburbanization; a heavy cultural emphasis on the nuclear family (where father knows best) as the centre of every healthy life; and that newly pervasive collective experience: television.

Those who came to Canada as children in the post-war years often recall uncomfortable feelings of being different. An experience that seems to have marked many was the longing for such North American delicacies as peanut butter and jam sandwiches in school lunches: tidy, odourless, normal. Instead, many young newcomers opened their lunch bags to find lovingly prepared meatballs, homemade pasta, cabbage rolls, sardine sandwiches, and other staples from "back home." Why, these kids wondered, must these terrible reminders of their difference send out aromas for the whole class to smell? Today, most Canadians of any background would likely prefer that container

---

"Today, migrants and 'the mainstream' influence each other—not only because immigrants in Canada are so numerous ... but also because they're more confident about expressing and displaying what makes them different."

of old-country cooking to industrially produced bread and spreads—and this in itself shows not only our altered taste in food, but our altered understanding of what it can mean to be different. These days, when the smell of homemade dumplings or curry wafts across the lunchroom, jealousy is a more likely response than disdain.

Deep changes in our attitudes to social difference are one reason why multicultural marketing has grown in importance over the past couple of decades.

Environics' social values surveys have found Canadians increasingly attracted to such concepts as *Social Learning* (learning by interacting with people of diverse backgrounds), *Cultural Fusion* (the belief that intercultural contact is enriching, not threatening or damaging), and *Search for Roots* (an interest in one's own background and heritage, and a belief that it's preferable to preserve—not erase—regional particularities).

Immigrants used to either fit themselves forcefully into the mainstream or resign themselves to being culturally marginal. Today, migrants and "the mainstream" influence each other—not only because immigrants in Canada are so numerous (especially in cities) but also because they're more confident about expressing and displaying what makes them different.

Some politicians, concerned about social marginalization and extremism among some groups, have proclaimed the "death of multiculturalism." But on the streets and in the shops multiculturalism has never been more alive—and most people quite like it. In Environics' 2011 Social Values survey, 83% of Canadians agreed that "I would like to expose my children to as many different cultures as possible, Western cultures as well as those from other parts of the world." Nine in ten (91%) agreed that "If you want to learn and grow in life, it is essential to meet and converse with different kinds of people, who come from all kinds of backgrounds."

Interacting with a diverse range of people isn't just an aspiration for most Canadians; increasingly, it's the reality of their daily lives. Since 1984, Environics' Focus Canada survey has been asking Canadians how frequently they interact with members of various ethnic and religious groups. As Figure 2.2 indicates, the numbers have risen steadily over the past three decades for all groups. Canadians of all backgrounds are mixing more.

Multiculturalism can be difficult: it's not all smiles and kebabs. Canadians do debate what works and what doesn't in a multicultural society. Generally speaking, however, Canadian attitudes toward social difference are increasingly positive, and this growing ease with diversity means that people of all backgrounds feel

FIG. 2.2

Canadians reporting more contact with minority groups over time

Often/occasionally, 1984–2011

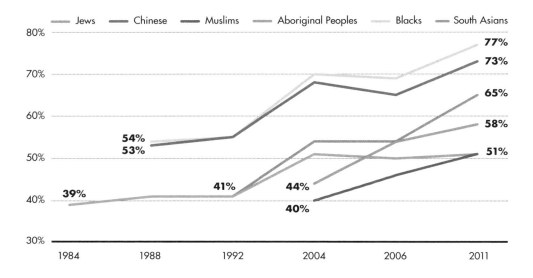

freer to express themselves. As a result, people are more likely to rub up against each other's cultural particularities in the course of daily life, and even sample bits and pieces of each other's practices, foods, and fashions. By and large, Canadians find these experiences enriching, not intimidating.

"Back home" isn't what it used to be

A Canadian prime minister has said, "Our multicultural nature gives us an edge in selling to the world. Canadians who have cultural links to other parts of the globe, who have business contacts elsewhere, are of utmost importance to our trade and investment strategy for economic renewal." Although these words wouldn't have been out of place in a Stephen Harper speech in the post-2008 period, they were in fact spoken by Brian Mulroney in 1986. And if Mulroney's statement was true over a quarter-century ago, it's doubly true today. Canadian diversity not only gives Canadian businesses access to what were once called "emerging markets" (some have by now decidedly emerged), it creates collaborative international networks of entrepreneurship, innovation, and knowledge sharing whose importance is difficult to overstate.

Most of us are familiar with the old story of the migrant getting off the boat in a new land with just a few dollars and a dream. Versions of this story have happened many times in Canada. But for contemporary migrants, this is not how it usually goes. For decades, Canada's immigration system has aimed at attracting upwardly mobile people with high levels of education, skills, and professional accreditation. (Immigration rules are discussed at greater length in the Introduction and Glossary.)

Partly as a result of these policies, Canadians tend to view migrants not as downtrodden people escaping from bleak circumstances elsewhere but as talented people who help to fuel Canadian economic growth. This perception is one of a number of reasons why Canadians have generally stood out from other societies in their positive attitudes toward immigration. As of late 2010, eight in ten Canadians believed that immigrants help the economy grow. When asked whether immigrants "take away jobs from other Canadians," the public rejects this idea by a ratio of nearly three to one (73% disagree, 24% agree).

Today, not only are migrants bringing their skills and energy to Canada, but in many cases they're arriving from rapidly growing economies—and bringing valuable networks and experience with them. The very act of migrating signals a certain amount of get-up-and-go; people who travel halfway around the world in search of opportunity are likely to be more resourceful and industrious than average. But the contexts from which migrants are arriving are even better launching pads than before. More migrants are arriving from societies with more wealth and entrepreneurial activity than in the past, as well as top-flight educational institutions.

Some of the countries that have sent the largest numbers of migrants to Canada in the past few decades are those that are now making huge economic strides, exerting increased global influence both in the goods and services they offer and in their cultural exports. For instance, China and India—whose rapid economic growth needs no summary here—were the top source countries for migrants to Canada for many years before the Philippines overtook them both in 2010. Together, people born in these two countries account for more than a million Canadians—and people who claim "Chinese" or "East Indian" as part of their ethnic heritage account for more than 2.6 million Canadians.

Moreover, Gallup research has shown that the desire to immigrate to the West is significantly more prevalent among the richest top 20% of people living in countries with relatively low GDP. It's those who are already successful or well positioned to succeed who are scanning the globe to find the best places for them and their children to flourish, both economically and in terms of quality of life.

In short, major source countries of migrants to Canada are thriving economically, and often it's people who are already doing well in those countries who are interested in migrating to places like Canada. (Others choose instead to stay home and ride waves of economic growth in their countries of origin.) These trends have two major implications. First, upon arriving in Canada, migrants and/or their children are perhaps even better poised for success than in the past. Immigrants certainly seem to stand out in their entrepreneurialism. *The Economist* has reported on a study from Duke University that found that "while immigrants make up an eighth of America's population, they founded a quarter of the country's technology and engineering firms."

The second implication has to do with the networks in which these new arrivals are embedded when they arrive. Along with high levels of education and in many cases above-average professional experience, migrants are likely to have contacts in their nations of origin with backgrounds similar to their own. This in turn is likely to help Canadian businesses connect more efficiently to fast-growing Asian economies.

"Back home" isn't as far away as it used to be

In the 19th and early 20th centuries, immigrants to North America would board a boat and say goodbye to their families and friends, in most cases forever. Letters ferried some news back and forth, but slowly. Moving to a new country across the ocean was an all-or-nothing proposition. Even as recently as a few decades ago, long-distance telephone calls were so costly that a few minutes of conversation on a birthday or a major holiday were as much as the average person could afford. Air travel remained prohibitively expensive. An immigrant in 1960 was more likely than an immigrant a century earlier to keep in touch with and even visit their country of origin, but the gulf between the old country and the new remained vast.

Today, most migrants who wish to can not only expect to visit their nations of origin in person many times, but can be in daily contact with their friends and families abroad at almost no cost. Missed a family wedding? Your cousin will send you the link to some highlights on a video-sharing site. Need advice from a friend on a home repair? Walk him through your problem via webcam. Social media will help you keep tabs on political and cultural news from back home (filtered through your friends and family who are still immersed in local media), and you can update your network on your daily triumphs and setbacks as you settle in your new country. Take a picture of a local oddity with your phone, share it with friends for instant laughs or sympathy.

This new ease of communication means that migrants to Canada aren't just people who hail from other contexts. Immigrants channel those contexts into Canada—and channel Canada outward—week in and week out. Of course, you don't have to be a migrant to be globally connected; anyone can use the internet to follow the news from Lagos or Mumbai or Lima. But the knowledge and networks immigrants bring with them when they arrive in Canada make them especially vital figures in global flows of ideas and trends, including consumer trends.

Young people in Canada who are migrants or the children of migrants are well positioned to maintain strong connections to their home countries and facilitate cultural flows between their home countries and North America. Our survey of migrant youth in Canada found that 97% of Chinese and 83% of South Asian migrants had a social networking account, and had an average of 337 and 315 friends, respectively. Thirty percent of the Chinese-Canadian youths' friends and 36% of the South Asian Canadian youths' friends on these sites were overseas. Substantial proportions of both Chinese Canadian (39%) and South Asian Canadian (33%) migrants communicate with friends overseas on a weekly basis. Given their ethnically diverse friend networks in Canada, the potential for cultural exchange as a result of these connections is enormous.

3.

The Settlement Journey

All newcomers are alike. This may sound like a ridiculous statement, given the diversity of Canada's migrant population. But when people first arrive in a new country there's a certain universality to their basic needs: they need groceries, a phone, somewhere to sleep.

When we say all newcomers are alike, we mean that a certain sameness is imposed upon them by the life stage in which they find themselves. You could say that all newcomers are alike in the way that all new parents are alike. Both groups are diverse and both are going through an intense, challenging experience that feels unique. But the nuts and bolts of the experience are largely the same: parents need to worry about keeping a baby fed, clean, and comfortable, and newcomers need to worry about such basic material concerns as food, shelter, and transportation.

Once they've caught their breath, newcomers need to find employment, the kids need to get to school, and gradually everyone must begin to pursue the other goals that help to build a happy, fulfilling life. Of course, the ingredients of happiness and fulfilment aren't the same for everyone, so as migrants settle into their new society, their diversity begins to reassert itself. They start to navigate subtle questions of identity, belonging, and self-expression, and along the way their outlooks and priorities shift profoundly.

Through our work with newcomers and more settled migrants, we've come to see the settlement process as a journey with four main stages:

1. Disorientation
2. Orientation
3. Belonging
4. Independence

All migrants experience the first two stages, and most experience all four. People move through these stages at different rates, however, and there are almost as many end points to the Settlement Journey as there are migrants.

If your organization is trying to connect with migrants, it's important to understand where your offering fits into the Settlement Journey. At what stage are migrants likely to seek out your offering—is it an urgent need that they'll look to satisfy right away, or something they might aspire to down the road? Is your message reaching them at a time when they can absorb it, or is it lost in the chaos of Disorientation?

We touched on the idea of the Settlement Journey when we introduced the Cultural Lens in Chapter 1. We argued that understanding where people are on their Settlement Journey is as important as understanding their ethnic culture and the consumer experiences they've had prior to migration. In this chapter, we take a closer look at each phase of the Settlement Journey to see how the settlement process shapes people's needs and outlooks.

PHASE 1: DISORIENTATION
Dominant Mindset: Lack of trust, short-term thinking

Suppose you just arrived in Canada, and although you're highly educated, your English or French isn't perfect. Which cellular contract is the best for you? Can you trust the car dealership near your apartment building? Should you hire the smooth-talking "consultant" who promises to find you a job commensurate with your qualifications? These are the kinds of dilemmas that rain down upon newcomers. Every decision takes time, and every wrong choice carries the risk of lost time and money. It's little wonder that the initial phase of settlement is a profoundly stressful and disorienting one.

The stress and uncertainty of the Disorientation phase also tend to have the effect of suppressing individual and even cultural differences. The Pakistani engineer, the Filipina bookkeeper, and the Brazilian dentist may differ in a thousand ways—but all will sit at the kitchen table with the same brochures for mobile phone plans and mutter their confusion. All are operating in a new (or less solid) language, all have been uprooted from their familiar frames of reference.

Naturally, people are individuals and their personalities don't disappear altogether. Some will have a greater tolerance for change and uncertainty than others. Nevertheless, the Disorientation phase is difficult enough to foreshorten almost everyone's outlook and planning. Where are the groceries? Where do I put my money? Where am I sleeping next week or next month? These are the bare-bones preoccupations of the newest of newcomers, and they induce justifiable feelings of vulnerability and lack of trust.

Because newcomers, quite rationally, tend to be wary of advice and promises, word of mouth from such trusted people as friends and family members is likely to have a very strong influence on consumer behaviour at this stage. Not only does a good tip provide some reassurance, it saves time the newcomer might otherwise have invested in comparison shopping.

Notably, while one might hypothesize that newcomers will reflexively trust people from their own country, religion, or language group, our qualitative research tells us that this isn't a given. We've found that newcomers are so uncertain about where to place their trust that the most credible people are sometimes those who share their predicament: other newcomers.

Understanding the Disorientation phase is an important challenge for organizations whose products and services newcomers are seeking right away, such as banks and wireless service providers. Newcomers need to get themselves established in these areas at a very early stage of their settlement, and service providers who reach out early and do a good job may reap the benefits of a long-term relationship. And yet while the reward may be substantial, communicating with those in the Disorientation phase is difficult. New arrivals are wary of striking bad bargains in an unfamiliar commercial environment, particularly when Canadian norms differ from those back home (for instance, higher banking fees). Although newcomers may be getting the same deal as other Canadians, they may suspect they are in fact getting charged extra because of some naive mistake or because they're dealing with an unscrupulous business.

The Disorientation phase is intense, but for most it's mercifully brief.

PHASE 2: ORIENTATION
Dominant Mindset: Exploration

After a period of weeks or months, newcomers make their way into the next phase of settlement: Orientation. They're not yet at home in their new society, but they've caught their breath and the sheer logistics of the next meal or phone call are no longer top-of-mind. Although many challenges lie ahead, people tend to be able to take more pleasure in the process of exploring their surroundings, sampling new products and services, and adjusting to a new rhythm of life.

Not only does the Orientation phase tend to find migrants exploring consumer choices, it also finds them thinking about Canadian society—professional life, different neighbourhoods, leisure activities—and imagining how they might ultimately fit into it. The anxious "short-termism" of the Disorientation phase falls away, and migrants can begin to consider their longer-term plans for their lives in Canada. The aspiration that may have driven their migration in the first place begins to reassert itself.

The Orientation phase can be an exciting time: newcomers often feel a sense of confidence and accomplishment as they transcend the vulnerability of their early weeks or months in Canada. This mindset, alongside increased familiarity with retail channels, encourages retail exploration in a variety of product categories. Even a trip to the personal care aisle at Walmart can be a voyage of discovery. Whereas in the Disorientation phase a newcomer might have felt pure frustration at not being able to find *his* toothpaste, he may now consider a range of exotic toothpastes. Which one will become his new Canadian toothpaste for his new Canadian life? Micro-adventures present themselves; adaptation becomes fun instead of arduous.

Children in the household can be very influential at this time. In fact, through school, they may well be the household members most engaged in Canadian society and most exposed to various cultures and influences. They could be the ones providing their parents with snippets of Canadian history or even the words to the national anthem. They're also more likely to be introduced to new products and brands, especially food. After having Kraft Dinner at a friend's house or pizza at a school function, they may start to request these products at home, sending parents for the first time into the unfamiliar freezer section at No Frills. And prompted by their children, the parents may try these new products themselves.

Orientation isn't only a metaphor for a psychological state. It's also literal and geographical. Migrants at this time begin to get their bearings in their neighbourhoods and cities, choosing shops, routes, and services according to calculations about price, quality, and convenience.

PHASE 3: BELONGING
Dominant Mindset: Confidence and routine

Almost every migrant to Canada will experience some version of the Disorientation and Orientation phases. The Belonging phase is common but not universal. A migrant has reached Belonging, as we mean it here, when he or she has found some basic anchors for life in Canada: personal and professional networks, a home and routine that are fairly comfortable, and, critically,

---

"Orientation **isn't only a metaphor for a psychological state. It's also literal and geographical. Migrants at this time begin to get their bearings in their neighbourhoods and cities, choosing shops, routes, and services according to calculations about price, quality and convenience."**

stable employment—ideally in his or her field of training. Some migrants may live in their adoptive country for years but never find work that feels worthwhile and never truly feel they belong.

Back to being me

It's important to note that Belonging doesn't mean being assimilated. Immigrants at this stage don't reject their culture of origin or hide it to fit in; indeed, as they emerge from the Orientation phase, they often place a new emphasis on the cultural identity in which they were raised. The shift from Orientation to Belonging is instead a shift from the suspension of personal preferences and expectations ("I'm in a new place and so must be completely adaptable in order to make the best of it and succeed") to greater confidence about Canadian culture and a recognition of which changes are necessary and which are optional ("Lots of good Canadians love dumplings and hate frozen pizza— I guess I'm one of them").

Similarly, migrants at this stage may feel more comfortable consuming media specific to their ethnic and language group. Whereas during Orientation they may have forced themselves and their kids to explore Canadian media offerings, they may now just watch and read what they feel like, confident that they can move easily among the different offerings without shutting themselves off from the wider culture. Our data have shown that longer-tenured migrants are more likely to consume media in their own languages. At this phase, a South Asian family may settle into watching the Bollywood Freetime Movie together on Omni TV on Saturday morning. A Chinese migrant who'd been switching between various free English- and Chinese-language newspapers may start to regularly read one of the popular Chinese daily papers, for example *Sing Tao* or *Ming Pao Daily*.

For many migrants, their sense of cultural confidence comes in part from their growing awareness of the sheer diversity of Canadian society—their recognition, for instance, that people all around them speak with different accents. At the Belonging stage, immigrants tend to feel more confident about the levels of social and cultural capital they've accumulated and freer to let the pendulum swing back from All Canadian, All The Time to a more personal balance between rhythms and habits from their old home and new home. This personal balance varies from person to person; some will settle into a diverse group of friends and activities, while others will choose to immerse themselves more in their own ethnic and language communities. But whatever choices they make, the balance they strike during the Belonging phase tends to be fairly permanent.

We made it

It is not that settled immigrants have overcome all the challenges of migration. Many will still feel overwhelmed and discouraged at times. Perhaps a fair way of describing the Belonging phase is that, if a good friend from back home asks, "So? Do you have a life in Canada?" the answer will be yes.

An important characteristic of the life Belonging migrants have built is that they've built it on their own, or with the cooperation of their immediate families. The vast majority of newcomers arrive as part of a family (in the decade leading up to the 2006 census, the proportion was 84%). But for many of these people, the immediate family that accompanied them in their migration was only a small subset of the family they would have had regular contact with—or even shared a home with—in their country of origin.

Because they tend to be part of a nuclear family uprooted from a larger web of kinship and friendship, migrants often have two key emotional experiences during Belonging. The first is pride in personal accomplishment: having built a new life in Canada without any of the usual support from family networks or friends. The second is a strong sense of immediate-family togetherness. Isolated from the wider extended-family network, spouses may rely on each other more, children may be listened to more, and all may emerge with a new-found sense of solidarity and intimacy after having overcome such a big challenge together.

From dreams to reality

The Belonging phase is a time when a newcomer's life in Canada has begun to resolve into a clear picture. During Belonging, migrants are justifiably proud of having found jobs and homes, helped their children settle in at school, made some friends, learned the ropes of a daily routine, and even made the first strides toward long-term improvements in their standard of living.

But while these hard-fought achievements bring satisfaction, they can also provoke a certain ambivalence, because life in Canada has gone from being a vague dream to a concrete reality—inevitably with some disappointments. Whether it's a job that's less elevated than one had hoped or a home less charming or a climate more uncomfortable, day-to-day life is bound to fall short of the hopes that drew migrants to uproot their families and move half-way around the world. This is not to say they regret the decision, but they may find that the reality of life in Canada falls short of their early aspirations. The Belonging phase is a time of realism and recalibration. Migrants are often re-vising their goals and expectations at this point, and in many cases their plans become both more modest and more attainable.

The relief of routine

As far as consumer orientations are concerned, the Belonging phase is a time of hard-won habit and routine. Migrants in the Belonging phase are no longer looking for their new, Canadian detergent brand or pausing to taste the sample crackers at the grocery store. They're less likely to tune in to advertising and promotions for ideas, and like longstanding Canadians, most are simply trying to power through their shopping list and get home. They've established relationships with service providers, and are either locked into their cellular service plans or have been convinced that all providers are the same.

But while the Belonging phase may be less fertile ground for, say, consumer packaged goods (CPG) companies, it's also a time when migrants are more likely to be involved in larger purchases, including investing, travel, home (or second home), home renovation, and children's education (private education and/or after-school programs). For those categories, the Belonging stage is the optimal time to build connections: migrants have stabilized financially and are making more concrete preparations for the future.

The new confidence and understanding of migrants in the Belonging phase has important implications for marketers. Whereas consumers at the Disorientation and Orientation stages are often confused and looking for information and guidance, those at the Belonging stage understand both their own requirements and the Canadian marketplace better. Having emerged from a period of particular vulnerability after they first arrived, they may also be especially sensitive to the feeling of being pushed or misled by businesses ("Now that I know my way around, I'll never fall for that again"). Marketers, advertisers, and retailers must therefore do more listening and less talking in order to reach these migrants.

PHASE 4: INDEPENDENCE
Dominant mindset: Satisfaction, stock-taking, legacy

Independence is the end of the Settlement Journey. To some extent, it's the goal of the journey. As the name implies, the Independence stage is defined by freedom and autonomy. Like the Belonging stage, not all migrants will reach the Independence stage. Those who reach this final stage of the Settlement Journey have accumulated a degree of social capital and comfort with themselves and their society that not everyone achieves.

As with the Belonging stage, it's important to note that reaching the Independence stage doesn't mean being "fully Canadian" in the sense of being indistinguishable in language, culture, and attitudes from a multi-generational Canadian of British or French heritage. The Settlement Journey as we conceive it isn't a linear process of leaving one's ethnic culture behind and adopting something else. That process exists for some people, but the linear model of acculturation isn't universal and isn't the best way to understand Migration Nation. Because of multiculturalism, technology, and globalization, migrants can stay connected to their countries of origin in unprecedented ways. This means the Settlement Journey can lead to many "final destinations."

Consider an Indian immigrant from the Punjab who arrived in Canada in 1983 and settled in Abbotsford, British Columbia, at age twenty-three. She's spent most of her life in Canada, and at age fifty-four has clearly travelled the full length of her Settlement Journey. She's very secure in her role in Canadian society as a citizen, an Indian-Canadian, a Sikh, a mother, and a member of her community. Yet she wouldn't meet many of the criteria for "acculturation" in traditional models. She still speaks Punjabi most often at home. Almost all her friends are Indian immigrants. She's heavily immersed in Punjabi-language media—both from India and Canada. Almost all the food she prepares is Indian, and she still prepares fresh roti for her family daily. This woman is in the Independence phase of her Settlement Journey. For all intents and purposes, her relationships with Canada, India, the culture of her grandparents, and the culture that will soon belong to her grandchildren are largely set.

Or consider a Chinese migrant who moved to Markham, Ontario, during the handover of Hong Kong sovereignty from Britain to China in 1997. After close to twenty years in Canada, he still reads *Ming Pao* daily and speaks Cantonese at home. He still maintains strong ties with Hong Kong. Indeed, today, owing to Skype, Facebook, Weibo, and IPTV, his connection to friends, family, and current events back home is even stronger than it was when he first arrived in

---

"The Settlement Journey as we conceive it isn't a linear process of leaving one's ethnic culture behind and adopting something else."

Canada. His son, who grew up in Canada, is a young adult now and works in Hong Kong and China. This man is also at the Independence phase of his Settlement Journey.

Migrants adapt—but the world around them also changes

Just as technology and globalization are changing the settlement experiences of people living in Canada, they're changing the pre-migration experiences of those who will eventually land in this country. Migrants from China and India who've arrived in the last two years may well meet more of the traditional acculturation criteria (language use, media consumption, and so on) than the two preceding examples of Independence-phase migrants. That's because migrants arriving today—especially young ones—are likely to be more globalized: they're likely to be cosmopolitan, exposed to global brands, and immersed in a global workplace. On arrival, they may be vastly more comfortable speaking English and consuming English-language media. They may also be more familiar with the brands on the supermarket shelves than were previous waves of migrants.

Nevertheless, even for highly globalized people, not everything is portable. It still takes time to settle in a new society, become accustomed to local geography and conventions, and especially to develop local relationships—both personal and professional. The Independence phase is one at which these are firmly in place. This phase is characterized by freedom to choose, and one can only have freedom to choose if one understands the landscape well enough to fully understand one's options. At the Independence stage, migrants have built up sufficient knowledge and social capital to have a strong identity and confidence in their roles in Canadian society—and to be able to decide where they fit and feel most comfortable.

The right balance for me

For most, the Independence phase is all about finding the right balances and combinations. The Punjabi immigrant in Abbotsford will have settled into a routine that involves shopping at Sabzi Mandi for spices but knowing she can get better deals on atta (Indian flour) at the Real Canadian Superstore. And while she's there she may pick up some Bick's pickles, a taste that her son introduced her to and that she now loves. She may spend a lot of time watching South Asian programming on ATN, but she also reads the copies of *Metro Vancouver* that her daughter picks up on her commute home from university. This is what Independence looks like for her, and from this point on, more time in Canada won't mean more Bick's pickles or fewer trips to Sabzi Mandi. She's found her mix.

The exploration that characterizes the early stages of the Settlement Journey has ceased at the Independence phase and routine has set in. Migrants typically feel confident in the way they participate in Canadian society, both in their own ethnic communities and in their wider communities. We've observed that migrants at the Independence stage often act as cultural ambassadors: they feel good about the ways their cuisine, rituals, entertainment, and religious practices differ, and this sense of confidence and positive identification makes it easy and pleasurable for them to share their ethnic cultures with people from elsewhere, whether other migrants or the Canadian-born. Many migrants also feel good about the aspects of their lifestyle they've adopted since being in Canada, and like to discuss their evolution in this regard. At this stage community involvement is likely to be stronger.

Passing the torch

Finally, at the Independence phase, migrants tend to have a sense of what they've achieved or are likely to achieve professionally in Canada. This results partly from the stage they've reached in the Settlement Journey, and partly from life stage (people often migrate as young adults or parents of young children, but by Independence they're at the height of their careers and parents of teenagers or young adults). As migrants begin to feel they can fully see the outlines of their own economic lives, their focus tends to shift to the next generation—their own uncertainty and striving are done and they're free to focus on other things, and they have a stronger sense of the resources they're able to devote to their children's early adulthood (whether it's education, or helping with a first home, or other priorities).

During the Independence phase, therefore, legacy often asserts itself as an important consideration: ensuring that children have the right education and social capital to prosper in Canada and globally, and laying the groundwork for grandchildren and the next generation in the extended family. These emerging concerns have implications for wealth management, charitable giving, remittances to family back home, and investments in education—especially post-secondary education.

4.

Products and Services
Through the Cultural Lens

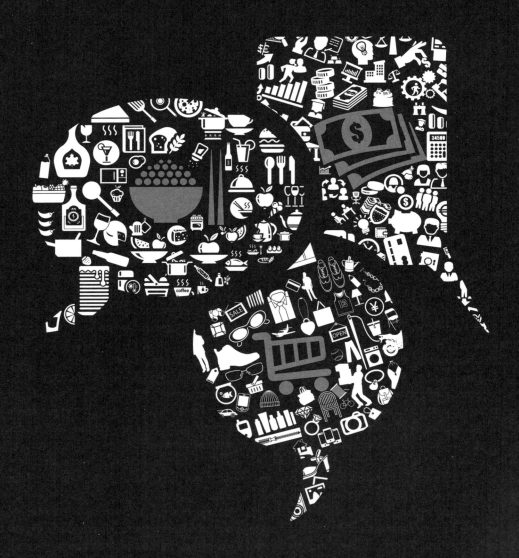

Food and Consumer Packaged Goods

When you were five, what foods do you remember your mother making? How about your grandmother? The food preferences we develop in early childhood seat themselves deeply in our palates. Our early experiences of food also exert emotional power over us later in life. What's offered as "comfort food"? Is dairy a staple or an oddity? Is spicy food a pleasurable part of the daily routine?

Because our tastes tend to be formed by our families, with recipes and cooking tips passed down from parent to child, our ethnic cultures generally influence our food choices much more than our choices in other product categories. For this reason, understanding and adapting to migration and ethnic diversity in Canada are especially vital imperatives for those in the food business.

Despite the clear link between ethnocultural diversity and the market for food, Consumer Packaged Goods (CPG) companies are relative newcomers to multicultural marketing in Canada. Banks have been courting immigrants for over a century, and telecom firms have been selling overseas communications services to new Canadians for decades. But it's only within the last ten years or so that CPG firms have begun to make serious investments in connecting with Migration Nation.

Two related trends provoked the big CPG firms to make this shift. The first was pressure from retailers, who were looking to adapt to the changing Canadian market and were seeking help from their suppliers to do so. The second trend was one we discuss in this book: the fact that Canadian-born people of French or British descent constitute a shrinking customer base, and offer little opportunity for growth. Newcomers are where the potential lies—and newcomers' tastes are also influencing the tastes of the Canadian-born as Canadian palates become more and more adventurous.

Loblaw and T&T: More evidence that multicultural is mainstream

A large grocery chain buying a smaller one isn't the kind of thing that tends to get splashed all over the business pages. But it was big news in 2009 when Loblaw Companies Ltd. purchased Chinese specialty chain T&T Supermarket Inc. for $225 million.

During its sixteen years in business, T&T had earned the nickname "the Asian Loblaw." It carried an extensive list of Asian grocery offerings, but it had the glossy look and feel of a major North American grocery chain—not of an independent shop nestled in Chinatown. The fact that Loblaw paid such a high price for the chain was a major signal to the food industry that the diets of Canadians new and old had gone global. Loblaw's then-president Allan Leighton described the strategy behind the acquisition this way: "Immigration to Canada is driving long-term growth over the next twenty years and will have a defining impact on retail grocery.... Our objective is to be the No. 1 ethnic player in Canada." Keeping Canadian kitchens stocked with noodles, coconut milk, fish sauce, and chilies was big business, and Loblaw wanted be at the centre of it.

Retailers—especially large ones like Loblaw—are powerful players in the food business. So when they state an objective, their suppliers (the large CPG companies) tend to listen closely. Retailers also turn to their suppliers for help building successful marketing approaches. When Loblaw needs to determine the best assortment of products for the Markham, Ontario, No Frills store, where the trading area's population is over 50% Chinese, they count on suppliers to help them assemble the best product mix. It's in the interest of CPG companies like Kraft and Unilever to show they understand these consumers deeply and are able to offer products to meet the needs of a Canadian marketplace that is changing profoundly.

Globalized palates and Asian flavours:
Mutual acculturation through food

To begin to see the contours of this change, one has only to look at such data as the NPD Group's 2011 *Eating Patterns in Canada* report. The report tells us that by 2011, Canadians were consuming 703 million fewer servings of

"The food habits that more recent newcomers bring from Asia are accelerating the Canadian population's embrace of an increasingly globalized Asian cuisine."

potatoes than they had in 2001. Meanwhile, the number of rice servings being consumed annually was up by 297 million. During the same ten-year period, consumption of other Asian favourites like pork and seafood increased while consumption of beef declined.

These changes may be driven primarily by people who are themselves Asian—either migrants or the descendants of migrants—but those populations aren't the whole story. Canadian-born consumers of all backgrounds are exploring new cuisines. Long gone are the days when Canadian menus revolved around beef and potatoes, tourtière, and other traditional rural staples that nourished English, Scottish, and French settlers. The pasta and perogies favoured by later waves of European immigrants are well loved, but they too are making room for new flavours. The food habits that more recent newcomers bring from Asia are accelerating the Canadian population's embrace of an increasingly globalized Asian cuisine.

Even as multi-generational Canadians embrace Asian flavours—from sushi, samosas, and dumplings to ramen, pho, and curries—many Asian migrants are embracing Western dishes that are popular in Canada. Some are also adapting their own cuisine to use Western flavours and ingredients. In Migration Nation, food is a powerful vehicle of mutual acculturation. In addition to the sheer size of the Asian-born market in Canada, the cultural excitement around food is yet another reason why keeping pace with diversity is especially critical for food producers and retailers.

THE CULTURAL LENS
Pre-migration food experiences: Different products, different process

It's not only in Canada that tastes are increasingly global; the market environments people experience prior to migration reflect multiple tastes and influences as well. Palates around the world—particularly in cities—are being exposed to a greater diversity of flavours. Newcomers to Canada are increasingly exposed to multinational brands prior to their arrival here. In fact, our research has found that some newcomers from Asia have greater trust in certain Western CPG brands (including Nestlé, Unilever, and Kraft) than does the Canadian-born population.

For CPG brands, it's important to be aware not only of the tastes newcomers bring with them to Canada, but of the image their brands have outside Canada's borders. CPG firms can get some easy wins simply by leveraging the equity of brands in the company's portfolio that already exist overseas. (We discuss a few examples of this practice on page 71, including Nescafé instant coffee and Cadbury chocolates.)

Food and Consumer Packaged Goods

ETHNIC CULTURE

Strong Influence. Food is one of the categories where preferences are most heavily shaped by ethnic culture.

PRE-MIGRATION INPUTS

Strong influence. Brand loyalties persist—even deepen. Migrants are generally exposed to big global CPG brands in their countries of origin. Many seek these out after landing in Canada.

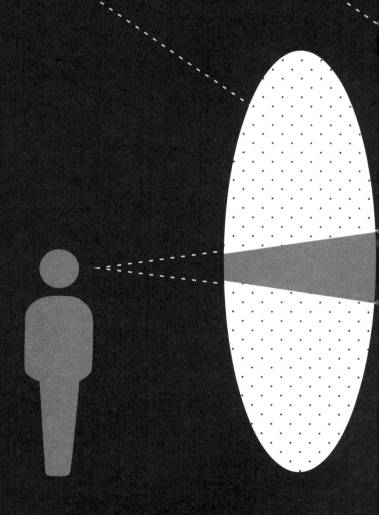

POST-MIGRATION INPUTS

Strong but variable influence. Through food, migrants both explore their new society and seek the comforts of their countries of origin. Different priorities emerge as settlement progresses.

CULTURAL LENS

Food is a strongly globalized category. Migrants integrate into a food land-scape full of international influences. The habits of the Canadian-born are changing as much as those of migrants.

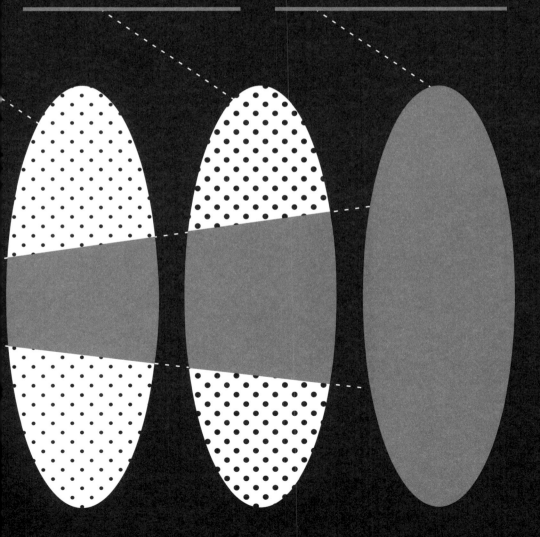

It is important to remember that, for many migrants from Asia, the very process of shopping and cooking might not have been a big part of their pre-migration life. Domestic servants who perform these tasks are much more common in parts of Asia than in Europe and North America. Immigrants from India in particular are likely to come from an environment where groceries are delivered to the door and prepared by a cook.

Even Asian migrants who didn't have servants in their countries of origin are more likely than the average North American working-age adult to have had live-in parents or in-laws who helped substantially with groceries and meal preparation. This kind of multi-generational labour-sharing is particularly common in Chinese households. The sudden withdrawal of such support, combined with new products and conventions of shopping, can make the mundane task of buying groceries a very daunting one for newcomers.

THE SETTLEMENT JOURNEY

It's not easy to make cassoulet with salt cod. Early Acadian settlers in Canada quickly accepted that recreating their native French cuisine in the New World was a losing battle. Like good migrants, they adapted: stirring their old knowledge together with the ingredients available in their new land, they cooked up a brand-new cuisine featuring poutine râpée, râpure, and fricot—inventions of necessity that over time became beloved classics in themselves.

Things are easier in the kitchen for today's migrants; many of the products and ingredients of their homelands easily available in Canadian stores. But shopping and cooking are activities that tend to rely on habit and routine, so any amount of disruption can be disorienting. Not only do migrants face new brand choices and ingredients, but language issues and even the layout of the grocery store can make food shopping feel like a hassle.

The Disoriented kitchen

Like financial services firms, Canadian food, grocery, and personal care companies have an opportunity to build relationships at the Disorientation stage of settlement. As discussed in Chapter 3, during the Disorientation phase migrants are looking for simplicity and reassurance. When they first arrive, they're likely to seek basic meal solutions and familiarity. This is no time for sampling the culinary riches of the Canadian mosaic: recent arrivals want to get their families fed, and they have relatively little time, energy, and money to devote to the task. Ideally, a trip to the grocery store during Disorientation will not only yield food, but also a sense of competence and accomplishment: "Life is crazy right now, but this is something basic I can get done for my family— without wasting time or money."

PRE-MIGRATION FAVOURITES:
HELPING NEWCOMERS FIND TREATS FROM BACK HOME

For firms that already have an international presence, connecting with migrants in Canada may be as straightforward as helping them bump into familiar brands from home. A few examples:

Indo-Canadians and Cadbury. The Cadbury brand is strong in Canada, and even better known in India. Indians are among the largest migrant groups in Canada: there were 1,165,145 people classified as having "East Indian" ethnicity in the 2011 National Household Survey. Two-thirds of these (67%) are first-generation Canadians, so many of their preferences will have been shaped by pre-migration experiences in India. Kraft, therefore, has a significant opportunity to promote Cadbury products to Indo-Canadians, particularly during celebrations like Diwali, a festival of lights whose rituals include the sharing of sweets. And the task of connecting Indo-Canadians with a brand they already enjoy is made easier by the fact that this group tends to be residentially concentrated and to patronize fairly predictable retailers, including Indian-focused shops as well as mainstream discount chains like No Frills. Many Indo-Canadians also tend to consume media specific to their own community. In short, it's not hard to find ways to communicate with these Canadians.

Chinese Canadians and Ferrero Rocher. Similar rules apply to Chinese Canadians and the Italian-made chocolate Ferrero Rocher. Ferrero Rocher chocolates are popular in southern China, and particularly in Hong Kong. The candy's long-running advertising campaign has emphasized romance and drawn parallels between Ferrero Rocher and flowers; the little round treats are sometimes even sold in bouquets rather than boxes. Ferrero Rocher chocolates are also popular New Year gifts, their gold paper carrying associations of prosperity in Chinese culture. As in the case of Cadbury chocolates, the challenge of getting Chinese Canadians to find their way to a brand they already like from back home is a modest one: Turin-based Ferrero Rocher already has a presence in Canada, and there are many well established means of connecting with Chinese-Canadian consumers, who tend to be residentially concentrated and attuned to media aimed at their communities.

Asians and instant coffee. Instant coffee is popular in both the Chinese and South Asian markets. Coffee brands that have an instant product to offer may do well to simply put it in the path of Asian customers, whether in shops catering to particular groups or in mainstream grocery stores in areas with high concentrations of Asian residents. As with the chocolates discussed above, instant brands that already enjoy some popularity in Asia (such as Nestlé's Nescafé brand) will likely get an especially good return on investment in connecting with Asian-born coffee drinkers in Canada.

No Frills is the leading grocery store among South Asian immigrants in Ontario: in a 2013 survey, Environics found that 77% had visited a No Frills location within the previous three months. The store's ads specifically target South Asian and Chinese newcomers, employing techniques that are well pitched at those in the Disorientation stage of settlement. First, No Frills ads inform newcomers that familiar products like bok choi, atta, and live fish are available in its stores. Second, No Frills consistently reminds shoppers that they're getting a good deal, with its "Won't Be Beat" policy guaranteeing the lowest prices. This approach not only appeals to newcomers' budget consciousness but also reassures them that they can relax; they don't need to worry about searching around an unfamiliar landscape to comparison shop. A guarantee of the lowest price is music to the Disoriented migrant's ears.

No Frills succeeds with newcomers in part by carrying familiar Asian brands. But there's another path to success as well: helping Disoriented newcomers develop new brand relationships by explicitly linking a product available in Canada to a product they knew back home. Reckitt Benckiser, for example, has targeted South Asian newcomers with the message that its Lysol brand of disinfectant and household cleaner is similar to the trusted Dettol brand popular in South Asia. This approach leverages Dettol's strength and helps newcomers make one more step toward feeling they've gotten their bearings in Canada.

Building relationships during the Disorientation phase

Grocery shopping happens frequently and consistently, with many opportunities to try new products and retailers. A newcomer can test out the mom-and-pop shop around the corner, the big-box discount store, and the ethnic specialty shop—all within a few weeks. This potential for experimentation means that

"The Disoriented phase of settlement is not a time of habit formation. Disoriented newcomers' thinking tends to be short-term and reactive: it is about getting by for now."

engaging newcomers in the grocery aisle is a different challenge from engaging them in industries where "shopping" is more sporadic—in financial services or telecoms, for instance.

For banks, forging a strong relationship with newcomers when they first arrive often yields significant returns. If a bank can connect with a newly landed migrant and provide her with the basics, it has a good chance of expanding the relationship down the line as the newcomer gains ground financially, requires credit and investment vehicles, wants to save for her children's education, and so on. The same is true for providing a new arrival with his first mobile phone. Unless you make a mistake, you're likely to still be receiving a monthly payment from him in two years—maybe with an upgraded device. So in cases like these, where "first relationship" is a major advantage, it's worth making a significant investment to understand and engage customers in the Disorientation stage.

Although it benefits CPG brands to engage consumers at the Disorientation stage, being the first place where a newcomer buys a bag of groceries doesn't necessarily mean you're at the beginning of a beautiful friendship. It's easier to experiment and mix and match in the grocery category, so forging an early connection doesn't provide the same return on investment as it does for businesses where relationships are stickier. CPG firms are therefore better advised to pay moderate attention to Disoriented newcomers, and instead work hard to understand the Orientation phase.

The opportunities of the Orientation phase

Since food and grocery shopping is habitual, CPG marketers strive to make their offerings part of consumers' habits. And yet the first, Disorientation phase of settlement isn't a time of habit formation. Disoriented newcomers' thinking tends to be short-term and reactive: it's about getting by for now. These shoppers are typically responding to immediate needs, not building routines that meet such considered goals as finding the best product, creating a pleasurable family ritual, or even saving money. (Disoriented consumers are highly price-sensitive but often not in a position to be strategic about getting a good deal.)

All of this changes during the Orientation phase: consumers are beginning to form the habits that will stay with them over the medium to long term. They're finding their bearings, gaining confidence, and exploring their options. Since exploration is part of the pleasure of shopping, trips to the grocery store during the Orientation phase can be remarkably entertaining. The grocery aisle becomes a safe, easy, fun way to find new things and try them out. Consumers are likely to be very open to samples and in-store experiences, especially those that engage kids and deliver a bit of light education. The risks are low—

"That breakfast cereal wasn't so hot; we'll try something else next week"—and the rewards are multiple: meeting household needs, learning about local tastes and offerings, and feeling a sense of empowerment at being able to navigate this new environment a little better each week. And as newcomers develop their Canadian habits, loyalty programs that help them build up points and earn rewards quickly may catch their interest (many migrants are arriving from markets where loyalty programs are very popular).

So the Orientation phase presents a significant opportunity for food and CPG companies targeting newcomers, provided they can align their strategy with the needs and mindsets that are characteristic of this stage of the Settlement Journey when it comes to food:

1. Openness and excitement about new choices

When was the last time you felt curious and stimulated at the grocery store? Unless you've recently been in the Orientation phase yourself, your answer may be "never"—or not since you were a kid. For most adults who are familiar with Canadian brands and retailers, a trip to the supermarket tends to happen on autopilot: you check the items off your list (often the same ones as last week or two weeks ago), pay, and get out. You may do all this while paying little attention to your environment.

By contrast, the newcomer in the Orientation phase will shop with eyes wide open, looking for new products and ideas. Our data shows that migrants who've recently arrived try a wider range of brands and categories than do more established migrants. While the Disorientation phase is usually a kind of survival mode ("Don't distract me—this is hard work"), Orientation is a time of openness and curiosity. And with that openness comes a tendency to notice and pay attention to multiple influences, including store promotions and displays as well as flyers or other communication.

2. A need to manage changing and sometimes contrasting tastes in the household

Changing household dynamics can contribute to this spirit of exploration. Children can exert considerable influences on a family's purchases—especially of food—during the Orientation phase. As we've seen, kids are sometimes more engaged with mainstream Canada than their parents are early in the settlement process. They virtually act as scouts in the new society, going out into mainstream

UNILEVER'S LUX AND KNORR:
BRANDS THAT MIGRATE WITH THEIR FANS

Multinational firms that know they have a winning brand in a major source country of migrants to Canada might consider migrating the brands themselves. CPG giant Unilever, founded in India in 1933 under the name Lever Brothers India Limited (later known as Hindustan Lever), provided the Indian market with such favourite brands as Brooke Bond tea and Sunsilk shampoo. As in many developing markets, Unilever's international presence has given its brands a certain glow in the eyes of consumers: suggesting premium quality. Unilever's soup and its seasoning brand Knorr have enjoyed a similar reputational advantage among consumers in Hong Kong and across greater China.

As consumers from those markets have migrated across the world and to Canada, Unilever's international presence has yielded still more benefits. Its North American Multicultural Business Unit identifies brands from the company's global portfolio that might make a successful trip from Asia to North America; it then reconnects migrant consumers in North America with popular brands from their pre-migration days. For example, after Unilever's North American launch of its popular Asian personal care brand Lux, it found that many Asian-born consumers preferred it over established North American brands. Similarly, Unilever has courted Chinese North American consumers with Knorr products that were previously available in China but not in North America. Notably, the marketing approaches for both Knorr and Lux have combined creative from Asia and North America.

How to determine which brands will best make the journey from Asia or elsewhere to Canada? One way of gauging demand for these brands is observing what's being imported via the "grey market" and sold in ethnic shops. It's common for small trading companies to bypass multinationals' Canadian offices and bring in popular products on their own. Take a stroll through Ontario's Pacific Mall or B.C.'s Aberdeen Centre and you'll find a range of Asian products imported in this manner, including confectionery products from Nestlé and Mars.

Canada through the school system (soaking up both classroom messages and their peers' informal chat) and reporting back on the habits and culture of Canada.

Children can begin to develop a taste for things like pizza and hot dogs at friends' houses and school events. TV ads and friends' lunch bags can also spark their curiosity about popular products. When kids make requests at home for the new, "Canadian" foods they've tried elsewhere, they can find a more ready audience than one might expect because the Orienting newcomer parents are seeking to learn and explore. Far from being automatically rejected ("No, you can't have chocolate breakfast cereal"), requests are often welcomed as opportunities to try out local offerings.

Newcomers tend to be open to their children's food requests for a few reasons. First, while newcomers generally want their children to value their own ethnic culture, they've typically come to Canada to expose their children to new influences and opportunities. Acculturation is an explicit goal for many, and that includes exploring new tastes. Second, providing a better future for one's children tends to be a primary motivator for migration; as parents and kids confront the stresses of settlement together, migrants may feel indulgent toward their children: "We're all working hard at adapting—why deny them a small treat?" Third, pursuing new experiences as a family can be gratifying for newcomers in the Orientation phase. Migration is both stressful and stimulating; the sense of family togetherness and shared effort it engenders can be powerful. The altered rules of the new environment can also put children and adults on equal footing—or even give children the upper hand!—in a way that can produce fun and bonding.

3. A need for convenient solutions to overcome possible lack of skill in the kitchen

Many newcomers, especially those from Asia, cook much more after migrating than they ever did back home. One reason is that restaurant meals in both China and India are extremely cheap; eating out is an affordable part of the routine for many people.

More importantly, though, as we discussed earlier, many migrants from Asia have had considerable support in the kitchen prior to their arrival in Canada. Not only is domestic help more common and affordable, but extended family members are more likely to live together or close by and provide help in caring for children—and often this means grandmothers cooking for the busy young family.

One mother from China told us in a focus group that she tended to prepare about two meals per week before moving to Canada; the rest came from domestic helpers and grandparents. A newcomer from India told us that not only did she not have to chop vegetables in India, she rarely even poured herself a glass of water. So moving from either of these scenarios to a three-meals-a-day kitchen routine with minimal support from relatives—all with an unfamiliar set of grocery offerings—presents a major challenge. People who may have had little responsibility for feeding themselves now have to learn about ingredients and recipes, plan meals for the week, and in some cases even learn the basics of cooking—from boiling water on up.

Given the stress of this experience, it's hardly surprising that many newcomers welcome convenient solutions in the form of processed foods and frozen meals. To some Indian mothers, having a child ask for a frozen pizza instead of a lovingly prepared roti might feel like the end of the world; to others, on a busy Tuesday night in February, it can feel like a gift.

4. A need for some continuity with pre-migration experiences

Although experimentation and exploration may be important parts of the Orientation phase of settlement, familiarity is fundamental to most people's relationship with food—from tastes to cooking rituals to grocery shopping. As well, while kids may want to try new things and parents may want to join in the fun, some adults in the household may be less enthusiastic as they watch pizza bagels and chicken nuggets come through the front door.

Because of these dynamics, the newcomers responsible for shopping and cooking may find themselves balancing competing desires in their households: for exploration on the one hand, and for familiar tastes—and culinary cultural touchstones—on the other.

The Orientation phase isn't all fun

Canadian grocers are aware of newcomers' desire to balance old and new and have taken many steps to meet their needs, for instance by stocking products widely available in major migrant source countries. Retailers and CPG firms can bridge some of the simple product gaps, but in the end newcomers are buying and preparing food in a completely different environment: different climate, different infrastructure, different socio-cultural rhythms. Try as Canadian retailers might to ensure a full range of global ingredients, they simply cannot achieve the quality and freshness available in migrants' home countries (often considerably warmer than Canada, with totally different growing environments).

Moreover, the retail environment in many Asian contexts is completely different. Compare the daily trip to the "wet market" in China to buy vegetables, fish, and meat with the weekly stock-up at a Canadian supermarket. Compare buying atta unbranded at an open market or even direct from the flour miller with picking up a branded package at Walmart. Add to these differences the absence of support from extended family networks that migrants may have been used to before migrating, and it's easy to see why food retailers can replicate only a small proportion of the back-home food experience.

The people responsible for feeding the family (generally women) are doing a job that lies at the intersection of a lot of strong emotions (including nostalgia and homesickness). Trying to keep everyone fed and happy can be very stressful. Just one example: in many Indian households, it's a basic expectation that flat breads such as roti and chappati be made fresh daily. This practice is much more feasible in India than it is in Canada—which may or may not change family expectations. In other words, newcomers can find themselves trying to meet expectations for fresh and authentic food from their homeland in an environment where achieving this isn't easy.

Anxiety about the failure to meet family expectations—and, conversely, the deep satisfaction at meeting them—can be powerful emotions. Food marketers

"The people responsible for feeding the family (generally women) are doing a job that lies at the intersection of a lot of strong emotions, including nostalgia and homesickness. Trying to keep everyone fed and happy can be very stressful."

ATTA LOYALTY:
UNDERSTANDING GULFS IN ETHNIC CULTURE

Sometimes a product seems as though it should connect fairly easily with newcomers—but doesn't. When this happens, it's often because marketers haven't fully understood the nuances of the product category or the depth of migrants' attachments to their pre-migration practices. This is a challenge that has its roots in ethnic culture: the emotional, familial relationships most people have with food and household rituals.

For instance, Indians around the world (especially those from the Punjab) are heavy users of flour, which they use in homemade flat breads like roti and paratha. But although this large, flour-loving market may seem an excellent target for Canadian brands like Robin Hood, in fact it will be very difficult—maybe impossible—to persuade Indians to shift away from Indian-style atta. The fact that atta is essentially the same as products offered by Canadian flour brands is irrelevant.

Similarly, the fact that the Chinese are heavy consumers of soup doesn't necessarily represent an opportunity for Campbell in Canada, even if its product offering is adapted.

Marketers looking for opportunities to connect with migrant communities must solve two problems. First, they must determine whether members of the community are heavy users of the product category. If so, they must determine whether switching brands is a possibility—or whether something about the group's relationship with the category will be a barrier to change.

communicating to these consumers need to account for and address these emotions. Advertising by Real Canadian Superstore (a Loblaw company) aimed at South Asian Canadians does exactly that, reassuring the South Asian shopper that "all Daddy's favourite foods" can be found there and blessing the female shopper with approval from a visiting mother-in-law (a powerful figure in more than one culture, best known for exacting standards and disapproval).

The Belonging phase: Settled in some ways, still seeking in others

Following the Orientation phase, migrants enter the Belonging phase. At this point, grocery shopping and meal plans will be less experimental and the household will have settled on preferred stores, products, and brands. The routines and loyalties evident during Belonging will have been forged out of the experimentation of the Orientation phase: loyalty to brands that were present and helpful during that phase tends to remain strong.

The mindset of migrants at the Belonging phase is similar to that of the Canadian-born—but that doesn't imply complete assimilation. Migrants at the Belonging phase aren't likely to be shopping, cooking, and eating in exactly the way a multi-generational Canadian household might: they'll still be seeking out ingredients associated with the cuisines of their ethnic cultures. But they're no longer new to Canada or navigating an unfamiliar marketplace; they now resemble other Canadians in the stability of their routines, their openness to new products, and their interest in samples and promotions.

Besides some notable product preferences associated with traditional cuisines from their regions of origin, there's another important area in which migrants at the Belonging stage stand out from other Canadians: they continue to seek ways to bridge the gaps between Canadian cooking habits and the culinary demands of their ethnic culture—and any help they can get is welcome. For example, people responsible for meals in Indian households may no longer feel guilty about not making fresh roti every day. But they may be quite actively poking around South Asian grocery stores to see which of the frozen flat breads most closely approximate the fresh. Similarly, Chinese families may be accustomed to falling a bit short of the freshness standards that daily trips to the wet market allowed—but they might be quite dedicated to exploring the prepared and frozen foods at T&T (scallion pancakes, meat buns, savoury dumplings) to see which convenient options might act as passable substitutes for favourites from back home.

Opportunities lie in providing migrants at the Belonging phase with innovations that help them enjoy some of the tastes of home in a Canadian environment where shopping habits are different (and family routines are often more pressed, partly due to the lack of intergenerational support). At this stage of the Settlement Journey, less guilt and anxiety is associated with trying to replicate favourite flavours from home. Generally speaking, migrants at the Belonging phase have expanded their repertoire of dishes and have plenty of things they enjoy. Many have incorporated Canadian ingredients and dishes. They've steered their household through a new culinary environment and have a justifiable sense of competence and achievement. If they get a little help from the frozen-food aisle or a takeout box from T&T as they work to provide some authentic tastes of home, they feel they've earned it.

Settled in a Canadian kitchen, but not assimilated

To reiterate, Belonging does not imply assimilation. Our research shows that the majority of food prepared in Chinese and South Asian Canadian households, for example, are dishes from migrants' countries of origin. This is especially true of Chinese Canadians. The tendency toward food from home may diminish over time—but not much. We've found in numerous studies that a strong majority of meals prepared in Chinese-Canadian homes—including those led by people who've been in Canada for a decade or two—consist mainly of Chinese cuisine. Moreover, in a 2013 survey we found that roughly a quarter of Chinese Canadians, regardless of their tenure in Canada, rely on T&T and other Chinese grocery suppliers as their primary source of groceries (most others will supplement grocery trips to other stores with Asian specialty products from T&T or elsewhere).

Tastes can evolve, and children, as we've seen, will often nudge families toward popular Canadian foods, but taste preferences are formed early in life and are not easily altered. Nor is there an urgent need to change, since multiculturalism and the sheer diversity of Canadian communities make it practical and socially acceptable for people of all backgrounds to eat what they most like to eat.

Traditional food, new habits

In most migrant households, most food will continue to be of the kind associated with family members' ethnic culture. But with time in Canada, change does happen around the edges.

One example from our research into the eating habits of Chinese and South Asian Canadians: breakfast. The first meal of the day is the one where families are most likely to adopt foods that aren't traditional for them. Not only do children tend to be enthusiastic about sugary cereal, but lack of time in the morning also favours the kind of convenient foods (boxed cereals, yogurt cups, granola bars, and so on) that are prevalent in Canada. And unless you're coming from Britain (where it's said that to eat well you should eat breakfast three times a day), breakfast is unlikely to be a cherished part of your ethnic culture's cuisine.

Snacks are another area where many migrants adopt foods that aren't traditional or prevalent in their countries of origin. Snacks are a way of exploring new tastes and pleasing children without interfering too seriously with the family's core cuisine.

It's at the dinner table that the ethnic cuisine of the family is most likely to be maintained. The evening family meal is the heart of the day's food routine, and the meal for which the most time is dedicated to preparation. Even at dinner there may be compromises—depending on the availability of key ingredients or varying tastes across generations—but more than at breakfast or lunch (especially bagged school lunches), parents are likely to hold the line and serve food their own grandparents would recognize.

KRAFT DINNER MASALA:
ADAPTING THE PRODUCT ITSELF

There's probably no more iconic Canadian packaged food brand than Kraft Dinner. Like all top brands, it generates strong feelings among consumers. It's associated not only with convenience but also with comfort, childhood, and a kind of small-town simplicity that it leverages in its promotions, which are "Canadian Hockeyville" in tone and style. But although Kraft Dinner has a devoted constituency in multi-generational, culturally homogeneous Canada, this constituency is a diminishing part of Canada's demographic landscape.

Migrants haven't grown up with the blue-and-orange box in their pantries, and in many cases they aren't predisposed to the taste of original "KD." According to research we conducted for PepsiCo in 2011, 64% of the general Canadian population find cheese as a flavour "very appealing." But only 34% of Chinese Canadians agree (49% among second-generation Chinese Canadians born in Canada). Among South Asian Canadians, the proportion who find cheese flavour appealing (57%) is closer to the general population but still lower than the national average. These differences in palate (rooted in ethnic culture), alongside a lack of familiarity with the brand and even a lack of knowledge about how to prepare the boxed pasta (resulting from a total lack of pre-migration experiences with Kraft Dinner), represented clear barriers for the growth of the KD brand in Migration Nation. Kraft needed to find a way to encourage migrants to make KD part of their Settlement Journey in Canada.

Kraft went about this in two ways. First, it launched campaigns targeting Chinese and South Asian Canadians. Spokespeople Oliver Li and Smita Chandra were hired to speak to their respective communities and promote Kraft products in the kitchen through TV ads and other media. Kraft also built websites that appealed to Chinese and South Asian preferences and palates, while incorporating Kraft products. One notable recipe on the South Asian–focused Kraft Ka Khana website was for "KD Masala"—a formula for preparing Kraft Dinner with ingredients like garam masala and ground coriander. KD Masala epitomizes the "adaptation strategy" whereby core products and brands are adapted for continued relevance in a changing demographic and socio-cultural landscape..

> **"KD Masala epitomizes the 'adaptation strategy' whereby core products and brands are adapted for continued relevance in a changing demographic and socio-cultural landscape."**

Charitable Giving

Imagine you're a new migrant to Canada who attends church weekly. You always drop as much as you can spare into the collection plate because helping the poor is an imperative of your faith. This has always been your practice, back home and now in Canada. One day at work, a colleague approaches you and asks for money. You hesitate. Seeing your confusion, he explains that the money isn't for him. Next weekend he'll be riding his bicycle over a great distance. Somehow, he claims, this exertion (and your kind support!) will cure cancer or save an endangered species. Do you reach for your wallet or call security?

This kind of fundraising, a familiar experience for many Canadians, is by no means universal. Approaches to charitable giving vary around the world. All societies have ways of encouraging people to contribute to the common good, but the forms this encouragement takes depend on cultural factors as well as such institutional factors as the size and role of government and the activities of religious groups. According to the 2013 World Giving Index, Canada is tied for the second most giving society. So although newcomers to Canada may be extremely generous and civic-minded, they're arriving in one of the most formally charitably active societies on earth—and much of the machinery of Canadian giving may be unfamiliar to them.

THE CULTURAL LENS

When we try to understand migrants' Cultural Lenses as they relate to the offerings of the consumer marketplace, we consider their ethnic culture, the experiences they've had before arriving in Canada, and the environment they're encountering in Canada (including the stage they're at in their Settlement Journey). We apply the same tools for understanding migrants' Cultural Lenses onto the world of charitable giving. Indeed, when it comes to philanthropic activities, all three of these factors can be even more powerful than they are in the consumer world.

Ethnic culture: Religion and solidarity with people back home drive giving

In the case of charitable giving, one aspect of ethnic culture that strongly affects people's attitudes and behaviour is religious tradition. While three-quarters of the Canadian-born population have some religion affiliation, among migrants the proportion is slightly higher: 80%. The fastest growing religions in Canada are Muslim, Hindu, and Sikh—trends that clearly show the impact of immigration on the religious composition of the country. But even though migrants are only moderately more likely than other Canadians to have a religious affiliation, they're much more likely to participate actively in their faith. For instance, about a quarter of non-visible-minority Catholics (23%) attend mass at least weekly. Among two major groups of mostly foreign-born Catholics, attendance rates are nearly three times that high: two-thirds of Filipino-Canadian Catholics attend mass weekly, and a similar proportion of South Asian Canadian Catholics (67%) hit the pews as often.

The stronger religiosity of the foreign-born does a great deal to shape their charitable giving patterns. According to Statistics Canada's 2010 report, *Giving and Volunteering Among Canada's Immigrants*, migrants gave 50% percent of their total charitable donations to religious charities. By contrast, Canadian-born donors gave 37% to religious charities, while giving a larger share to charities related to health and social services. Four in ten migrants (41%) cited fulfillment of religious obligations or beliefs as one of their motivations for charitable giving, compared with a quarter (23%) of Canadian-born donors. In short, migrants are more religious, their religion is more likely to be their reason for giving, and religious organizations are more likely to be the beneficiaries of their generosity.

Although religion is clearly a powerful force in shaping migrants' attitudes and behaviour related to charitable giving, it's not the only aspect of ethnic culture that matters. Broader social values also have an impact. Ethnic cultures that emphasize collectivist values will produce different motivations for giving than will more individualistic cultures. As well, some societies are more fatalistic than others, while others believe more strongly in the power of human agency. If you're poor in one place, you might be seen as suffering as a result of forces outside your control and therefore deserving of help; if you're equally poor in another place, you might be seen as a lazy person receiving your just deserts.

One final and rather obvious way in which ethnic culture shapes people's giving habits is migrants' willingness to contribute to causes in their countries of origin. For many, these contributions go directly to family (see Chapter 6 for a discussion of remittances). For others, the desire to contribute to their societies of origin is a matter of more generalized solidarity. When the 2004 tsunami struck in South Asia, over 400,000 migrants from the affected societies (including India, Sri Lanka, and Indonesia) were living in Canada; many of these responded directly and also lobbied the Canadian government for matching support. In 2008, Chinese Canadians mobilized quickly and powerfully to raise money to help victims of the earthquake in Sichuan. And when Hurricane Haiyan hit in 2013, Filipino Canadians likewise mobilized money and other support, with the Canadian government offering matching funds to help with relief efforts. These are just three cases among many where ethnic diasporas in Canada have donated to—and attracted other Canadian support for—causes in their homelands.

So ethnic culture certainly plays a role in shaping people's attitudes and behaviours in the charitable arena—but here again, ethnic culture is only one of three aspects of the Cultural Lens migrants have onto charitable giving.

Pre-migration influences:
From communism to corruption, trust varies according to experience

Migrants from some cultures (Eastern Europe and the Caribbean, for example) arrive in Canada with relatively little experience of charitable institutions; understandably, they feel below-average levels of trust toward charities. (The Canadian-born can be skeptical, too, but their skepticism is likely to revolve around questions of the organizations' efficacy or the management of their finances—not a sense that those seeking support are hucksters.) Canadian nonprofits may not only suffer from migrants' lack of familiarity with Canadian-style charitable giving; they may also be running against other headwinds, including migrants' experiences of corrupt institutions in their countries of origin and even stigma about independent charities in communist or strongly socialist countries (where people are more likely to believe that the government should be doing whatever socially minded work needs doing). When communicating with newcomers who've had these kinds of pre-migration influences, Canadian charities are faced with the task of motivating donations (uphill work at the best of times) as well as the imperative to build familiarity with and trust in the very idea of the charitable sector.

It's notable that although some charities operate across borders, international promotional efforts in the nonprofit world are much different from those in the business world. Big Macs, Frappuccinos, consumer electronics, and other products are ferried around the globe by huge firms that have powerful incentives to

"Adults' exposure to charitable organizations may come through their children's schools and extracurricular activities."

break into new markets. Charities, of course, operate by different rules and with different motivations. While consumer environments in the world's major cities might be converging in some ways, charities tend not to have global scope (or global marketing budgets!) in the way major corporations do.

THE SETTLEMENT JOURNEY
Disorientation: Not much money or attention to spare

The pre-migration mindset of many newcomers isn't the only challenge facing charities seeking their support. The early phases of the Settlement Journey aren't an easy time to attract donations. Just as newly arrived migrants at the Disorientation stage are difficult for business to reach, they're difficult for charities to reach. Not only are they preoccupied with creating their new life in Canada, but they're typically cautious with their money as they seek employment and dedicate their savings to home-buying and other expenditures associated with settlement. We noted earlier that simplicity and convenience are important to people in the Disorientation phase because this first stage of settlement is such a confusing and overwhelming time. And since most charities must communicate complex messages about unfamiliar concepts (not just their missions, but the entire model of charitable giving in Canada, including tax benefits), they're unlikely to find a ready audience among recent arrivals.

Orientation: A time to build trust

As newcomers' immersion in Canada continues, Canadian influences will begin to temper their attitudes from the pre-migration period. As migrants develop more relationships with other Canadians and encounter public messages about charitable organizations and initiatives—and as they emerge from the overwhelming Disorientation phase—they're likely to become more open and curious about charities.

Most migrants will learn about charities through direct personal connections and experiences, gradually building up their trust in these organizations. As with many things during the early phase of settlement, adults' exposure to charitable organizations may come through their children's schools and extra-curricular activities; these pre-existing relationships are likely to bolster newcomers' sense that the charities are legitimate and trusted by other Canadians. School-based initiatives in particular tend to resonate easily with newcomers.

In addition to the charities they encounter through their children, newcomers are likely to come across organizations through their own efforts at settlement and personal development. Many migrants get to know the YMCA, for example, because of its newcomer support programs, especially those related to English

Charitable Giving

ETHNIC CULTURE

Strong influence: All societies have mechanisms for generosity but the channels—extended family, religious organizations, government, independent charities—vary.

PRE-MIGRATION INPUTS

Strong influence: The Canadian charitable sector is more formalized and less religious than those in many source countries.

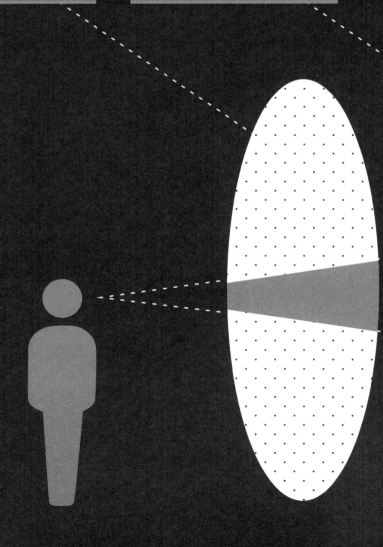

POST-MIGRATION INPUTS

Strong Influence: Openness to giving increases over time as migrants gain financial ground and build trust in the Canadian model of charitable giving.

CULTURAL LENS

Canadian charities cannot expect much from newcomers. But migrants grow more likely to give over time. Familiar and trusted organizations are likely to reap the benefits.

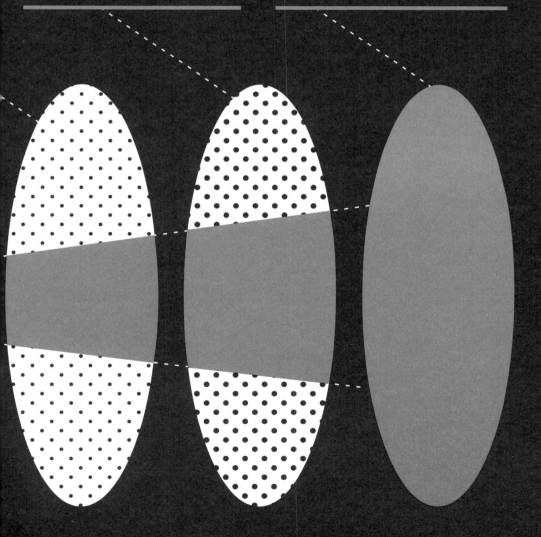

FIG. 4.1
Charitable giving increases markedly with tenure

Average annual charitable donations among immigrants, by tenure in Canada

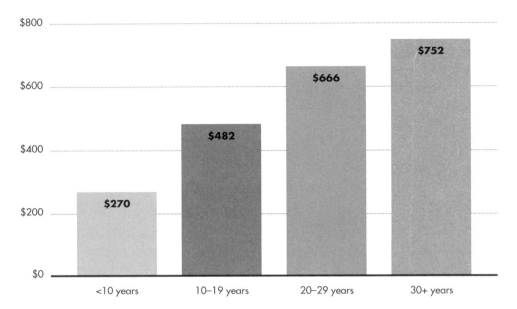

language learning. And like other Canadians, migrants are often exposed to United Way fundraising drives through their workplaces. In all these cases, a charity's association with a trusted institution such as a child's school or an adult's workplace can establish a basic level of trust that may eventually lead to an interest in charitable gifts. Donations are unlikely to come right away, however. Charitable giving is a habit that tends to develop at a later phase in the settlement journey.

According to Statistics Canada, the average amount donated annually by migrants who've been in Canada for under ten years is considerably lower than the average among the Canadian-born ($270 vs. $409). But after their first decade, migrants on average give *more* than other Canadians. Migrants who've been in Canada for ten to nineteen years give an average of $482 annually. And their generosity increases steadily throughout their tenure. Among those who've lived in Canada thirty years or more, average annual giving is almost double the average among the Canadian-born.

Aside from financial considerations and the unfamiliar Canadian charitable land-scape, there's another reason why many migrants will be slow to start contribut-ing to Canadian causes: many are already the benefactors of large kinship and community networks back home. At early stages of settlement, a strong aware-ness of the needs of their home communities can work in tandem with low levels of trust in Canadian charities, producing thinking along these lines: "This sports program for low-income kids might be a pretty good cause—I'm not sure—but I *know* this money would go a long way if I sent it back home to my sister's kids."

Belonging and Independence phases

As migrants' steadily rising donations suggest, their tendency to make charitable donations is influenced by discretionary income that increases with age and tenure in Canada. But for Canadian-born and foreign-born alike, the amount of money at one's disposal isn't the only factor affecting one's willingness to make charitable gifts. Social values, relationships with individuals and institutions, personal interests, and personal experiences all make a big difference. Did an organization help you at a difficult time in your youth? Did a hospital save your child's life? Do you like to kayak and therefore have a special interest in the health of your local waterways? Did your parents teach you to always give something—even if you couldn't spare much? All these considerations are powerful and have little to do with income. All come into play for both Canadian-born and foreign-born. In the case of the foreign-born, the phases of the Settle-ment Journey are one more influence on their ability and willingness to give.

Charitable donations aren't transactions with specific, tangible benefits in the way that purchases are, but they do confer benefits, including a sense of belonging and contribution, and a sense of emotional and even spiritual gratifica-tion. For migrants, intangible benefits related to social belonging can be espe-cially powerful. Contributing to causes in Canada can confer a sense of having "made it" that differs from the satisfactions of a high standard of living or even the success of an adult child. For those who become not just solidly middle-class but truly rich, a prominent donation (such as Jamaican-born Canadian Michael Lee-Chin's $30-million contribution to the Royal Ontario Museum, or twenty Italian families' collective gift of $10-million to the Art Gallery of Ontario) can be a way of highlighting not only one's personal success and contributions to the community, but the contributions of one's entire community. Contributing to a cause back home can also be a profound experience: it affirms and celebrates one's origins while making admirable use of the fruits of one's migration.

Those who enter the Belonging stage may have the financial latitude and the intellectual and emotional energy to think about and pursue these intangible rewards. But it's those who've reached the Independence stage who are most likely to be ready to really contemplate and appreciate the benefits of charitable giving. At the Independence stage, migrants have often accumulated a great deal of hard-won social capital and have forged an identity that is uniquely their own. It's during the Independence stage that people tend to reflect deeply on their relationship with Canadian society, their own ethnic diasporas, the factors that have shaped their development, and the legacies they'll leave behind for others. This mindset, along with increased financial security and greater trust in and familiarity with charitable organizations, combine to make charitable donations much more likely.

Still, in charitable giving as in all else, acculturation happens to everyone but does not lead everyone in the same direction. With more time spent in Canada, some migrants will become attached to Canadian causes and give locally. Others will give some in Canada and send some back home. Still others will remain keenly attuned to issues in their countries of origin and focus all their efforts there, appreciating their success in Canada but having a sense that their help is more badly needed elsewhere. Some migrants from developing nations, especially those that suffer from extreme poverty or conflicts, report a sense of guilt about enjoying a life of relative comfort in Canada while their compatriots (including friends and relatives) suffer. These feelings can cause them to tightly focus both activist and charitable efforts on their home countries. Such charitable giving patterns are not evidence of failure to integrate into Canada; these variations are inevitable results of the diversity of people's unique personalities, relationships, and moral reasoning.

Building trust as early in the Settlement Journey as possible

Nonprofit organizations seeking to attract donations from migrants need to be conscious of all three elements of the Cultural Lens through which migrants see charitable giving: their ethnic culture, their pre-migration mindsets, and their Canadian experiences (which encompass all phases of the Settlement Journey). Depending on the first two factors, some groups may arrive in Canada with a greater willingness to support charitable causes. But given the time it takes to get settled and feel financially secure, all groups—regardless of ethnic culture and pre-migration experiences—will probably be difficult to fully engage before the Belonging or (more likely) the Independence phase. Nevertheless, although the Independence stage may be the most fruitful for charities seeking donations, trust must be built up earlier, in the Orientation and Belonging phases. The most straightforward way to build trust is to be aligned with familiar and trusted institutions, which may be religious, educational, or associated with career guidance or mentorship. Finally, it's important to remember that while everyone has nuanced personal reasons for making the charitable donations they do, migrants have an especially delicate balancing act when it comes to expressing their multiple and overlapping identities, values, allegiances, and hopes for the future. As with all donors, understanding as much as possible about what drives them as individuals will enable stronger communication and deeper engagement.

Alcohol Beverage

In Japan, co-workers typically consume large quantities of sake or beer at Bonenkai, literally "forget the year" parties held in December. North American sporting events call for beer, while weddings call for champagne. In France, Italy, and Spain, a meal is not a meal without a glass of wine.

Just as food is a cornerstone of culture, in many cultures alcohol is a key part of social rituals—from big ones like weddings to quotidian ones like family meals. Alcohol is, of course, not just another beverage; it's also a drug. So over and above its status as food, alcohol is treated differently across cultures, depending on attitudes to things like personal indulgence and the shedding of inhibition.

Outside of Quebec, Canadian attitudes toward alcohol have historically been ambivalent: enthusiasm for the consumption of alcohol has struggled against an inclination toward temperance. In this way, Canada is similar to many Northern European societies whose values have been shaped by Protestantism. In these societies, alcohol is prevalent but treated with caution both legally and culturally. Although the official Canadian temperance movement of the early 20th century is long dead, it's left its traces in the relatively strict controls on where alcohol can be sold and consumed. Quebec's more relaxed approach to alcohol—both legally and culturally—arises from its French heritage and Catholic-influenced values.

THE CULTURAL LENS
Ethnic culture and pre-migration:
Less drinking overall, but Asian norms are changing

Most newcomers to Canada arrive from societies whose attitudes and behaviours regarding alcohol differ from those in Canada. These migrants' Cultural Lenses onto alcohol beverages are shaped by their ethnic cultures (deep-seated ideas about the role of alcohol, if any, in social life) and by the environments they've experienced prior to migration.

Most newcomers arrive from societies where alcohol is less prevalent than it is in Canada. According to the World Health Organization (WHO), the average Canadian aged fifteen and over consumed 8.1 litres of pure alcohol per capita in 2012. Canadians derive about half of their total alcohol intake from beer. Over three-quarters of Canadians (78%) have had an alcoholic drink in the past year, with men being only moderately (82%) more likely than women (74%) to say they'd bent an elbow.

The picture in major source countries of immigration to Canada is different. In China, alcohol consumption is lower than in Canada: 5.75 litres of pure alcohol per capita in 2010. The gender difference in consumption is markedly greater there, with one recent survey finding that in the previous year only 15% of women had had a drink compared with a majority of men (55.6%). Indian consumption is lower than either Canada or China, at 2.46 litres per capita (in 2010). According to the Indian Centre for Alcohol Studies, only a minority of Indians have at least one drink a year, with men being much more likely (30%) to drink than women (3%)—but with women embracing alcohol at a faster rate.

Despite the relatively modest levels of alcohol consumption in much of Asia, in this as in so many other aspects of life, economic growth is transforming the region's tastes and expectations. This is especially true in India and China. Although they don't sip wine and beer in the quotidian way of North Americans or Europeans, Asian consumers—particularly those in East Asia—are beginning to flex their muscles as consumers of premium spirits. Cognac houses like Remy Martin and Hennessy have long invested heavily in markets like Taiwan and Hong Kong and have been rewarded with strong sales, especially for their premium and super-premium brands. According to International Wine and Spirits Research, the Chinese market has been a vital growth area for the leading cognac houses over the past several years.

Chinese interest in high-end spirits extends well beyond cognac; purchases of Scotch whisky in China increased roughly tenfold between 2001 and 2011. China's growing middle class is interested not only in sampling the indulgences it can now afford, but in exploring the offerings of the world beyond China's borders. As a result, although domestic products account for most of the Chinese alcohol market, products with the cachet of heritage from abroad (such as Scotch whisky) are gaining ground. Tapping in to this demand for international beverage experiences, London-based drinks giant Diageo has invested heavily to create Johnnie Walker Houses in East Asia that act as showcases—"global embassies" in the firm's words—for their premium Scotch whisky brands. The first, a $3.2 million conversion of a Shanghai villa that opened in 2011, must have been well received, as the firm opened a similar facility in Beijing the following year, and a third in Seoul in the fall of 2013.

Indians haven't traditionally had the same appetite for high-end spirits, and cognac in particular, as East Asians. Nevertheless, India is the largest whisky market in the world and the second-largest spirits market. As in East Asia and Greater China, the growth in demand for premium spirits is disproportionately high in India, with the country's superrich starting to show the same enthusiasm for lavish alcohol spending as their Chinese counterparts. In 2012, in separate instances, two Indians bought two limited luxury edition bottles of Dalmore 64 Trinitas, worth £100,000 each. (India is also projected to have one of the youngest populations in the world over the next decade or so, which will contribute to an appetite for alcoholic beverages—although not every young adult out on the town will be in a position to splash out on six-figure bottle service.)

This strong and growing enthusiasm for spirits in Asian cultures might seem surprising. Even if Asian incomes are rising and consumers are now able to afford fine cognac and Scotch, why would newly middle-class people in China and India suddenly choose to spend their disposable cash on alcohol beverages that have traditionally played at best marginal roles in their ethnic cultures and social lives?

We think two factors are at work. One of these is the globalization of some strains of what might be called leisure culture; the idea of having an alcoholic beverage with friends has wider appeal. Even in Muslim-majority countries, where religious proscriptions against alcohol have meant that social drinking hasn't been widespread, sales of non-alcoholic beer have been growing rapidly over the last decade. *The Economist* reports that in Iran, non-alcoholic beer sales quadrupled between 2007 and 2012. The magazine suggests that the reasons are cultural: "As a statement of a globalised lifestyle beer, even if non-alcoholic, may be more potent than Coca-Cola."

Some of the increased market for alcohol in East and South Asia may also be driven by an interest in the "globalized lifestyle." But something else is also happening. The drivers of alcoholic beverage consumption in Asia differ from those in the West, which explains the different purchasing patterns in the two regions. Whereas North Americans drink relatively inexpensive products in such quotidian rituals as family dinners or an after-work beer with colleagues, in Asian societies, the demand for alcohol is driven more by the imperatives of status and hierarchy—hence the attraction to premium products. In China, it's common to "give face" with expensive spirits as gifts. In India, the purchase of alcohol for weddings is often more brand-conscious than it is in the West, with Johnnie Walker whisky being a star product. Elaborate toasting rituals and formalized exchanges of premium alcohol between employers, employees, clients, and associates all help to reinforce status hierarchies in Asian societies. Alcohol can also have status implications in North America—an expensive bottle of Scotch or champagne sends a message in Toronto just as it does in Beijing—but this dynamic tends to be stronger in Asian cultures. And it's the strength of that dynamic that makes Asian markets such attractive ones for those marketing premium and super-premium brands of alcohol beverages.

Alcohol Beverage

ETHNIC CULTURE

Strong Influence: Less consumption in many Asian societies, especially among women.

PRE-MIGRATION INPUTS

Changing Influence: High-end Western spirits increasingly play a role in reinforcing status hierarchies in rapidly growing Asian economies.

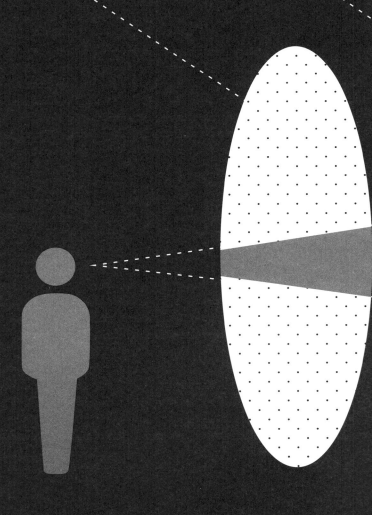

POST-MIGRATION INPUTS

Moderate Influence: Consumption increases moderately with time in Canada. Attraction to expensive spirits may be left behind.

CULTURAL LENS

Neither Canadian-style social drinking, nor Asian-style purchasing of premium products prevails. Marketers must find new ways to be relevant to migrants.

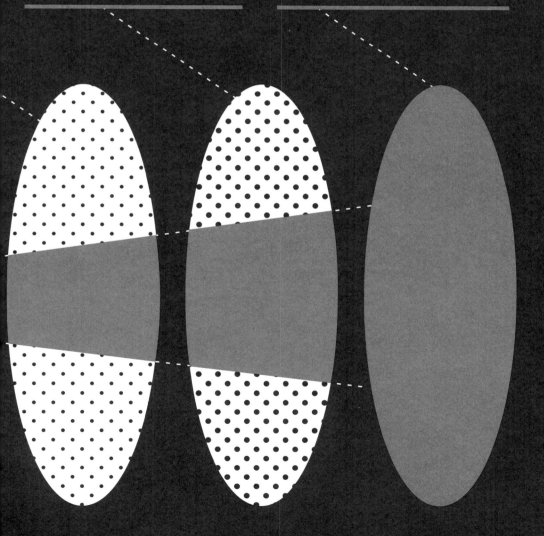

We saw in Chapter 3 that because Asian societies are changing so quickly, an Asian migrant arriving in Canada in 2013 will be travelling a different "cultural distance" than one who migrated from the same society a couple of decades earlier. With respect to alcohol beverages, this is true to some extent: among Asians who have migrated recently, their Cultural Lenses onto the alcohol beverage market in Canada will be influenced by a different set of experiences from back home. Still, while they may be arriving from societies in which alcohol-consumption levels are getting closer to those found in Canada, for most migrants the role alcohol plays in their home cultures and in Canadian culture will still be quite different. The drivers of alcohol purchase in Canada and in countries like China and India remain quite far apart. Consider how small a role status plays as Canadian consumers select a "two-four" to bring to a friend's place for a barbecue, or a $10 bottle of red wine to drink with a friend while watching a movie on the sofa.

Post-migration: Migrants don't get much thirstier with time in Canada

The key question for those marketing alcohol beverages in Canada is to what extent these pre-migration cultural and market traits shape behaviour as migrants land and settle in Canada.

According to Environics research, a little of the enthusiasm for drinking in Canada may rub off on newcomers: many will gamely raise a glass during social gatherings with colleagues or new friends (even if they only take a few sips). But self-reported rates of consumption suggest that Chinese and South Asian migrants tend to carry with them the relative lack of enthusiasm for alcohol beverages from their societies of origin. Research conducted by Environics in 2008 showed that the incidence of drinking alcoholic beverages is significantly lower among Chinese and South Asian Canadians than it is among the general population. According to Health Canada's 2011 Canadian Alcohol and Drug Use Monitoring Survey, 65% of all Canadians aged twenty-five or over had consumed some alcohol beverage in the past thirty days. By contrast, our research found that only 38% of Chinese Canadians and 32% of South Asian Canadians had done so.

The influence of ethnocultural norms comes through even more strongly when we look at alcohol consumption patterns by gender. In the general population, Canadian women are slightly less enthusiastic drinkers than their male counterparts. Still, Health Canada found that over half (57%) of Canadian women had consumed some alcohol beverage in the previous thirty days. This makes the average Canadian woman (an average that includes both the Canadian-born and foreign-born) almost twice as likely as Chinese Canadian women

(31%) and almost three times as likely as South Asian Canadian women (20%) to have had a drink in the previous month.

Those tasked with marketing alcohol beverages in Migration Nation may well be daunted by these numbers. This challenge of a growing, distinctly un-thirsty foreign-born population will be especially acute for the breweries that rely on young adults to consume large volumes of beer at bars, house parties, and public events. One response to this challenge is to simply wait and hope that the children of migrants (or those who migrate as children) will come to embrace Canadian-style drinking culture at the same levels as the general population. Such a change is not impossible—but a better approach than waiting and hoping is to develop a strategy rooted in an understanding of how and why these groups relate to alcohol beverages as they do.

As in other categories, familiar brands matter

In our discussion of food and consumer packaged goods, we described the advantage that international brands can enjoy with migrants to Canada when those migrants arrive from countries where the brands are well regarded. Without any special outreach in Canada, brands can benefit from the loyalty of migrants, who will happily snap up a detergent or chocolate bar they recognize and trust. This kind of advantage also applies to alcohol beverages: especially early in the settlement process, migrants will turn naturally to dominant brands from their countries of origin. Jamaicans will be attracted to Guinness. Chinese and Indian consumers will be drawn to the Western cognac and whisky brands that dominate in their home countries: Chivas Regal and Hennessy in China, for example, or Johnnie Walker and Teacher's in India. Aware of this dynamic, these brands have all made some investment in reaching migrant communities in Canada, mainly through tactical campaigns at festivals or on-site promotions. Teacher's Scotch Whisky's sponsorship of Cricket Canada, commenced in 2010, is an example of this kind of investment.

Consumption of high-end spirits: A casualty of the Settlement Journey?

If Canadian alcohol beverage marketers are discouraged by Asian immigrants' modest levels of consumption, they might well be heartened by news that high-end products are showing such strong growth in Asian societies. Are migrants from Asian countries like China and India holding on to the status orientations prevalent in their home societies, and can Canadian marketers appeal to those values in order to market premium spirits? If Chinese in China are splashing out on cognac and Scotch to show they know the good stuff and can afford to share it, might Chinese in Canada spend in similar ways?

The success of this strategy depends on whether migrants' values relating to status and hierarchy persist in Canada as they move through the stages of the Settlement Journey. Although many Asian migrants come from hierarchical societies, when they arrive in Canada they're immersed in a relatively non-hierarchical context. (Status hierarchies exist in all societies to some extent, but some societies emphasize and ritualize them more than others. Environics' Social Values research finds Canadians to be relatively egalitarian and anti-hierarchical in their values.) Migrants may retain many of the values of their home country, but they also absorb the norms around them—and their children do so even more.

As the importance of traditional status diminishes, the need to emphasize it in consumer behaviour declines. Our focus groups have found young Chinese consumers relieved that they no longer need to engage in hierarchical evenings out organized by their boss where heavy drinking of premium spirits is encouraged. They can relax and not drink if they don't want to. If they do drink, they can sip and enjoy the taste without worrying about offending anyone with what they do or don't imbibe.

Broadly speaking, migrants' values do tend to converge with those of other Canadians over time—and if high-pressure, high-end gifting involving alcohol is something people are rather glad to be free of (as opposed to other ceremonies and rituals they genuinely enjoy), they may well drift away from premium spirits as status markers. This means that many of the occasions that drive the volume of consumption of premium spirits in Asia will simply not exist in Canada. That leaves alcohol beverage companies needing to look more closely at how to engage and communicate with these consumers in order to ensure that whatever brand affinity they've brought from back home is leveraged in Canada.

Focus on context: Different social patterns mean different drinking habits

If migrants are unlikely to throw back beers at the hockey game as their Canadian-born compatriots do, and if they leave behind the spirits-purchasing habits of their countries of origin, what can marketers do to reach them? The first thing is to look at how alcohol is consumed. In many countries, alcohol beverages are much more closely associated with food. Of course, the Canadian-born also associate alcohol with meals, but beverage companies have relied to some extent on a young male demographic drinking at a bar or while watching sports or engaged in another leisure activity—not necessarily while sharing a meal.

Chinese beer drinking—including among young men—is more likely to take place at a restaurant over small shared dishes, not at a bar. And in China, as well as other source-country cultures like Brazil, buying beer at a restaurant tends to be a collective and social experience. Instead of everyone getting their own pint (the British way), large bottles of beer are purchased and shared in small glasses, the way several people at a table might share a bottle of wine. These habits are likely to persist even into the second generation and may gain traction with non-Asian millennials; sharing larger bottles of beer might even be seen as a variation on the move toward "small plates" in restaurants — where sharing and sampling are part of the pleasure of a meal together.

Brewers in Canada need to understand that their traditional communications may not be relevant given this frame of reference. The Yakitori Bar in downtown Toronto may provide a glimpse of the future of young adult drinking in Canada. The crowd is a mix of students from nearby University of Toronto, many of them large groups of young Asian international students alongside Toronto's young urban millennials. In some respects, Yakitori looks like many of the other pubs in Toronto. Coors Light is on tap and the Blue Jays game is on. But a closer look at the tables shows that the patrons may be sharing Korean fusion dishes or drinking soju cocktails. Many are drinking beer, but the way they're buying and drinking it is subtly different from what one might expect at a campus pub in a less ethnically diverse area or at a bar in monocultural rural Canada. This isn't an "exotic" environment, simply a place where Toronto's diverse young population can find something that suits them all. Companies promoting alcohol beverages in Canada need to attune to these cultural changes to ensure their product remains relevant.

Another contextual point to note has to do with the relationship between young South Asian men and their family networks. Of course young South Asian men will, like young men of other backgrounds, hang out with their buddies; the importance of social life with young age peers is fairly universal. But more of a young South Asian male's social life in Canada is likely to be spent with extended family. The weekend is more likely to find him hanging out with his cousins at a cross-generation family gathering than cracking open a two-four at a friend's place. The family gathering may also feature beer, but the context is different and the patterns of consumption will be different as well. To retain the business of an increasingly Asian-influenced youth market, brewers need to understand this new reality and communicate to these young Canadians in a way that speaks to the occasions and motivations they associate with the beer category.

Grocery Retail

For grocery retailers, adapting to Migration Nation means much more than offering the right flour for Indian papadams and the oyster sauce Chinese home cooks prefer. People who arrive from other parts of the world are not only used to different brands and produce, they're accustomed to entirely different shopping environments and distinct grocery-buying rhythms.

Wet market meets supermarket:
Chinese Canadians' pre-migration experiences shape Canadian retailers' offerings

Consider the experiences that migrants from Hong Kong, China, and Taiwan bring with them from Asian food markets, where modern grocery retail (in the form of supermarkets) has grown but is still fairly new. A large share of food purchases still take place at "wet markets," where fresh meat, seafood, and produce are sold. It's common for home cooks to make a daily trip to these markets, ensuring that the food they cook that day will be as fresh as possible. Western retailers entering the market in Greater China have struggled to make their proposition relevant in this context, where a weekly or bi-weekly stock-up trip (common in North America) is not standard routine.

In Asian societies, what North Americans might call takeout food plays a different role in families' domestic rhythms. It's common for Asians to purchase ready-to-eat food from markets, small restaurants, and street vendors. These vendors may be integrated into the grocery-buying context, operating more as a supermarket's prepared-food counter than the stand-alone fast-food restaurant North Americans might associate with the takeout category. Chinese-Canadian specialist retailers are well aware of this frame of reference. Some have designed their grocery retail experiences in a way that balances the pleasures of wet-market and food-cart shopping with some of the advantages (convenience and cleanliness, for example) of modern Western grocery retailing.

A visit to a T&T Supermarket gives insight into the distinct shopping model many East Asian customers expect based on experiences in their countries of origin. Canadian-born shoppers often marvel at the live fish available in T&T's seafood section—but the differences don't stop there. In most Western supermarkets, the first thing shoppers see as they enter is fresh produce. But at T&T it's ready-to-eat food, prepared on the premises, ranging from dumplings

FIG. 4.2

T&T the clear leader in Chinese grocery

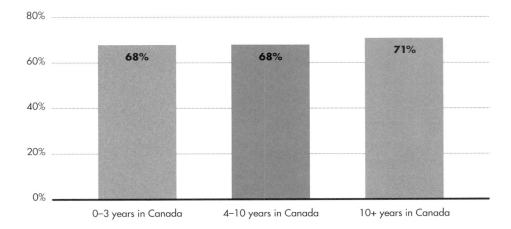

Proportions of Chinese Canadians who have visited T&T in last 3 months, by tenure

to barbecued pork to sushi. This setup mirrors the entrance to a wet market in China, where prepared food is available from small vendors. At T&T, the prepared-food section offers a familiar and enjoyable experience to the Chinese shopper, as well as food that can be purchased as a snack or to supplement a meal that's being prepared at home with regular grocery items.

Adjacent to the prepared-food section are the bakery and a large frozen-food section offering products similar to those available in the ready-to-eat section, such as frozen dumplings, scallion pancakes, and noodles. In Greater China these products are generally purchased fresh, but in Canada this frozen section offers a substitute.

Produce, which comes first in North American supermarkets, comes last at T&T. It's sold in a large, distinct section—arranged almost as a separate store.

In short, it's not only the products on offer but the flow of the entire shopping experience that's different at T&T—a store that successfully serves East Asian customers with a grocery experience similar to the ones they were accustomed to in their countries of origin.

Among Canada's migrant communities, the Chinese-Canadian community has by far the most developed specialty grocery retail environment: a result of the

FIG. 4.3
South Asian shoppers favour mainstream discount chains

Percent reporting visit in past 3 months

Ontario		British Columbia	
No Frills	**77%**	Real Canadian Superstore	**77%**
Walmart	**68%**	Safeway	**55%**
Food Basics	**52%**	Walmart	**48%**
Costco	**45%**	Save-On-Foods	**45%**
Shoppers Drug Mart	**45%**	Costco	**37%**
FreshCo	**42%**	Fruiticana	**37%**
Dollarama	**40%**	Shoppers Drug Mart	**28%**
Metro	**31%**	Dollarama	**28%**
Loblaws	**24%**	London Drugs	**27%**
Asian Food Centre	**24%**	Sabzi Mandi	**27%**
Sobeys	**23%**	Price Smart	**23%**
Fortinos	**20%**	No Frills	**19%**
Longo's	**19%**	T&T	**15%**
Real Canadian/Loblaws Superstore	**17%**	IGA/Foodland	**13%**
T&T	**14%**	Loblaws	**10%**

size of the Chinese-Canadian population, the length of their tenure, and the unique needs arising from the distinctiveness of their cuisine. Even after long tenure in Canada, most meals prepared in Chinese Canadian homes feature dishes and ingredients associated with Chinese ethnic culture—hence tenured immigrants' sustained patronage of specialty ethnic shops like T&T.

T&T is obviously the leader in Chinese grocery. According to our research, about 7 in 10 Chinese Canadians in B.C. and Ontario have visited a T&T store in the past three months. It's the store that Chinese Canadians are most likely to use as their main grocery store (25% do). But it's not the only game in town. The Foodymart Corporation has eight locations in Ontario, and gives T&T a run for its money; a quarter of Chinese Canadians in the Greater Toronto Area have visited one in the past three months. Oceans Fresh Food, meanwhile, has three GTA locations. Of course, these chains are complemented by many independent stores across the country.

South Asian Canadian grocery:
Still under construction, with a big gap between pre-migration and post-migration experiences

Food-shopping experiences in South Asian societies are also very different from the North American supermarket model. Although Western-style grocery retail is making inroads in parts of South Asia, it's even less common there than in China and other East Asian countries. (According to *The Economist*, less than 10% of grocery sales take place in "organized" shops in the style of North American supermarkets. Small, family-run stores dominate the grocery retail market for now, thanks in large part to government regulation.) The result is that migrants arriving in Canada from South Asian societies are likely to find their local supermarket even more jarring and unfamiliar than do their fellow migrants from, say, China. For many newcomers, the confusion of the supermarket is compounded by the fact that they may have had domestic helpers to do grocery shopping in their countries of origin. Perhaps because of these dynamics, South Asians on average make fewer trips to the grocery store but buy more when they go.

One distinctive characteristic of how South Asian newcomers shop for groceries is that men are more likely to be involved. It's common for a male head of household to migrate to Canada first and begin the process of establishing a life. Once he's settled to some extent, his wife and children will join him. And in families that have settled this way, the husband frequently acts as a guide to the routines of Canadian life. Even if the migrants' ethnic cultures may view feeding the family as women's work, in cases where men have come early to blaze the settlement trail, it's common for the grocery store to be a place

Grocery Retail

ETHNIC CULTURE

Strong Influence: Many cultural influences affect shopper behaviour. These include gender roles, attitudes to pricing, and the role of prepared foods versus ingredients for cooking at home.

PRE-MIGRATION INPUTS

Strong influence: Retail environments and shopping habits differ significantly. Specific features vary by society (e.g. home delivery in India, wet markets in China).

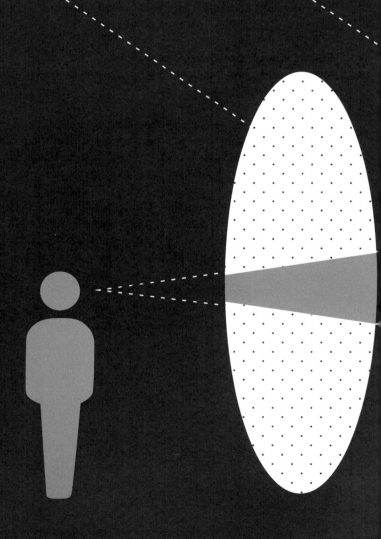

POST-MIGRATION INPUTS

Fluctuating Influence: After various phases of exploring new products and seeking out favourites from home, migrants usually find a repertoire of shops that meet their needs in various categories

CULTURAL LENS

Preferences for familiar shopping experiences are moderate, but ethnic culture drives strong demand for specific products/ingredients. Migrants experiment for months or years, seeking the right mix.

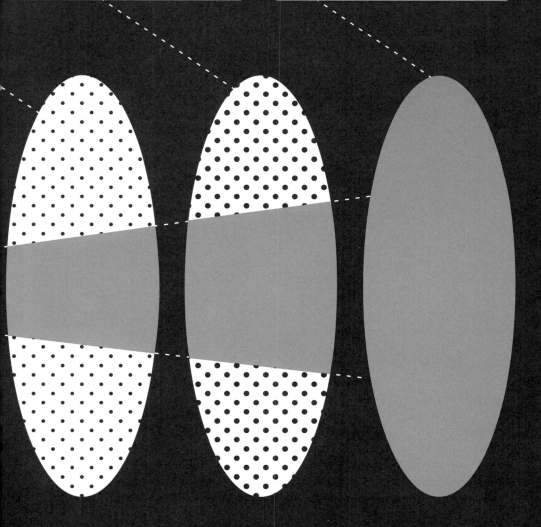

where men participate actively, helping their families navigate and adapt. For instance, in research we conducted in 2013, we found that in 56% of South Asian households in Canada, men bear either primary or partial responsibility for grocery shopping. Among newcomer households—in Canada for less than five years—the number is even higher: 72%. These are remarkable levels of male participation in grocery buying.

Like migrants from China, migrants from South Asia have expectations—both about products and about the grocery shopping experience—that have been shaped in another market. But South Asian–inflected grocery retail remains underdeveloped in Canada relative to Chinese-style offerings. Independent stores carry South Asian products, and there are even some regional banners with multiple locations, such as Sabzi Mandi Supermarket in British Columbia and Asian Food Centre in Ontario. But South Asians in Canada don't have anything on the scale of T&T to reliably bring them both the flavours and the food-shopping rhythms of home.

There are two reasons for this. First, Canada's large South Asian population is newer; Chinese migrants have been established in large numbers for longer. The second reason has to do with the nature of South Asian shopping norms. On one hand, these migrants' grocery expectations are sufficiently similar to those of other Canadians on many dimensions that they can be reasonably well accommodated by existing retailers, with moderate adjustments. On the other hand, where South Asian grocery norms do markedly differ from those in Canada—home delivery, for example, and bulk offerings of unbranded products like spices—they'd be impractical for Canadian retailers to replicate.

Will we see a South Asian T&T? It is difficult to tell. Even where a specialty South Asian grocery does exist, it doesn't always attract strong loyalty. Although specialty ingredients are important, for the bulk of their trips and needs, many South Asian grocery shoppers have been thoroughly won over by mainstream discount and general merchandise banners such as No Frills and Walmart in Ontario, and Real Canadian Superstore, Costco, and Walmart in B.C.

THE SETTLEMENT JOURNEY
Seeking made-in-Asia products, made-in-Canada retail experience

Throughout this book, we describe the three elements of the Cultural Lens through which migrants see the Canadian marketplace: their ethnic culture, their pre-migration experiences, and their post-migration experiences, including their Settlement Journey. In the case of retail, pre-migration experiences set expectations about grocery shopping and the Settlement Journey adjusts those

HIGH BRAND LOYALTY ≠ LOW PRICE SENSITIVITY

Marketers sometimes make the mistake of believing that because a consumer is brand loyal he or she isn't sensitive to price. But this isn't always the case—and newcomers to Canada offer an excellent example of a mindset that decouples the two. For reasons we described earlier in this book (high trust in specific global brands, belief that private labels are a last resort for those who can't afford better), brand loyalty is often very high among newcomers. At the same time, newcomers are above average in their price sensitivity. Environics' Social Values research shows that migrants who've been in Canada for ten years or less score high on the value *Importance of Price*. Sticker shock compounds this pre-existing sensitivity: about four in ten Chinese and South Asian immigrants (41% in a combined sample) say that their day-to-day living expenses in Canada are higher than they'd expected before migrating.

A shopper may, for instance, favour Tide detergent and shun lower-cost alternatives. But that doesn't mean he'll buy Tide at any price; he may watch like a hawk for sales, and stockpile Tide when the per-unit price goes down. This is a case of acute price sensitivity and strong brand loyalty working in tandem—and it's a phenomenon that occurs more frequently among migrants than among other Canadians.

It's no coincidence that discount grocery stores like No Frills and low-cost general merchandise stores like Costco and Walmart are popular among newcomers (as we discussed in the Food and Consumer Packaged Goods section). One reason for their success is that they enable consumers who are brand loyal and price-sensitive to stock-pile favourite brands at relatively low cost. The fact that migrant households tend to be larger than those of non-migrants also makes pantry stocking and bulk purchasing more attractive. The average Canadian household has 2.5 people, whereas the households of foreign-born people who've been in Canada for less than twenty years have over three people on average.

Why are migrants more price-sensitive than other Canadians? The most obvious reason is that they may need to be. Recent migrants—and even more settled ones—tend to have lower incomes on average than the rest of the population (despite higher levels of education). But labour market struggles may not be the only factor. Depending on their countries of origin, newcomers may bring with them a sense that frugality is an admirable character trait in itself. These factors, as well as the fact that migrant earners tend to have more mouths to feed (more kids and sometimes live-in grandparents), combine to make migrants more likely than other Canadians to look for the deals that enable them to keep buying their favourite brands without ringing up too large a bill.

expectations. Often this process is relatively painless; many migrants even prefer Canadian shops to the retail environments they experienced in their countries of origin.

But it's not all smooth sailing for newcomers in the grocery aisles. For all of us, food is deeply connected to our ethnic culture; there's simply no substitute for the foods and ingredients we've learned to find pleasurable. While many migrants quickly feel comfortable with the shopping experiences (and especially the discounts) big chains offer, their desire for food from home won't simply subside as they spend time in Canada and proceed through the stages of the Settlement Journey. And when it comes to many specialty ingredients, big chains are not yet a reliable source.

So, although Chinese and South Asian Canadians are typically seeking different ingredients associated with the cuisines of their respective ethnic cultures, they show a similar pattern of behaviour when it comes to grocery shopping: both groups turn to a combination of ethnic specialty shops and mainstream retailers to achieve the right balance of products, brands, prices, and shopping experience.

For South Asian shoppers, trips to ethnic shops are usually triggered by the need for specific product categories (like atta and South Asian sweets) in which retailers from their own ethnic cultures have a better range of offerings. But South Asian shoppers tend to try to minimize the number of items they buy at specialty stores, preferring to get as large a proportion of their groceries as possible at mainstream stores, often discount chains. South Asian Canadians in particular tend to be less trusting of South Asian specialty grocery shops than they are of mainstream retailers. In our research, we often find South Asian Canadians expressing doubt about the quality of products, the expiration dates, and the cleanliness of the specialty stores they visit. Trust is, of

---

"For all of us, food is deeply connected to our ethnic culture; there's simply no substitute for the foods and ingredients we've learned to find pleasurable."

FIG. 4.4
Chinese Canadians make more grocery trips

Basic trip types by ethnicity

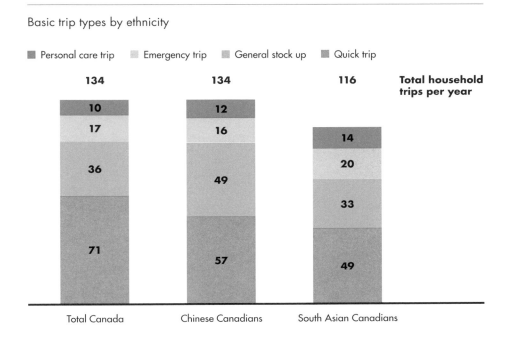

course, essential to building loyalty in retailing. So the trust gap that's currently a deficiency for many small South Asian retailers represents an opportunity for mainstream grocers, and perhaps even for a South Asian T&T.

Like South Asian shoppers in Canada, Chinese shoppers turn to ethnic shops for specialty products and use mainstream retail to meet some of their needs. Many first-generation Chinese Canadians distribute their shopping trips between specialist Chinese grocery stores (for specific ingredients) and mainstream, often discount stores for household goods and non-Chinese staples like milk. On average, Chinese shoppers are more at ease getting the bulk of their groceries from Chinese shops—but this group also harbours some doubts about ethnic specialty shops, both because of quality concerns and because mainstream shops are often seen as offering better value. In focus groups, for instance, we've heard Chinese shoppers claim that while they need to buy meat at T&T because it has the right cuts, they'd prefer to buy at mainstream grocery stores. One of the reasons for this lack of trust is the sense that these stores, even established chains, are still outside the mainstream and don't necessarily adhere as closely to the high standards that have become firmly ingrained in large North American retailers.

Not all of these quality concerns may be rooted in experiences of Canadian ethnic specialty retail. Memories of retail experiences in their home countries may cause some migrant shoppers to assume that grocers in Canada who hail from their countries of origin may have simply transplanted practices and standards from back home. Perceptions of a quality difference between mainstream North American retailers and specialty retailers will likely diminish over time, but for now they represent a weakness for ethnic retail and an opportunity for mainstream retail.

Different shopping trip types

Environics' research has found that most households take two kinds of grocery trips: quick trips and stock-up trips. Quick trips are more frequent, occurring about six times per month. The average quick trip lasts twenty minutes and rings up a bill of about $40. It fills in staples, most commonly milk, fresh produce, and bread or other baked goods. Stock-up trips are less frequent and more comprehensive. Occurring about three times per month, the average stock-up trip takes forty-five minutes and costs $130. On these trips, shoppers tend to acquire the same items as they do on quick trips, as well as meat, fish, and packaged goods.

Chinese and South Asian Canadian shoppers differ from Canadian averages in a couple of ways (see Figure 4.4). The dollar value of the average Chinese grocery trip is generally higher, driven by the larger average size of Chinese Canadian households. According to estimates by Environics Analytics, the average number of residents in a Chinese-Canadian household is 3.18, as compared with 2.5 for the general population. It makes sense, then, that Chinese Canadians spend about 9% more per week on groceries than the average shopper in Toronto and Vancouver. (This latter finding is from research conducted in 2008 by Solutions Research Group Consultants, which found that the average Chinese-Canadian grocery spend was about $136.) Research conducted by Environics in the same year illustrated the shopping behaviour behind this higher spending. Although Chinese-Canadian households take the same number of shopping trips in total (134 in the year), they take fewer quick trips and more stock-up trips. While the average Canadian household takes three stock-up trips per month, the average Chinese-Canadian household takes just over four. This disparity is driven by the larger household size as well as the likelihood of visiting multiple stores—both mainstream and ethnic grocery.

South Asian Canadians make fewer trips—especially quick trips—despite relatively large household sizes. Although the number of general stock-up trips they make is similar to the general population's, South Asian Canadians make only forty-nine quick trips in a year compared with the general population's seventy-one. One of the factors behind this is South Asian Canadians' reliance on large-format, mainstream banners, particularly discount stores like No Frills or general merchandise stores like Walmart. Even as newcomers, this population quickly adopts the stock-up shopping behaviour common in North America. They're not as reliant on ethnic grocery banners as are Chinese Canadians, and they tend to make fewer quick, ethnic-specific trips.

Retailers in search of their next move

The challenge for grocery retailers is, of course, to capture as many grocery trips as possible by stocking their shops with the right items at the right price. Deciding which products to stock is a central concern for any grocery retailer. But when a store's trade area contains multiple ethnic cultures, each with distinct tastes, habits, and preferences, the puzzle of what to stock becomes much more complicated.

The business environment for retailers in Canada is highly competitive, and their margins are thin. They rely on loyalty and can't afford to lose the slightest shopper traffic. Maybe more than any other business in Canada, they need to engage Migration Nation—but the knowledge gap they face is a challenging one. While focusing on the needs of one ethnocultural group may be viable for a small specialty store, it won't be for larger players. Serving only a narrow slice of the population—however well—will tend to inhibit growth for those seeking to build a national business from a particular ethnic base. So the Canadian retailer needs to develop a broad understanding of the range of ethnic groups across the trade areas in which its stores are located. Retailers need to develop a fairly detailed understanding of relevant migrant cuisine, which elements are adaptable, and which are non-negotiable. What role does atta, the flour used so frequently by Indian families to make flat breads, play in planning shopping trips in Canada? What about the cooking sauces used in Chinese cuisine? Fresh produce is clearly of universal importance, but which fruits and vegetables are essential to which groups? Which mainstream Canadian products will migrants wish to experiment with, and which are non-starters?

Ideally, retailers need to strive for a sweet spot where they primarily cater to "mainstream" tastes while offering just enough specialty product to attract the most populous minority groups in their areas. As we've argued throughout this book, however, in Migration Nation, mainstream is not a simple concept. If your store is in a trade area where almost half the population was born in East Asia, which products are your core offering, and which are specialty items? In some neighbourhoods, those seeking breakfast cereal and frozen pizza are a specialty market, while those seeking fresh dumplings or atta are mainstream.

As time goes by, this challenge will only grow muddier: the Canadian-born are ever more international in their food tastes, and many migrants (typically coaxed by their children) slip into the convenience routines of the North American kitchen, including processed frozen foods. Retailers more than any other business need to understand acculturation patterns. Why invest heavily in meeting ethnic preferences if those preferences are rapidly changing?

Currently, the ethnic food business in Canada is up for grabs. Traditional small-format ethnic stores are being challenged by slicker operations like T&T and Oceans. They in turn are challenged by mainstream players—especially the discount grocery and general merchandise banners that increasingly offer a diverse selection of products. A recent development in Ontario is multi-ethnic banners that are serving a combination of large ethnic groups. Al Premium Food Mart in Scarborough, Ontario, and Galleria Supermarket in Toronto are both examples of "ethnic" stores that cater across ethnicities to Chinese, South Asian, Filipino, and other groups. Nations Fresh Foods recently opened a store at Jackson Square Mall in Hamilton, Ontario, with the slogan "Where East meets West"; Nations is explicitly positioned as the store for Migration Nation.

Grocery retail is extremely dynamic, and the pace of change is unlikely to let up. Online ordering, U.S. entrants to the Canadian market, high levels of cross-border shopping, and many other factors are at play. The rapidly changing ethnic composition of the Canadian population is yet another factor that retailers need to develop strategies to address.

Telecoms

Students of psychology will recall Abraham Maslow's hierarchy of human needs: a prioritized list of the things that sustain human life. The hierarchy moves from fundamentals like air, water, food, and shelter at the bottom to higher-order needs like morality, problem-solving, mutual respect, and a sense of meaning at the top. A parody of Maslow's famous hierarchy circulated online recently; this one had a new bottom rung, even more fundamental to human life than air: WiFi.

Although this meme was a slight exaggeration, wireless technology is now pretty fundamental to basic functioning in North America—not least for new-comers, who urgently need internet connections and mobile phones to manage their many early settlement tasks, such as finding somewhere to live, map-ping routes to local shops, managing their new bank accounts, and seeking employment resources. Along with day-to-day banking, wireless services are among newcomers' most immediate needs. For this reason and many others, new arrivals present a clear opportunity to Canada's telecom providers.

THE CULTURAL LENS

How best to connect with recent arrivals? Like firms in other industries, telecoms need to bear in mind the three elements that make up migrants' Cultural Lenses: ethnic culture, pre-migration experiences, and the Settlement Journey. In partic-ular, understanding the Disorientation phase of the Settlement Journey will help providers orient themselves to newcomers' needs and priorities.

Ethnic culture: A relatively weak influence

Wireless products and services are sufficiently new that people's predispositions to them aren't heavily influenced by traditional ethnic culture. Our ethnic cultures certainly shape our outlooks on related matters like work, relationships, and even technology in general. But unlike, say, our food customs, our mobile-technology tendencies aren't flavoured by previous generations' habits and preferences, given that the wireless landscape is new to everyone. Ethnic culture has an influence around the edges; for instance, soon after Apple re-leased its iPhone5S, reports emerged that the model with a gold-coloured exterior was flying off the shelves in China, where gold is seen as an auspi-cious colour. In general, however, ethnic culture is less salient in the wireless industry than it is in many other product and service categories.

Pre-Migration wireless experiences:
In many countries, better and cheaper than in Canada

If ethnic culture isn't an important influence on our attitudes and behaviours toward technology, why is one of the main Chinese malls in Toronto, Pacific Mall, ground zero for innovative wireless technology and accessories? Chinese engagement with wireless innovation has more to do with the fast-moving wireless market in China than with cultural factors. Newcomers' Cultural Lenses onto wireless products are strongly influenced by the commercial environments they experienced prior to migration. In many of the major source countries of migrants to Canada, the wireless environment is much more advanced than the market people encounter when they arrive here. China is certainly one instance of this phenomenon.

Unlike financial services, where the pre-migration frame of reference is often a less developed market, for wireless and telecom services the frame of reference is in many cases a more developed one. Industry analysts at Canalys projected that Brazil, Russia, India, and China (BRIC countries) would account for over 70% of all smartphones shipped in 2013, and that China alone would account for 29%. Many newcomers to Canada are therefore coming from highly dynamic wireless markets. These are markets that are leapfrogging the West on a range of wireless consumer behaviours, from "social shopping" to openness to mobile wallet technology. According to a Worldpay 2012 survey, 17% of Canadian disposable income is spent online, as compared with 31% in China and 33% in India. And whereas in Canada 11% use a smartphone for online purchases, in China and India the figures are 46% and 40%, respectively.

"Unlike financial services, where the pre-migration frame of reference is often a less developed market, for wireless and telecom services the frame of reference is in many cases a more developed one."

Post-Migration wireless experiences: A step backward

As most of us have experienced, once you develop a convenient wireless habit, like banking with a handy app, it's frustrating to have to go back to the old way of doing things. Newcomers arrive in Canada with a strong desire for the full range of wireless services they used before migrating. Their expectations are often higher than those of the Canadian-born—and those expectations frequently go unmet. This isn't a new phenomenon. Newcomers from Hong Kong in 1990s had to wait until 2001 before getting the same GSM network in Canada that they'd had at home. The Philippines is known as "Text Capital of the World" because the affordability of SMS messaging there has led to a huge volume of messages being sent: 1.39 billion were being sent daily in that country in 2009. Filipinos are therefore shocked to arrive in Canada and see relatively low adoption of text messaging, not to mention mobile plans that charge users for every text message they send. The texting habit is hard to break: research conducted by Environics in 2012 showed that Filipino Canadians are spending an average of $91 per month on wireless services, as compared with $50 per month among the general population.

Newcomers tend to be careful about their spending across all categories; their employment situations are often unsettled and they're trying to make their savings last until they find their footing. But this tendency toward financial caution is compounded when it comes to wireless services, since many newcomers will have the sense of spending more for inferior service and will therefore be even more vigilant about protecting themselves. Confusing service agreements and the difficulty of comparing different firms' offerings can result in still more caution.

THE SETTLEMENT JOURNEY
Disorientation: Just get me connected

Getting telephone and internet access is a vital first step that enables newcomers to pursue other settlement goals, such as navigating their new city and finding work. They need to get set up quickly; as with banking, they're seeking a solution that's fast, convenient, and covers all their essential service needs. This may sound like a simple goal, but any established Canadian who's struggled to understand their own wireless plan can imagine the difficulty newcomers face in making similar evaluations, often in a language that is not their mother tongue and having recently arrived from a totally different market context. The urgency of newcomers' need for telecom services, combined with their often high expectations about the availability of affordable services (based on pre-migration experiences), creates a very specific newcomer mindset for the telecom category. The consumer mindset at this time is one of distrust and general confusion ("Why am I paying for services that were free in my home

Telecoms

ETHNIC CULTURE

Weak Influence: Wireless tech
and gadgets are too new for cultural
traditions to have much effect.

PRE-MIGRATION INPUTS

Strong influence: Many migrants
arrive from source countries with great
enthusiasm for technology and high
adoption rates. Pre-migration wireless
service is often better and cheaper.

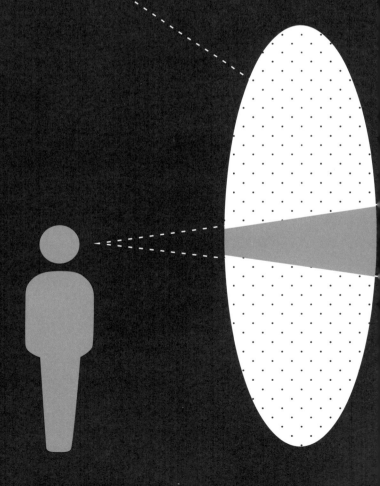

POST-MIGRATION INPUTS

Strong Influence: Newcomers are jarred—especially during Disorientation phase—by higher fees and costs, demanding service agreements, and complicated plans.

CULTURAL LENS

Upon arrival, newcomers are keen on connectivity but seek low-cost, low-commitment options. As the Settlement Journey unfolds, many adopt the same services other Canadians use.

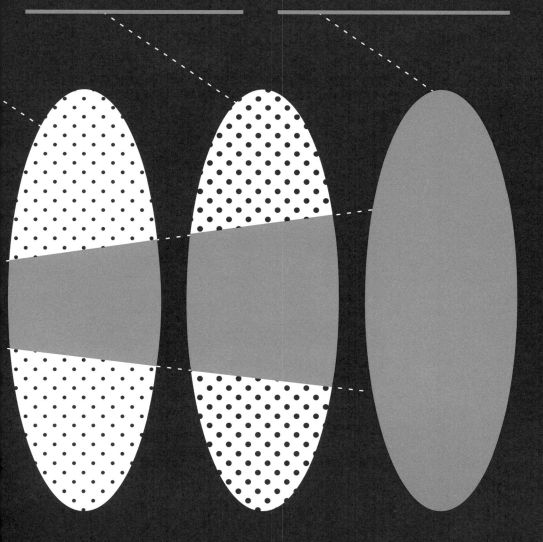

country? Am I getting a good deal? You want me to sign a contract for *how long*?"). So, as with banking, the needs arising from this frame of mind are simplicity and reassurance. Newcomers tend to rely on word of mouth at this stage. And given the high level of technical knowledge in many migrant communities, savvy advice isn't hard to find.

The wireless market is currently divided into three main offerings, two of which (numbers 1 and 2 below) are reasonably well matched to newcomers' mindset and needs at the Disorientation stage:

1. Low-cost providers, represented by recent entrants to the Canadian market such as Wind and Public Mobile. These offer cheaper plans and no-contract service—both desirable features for newcomers.

2. Value brands provided by the larger Canadian players like Fido (provided by Rogers) and Koodo (provided by Telus). These are essentially competing with the new entrants and should represent a similar proposition: simplicity, value, and limited need for credit history.

3. Premium brands like Telus, Rogers, and Bell that offer the latest devices and a fuller range of services, including bundled offerings with television and internet service. Given the relative complexity of the plans as well as their higher cost, these are more suited to migrants who've reached the Belonging or Independence stage.

The low-cost providers and value brands described in 1 and 2 weren't designed for newcomers and haven't invested too heavily in attracting them. Nevertheless, because they're structurally well adapted to newcomers' needs, they're successfully capturing business from newcomers and large segments of migrant communities. The key factors that differentiate them are the simplicity of their terms (no credit checks, no long-term commitments) and their competitive pricing. Low prices succeed in two ways among migrant communities. First, lower prices, combined with greater transparency about fees, appeal to newcomers who are accustomed to more affordable services back home. Second, even setting aside the actual cost, some newcomers arrive from societies that place high value on deals and discounts; for them, getting a bargain on a must-have service is especially desirable.

Low-cost telecom providers connect with newcomers in a number of ways. They use dealers that are well established in specific ethnic communities; they operate out of kiosks in shopping malls in neighbourhoods with high concentrations of migrants; and they develop targeted offers, including general-value propositions

A CANADIAN MARKET—BUT A GLOBALIZED CONSUMER

The foreign-born population introduces global influences into the Canadian market in many industries. And in the wireless and telecom industry, they amplify a global influence that's already strong. From a consumer perspective, this industry is already global—devices are launched and used across the world, and device brands and software providers are widely familiar. Service providers, however, are local, and it's this disjunction between global technology and local service that creates a tension. New devices available in other markets sometimes come late to Canada, and sometimes cost more here than elsewhere. So to many Canadians, the wireless service providers look like they're resisting globalization. There's a persistent belief that more competition from foreign companies in Canada would benefit consumers. In fact, Canadians' tendency to compare domestic providers with those outside the country is so strong that in 2013 the Canadian Wireless Telecommunications Association produced ads that defended its members' prices by arguing that they compare favourably with those in the U.S.

The foreign-born population isn't just a segment to be targeted through ethnic media; they're a driving force in a dynamic industry, a portal to advanced practices in other parts of the world. The line between the attitudes of foreign-born Canadians and the young urban Canadian-born population is blurred. Trends introduced from Asia into the Canadian market can and do spread—it's not only Chinese Canadians who'll travel to the small Chinese-run stores at Toronto's Pacific Mall for smartphone accessories or services. So any company operating in this sector needs to know that addressing the needs of multicultural consumers by being aware of their global influences will give it a competitive advantage within the entire Canadian market. Conversely, ignoring the preferences and expectations of foreign-born consumers can cause damage with a much wider swath of the Canadian population.

"The foreign-born population isn't just a segment to be targeted through ethnic media; they're a driving force in a dynamic industry, a portal to advanced practices in other parts of the world."

like unlimited plans and offerings that focus on contact with particular regions of origin, such as Wind's "World Saver International Talk and Text" and Mobilicity's "Asia Super Saver Long Distance." These approaches, alongside some small-scale, low-cost tactical communication in ethnic media and around key festivals, leave low-cost telecoms well positioned to attract newcomers.

Cultivating relationships in a churning industry

Such moderate investments in newcomer outreach offer a decent return — but not a spectacular one. Telecom providers don't get as much bang for their buck as banks do when they succeed in building the "first relationship" with new arrivals. If a bank can attract that first chequing account, it may well cultivate a highly rewarding lifelong relationship that includes mortgages, investments, and credit products. The lifetime value of a new wireless customer is not as high. This is one reason why some of the higher-cost outreach practices we see among the banks — such as targeting newcomers on arrival and even pre-arrival — may not be considered viable in the wireless market.

Another factor that causes banks and wireless providers to navigate the new-comer market differently is the huge stability gap between the two industries: the Canadian banking industry is staid and reliable, while the wireless industry is in a constant state of flux. The composition of the industry itself is unsettled. There is perennial speculation about new entrants into the wireless market being acquired by established players, and 2013 saw a major flurry (that eventually came to nothing) about the possibility of U.S. giant Verizon entering the Canadian market. The industry's product and service offerings are also constantly being revised. Changes happen at the micro level, with new devices entering the market at a predictable pace, and at the macro level, with major shifts in consumer needs from voice to data and entertainment offerings. The big three providers, Bell, Rogers, and Telus, as well as sub-brands Koodo and Fido, have to navigate these changes while at the same time attempting to engage multicultural consumers. As a result, their multicultural offerings must constantly change and evolve.

Current practice: Strong on ethnic culture, weak on Settlement Journey

At present, in addition to the newcomer-focused tactics we've just described, telecoms in Canada make some investments in targeted ethnic marketing, especially among Chinese and South Asian Canadians. These efforts include TV, radio, and print advertising, with targeted offers and sometimes pitches connected to cultural occasions. Lunar New Year campaigns are common; one example is an offer from Rogers of free calls home during New Year festivities.

Telus advertises heavily in South Asian media. For the most part, however, these efforts are aimed at repackaging existing "mainstream" offers for specific consumer groups. Their main focus is on ethnic culture: they make appeals in-language or at a particular time of year in order to increase their relevance to ethnocultural communities. There's nothing wrong with these initiatives, but the industry at large tends to miss opportunities to align their efforts on ethnic culture with post-Disorientation phases of the Settlement Journey.

Opportunities to target newcomers on arrival with the Fido and Koodo value brands using simple messaging and value offers aren't yet completely realized. These brands do target newcomers to some extent—but this sometimes arises as an accidental by-product of outreach to ethnic groups, not a deliberate pitch rooted in an understanding of the first phase of the Settlement Journey: Disorientation. There are also unrealized opportunities to build relationships established during the Disorientation phase into longer-term, higher-value relationships that endure through Orientation, Belonging, and Independence. Although the evolution of these relationships might not be as impressive as they are for the banks, the road from "unlimited texting" for a newcomer to HD TV, home internet, and the rest could be made smoother and more inviting.

Just as telecoms could benefit from deeper reflection on the Settlement Journey, paying more attention to migrants' pre-migration realities would also be worthwhile. The appetite for unlimited access to talk and data is developed in markets where such access is widespread and cheap. Is a "no fee" offer really a powerful draw for people who don't expect fees in the first place? It's critical for telecoms to understand that migrants arrive from specific and sometimes highly sophisticated market environments. Although on paper they may some-times look like simply a value-seeking sub-segment of the existing Canadian market, there's more going on in their orientations to wireless offerings—and firms that understand this dynamic will be better equipped to develop truly relevant and appealing offers.

Everyday Banking

A bank account is one of three things nearly all new-comers seek out at the very outset of their settlement process. The other two are internet access and a tele-phone. The to-do list for new migrants is very long, but phone, bank, and internet are generally top priori-ties, since accomplishing most other tasks depends on having these basic tools in place. When newcomers scan the Canadian banking landscape seeking a trust-worthy home for their money, what do they see?

THE CULTURAL LENS
Newcomers' expectations:
Pre-migration experiences trump ethnic culture

Although ethnic culture profoundly shapes people's relationships with money, when it comes to day-to-day banking, their deep-seated values are actually less salient than their experiences in the market environments of their countries of origin. Ethnic culture affects, for instance, people's orientation to saving versus spending—but when it comes to banking basics, differences across migrant groups are more likely to be rooted in differences in people's home banking environments. Were cash transactions the dominant mode of commerce? Were banks stable or shaky? What were banking fees like? Was credit normal or an elite privilege?

What newcomers look for in a Canadian bank is also shaped by their specific needs as migrants (such as establishing credit histories and sending money home to family). Here are a few notable patterns we've found through our research into migrants' day-to-day banking needs.

You want *me* to pay *you*? In focus groups, up until a few years ago we often heard newcomers complain about the fees and administrative headaches they encountered at Canadian banks. Those who come from countries where banks don't charge service fees understandably find it surprising and annoying to pay for the privilege of entrusting their money to a Canadian bank. Although abandoning fees would be a tall order for banks, making the account set-up process as friendly as possible (with special welcome rates and freebies) might help to cheer newcomers up as they embark on what may be a lifetime of paying Canadian-style banking fees.

Foreign exchange and remittances. Newcomers have their feet in at least two worlds, if not more. They have connections to Canada, connections to their home country, and often connections to intermediate countries where they've lived and worked prior to reaching Canada. And with business and kinship relationships across multiple borders, migrants need to move money—both to bring savings to Canada for themselves, and to send support to their families back home. (In fact, remittances sent home are a massive economic force: the World Bank estimates that in 2012 migrants were responsible for the movement of $529 billion.) Unsurprisingly, then, fluctuating rates of foreign exchange and international remittance fees alike create anxiety for newcomers. (Transaction fees on remittances add up to billions; at the close of 2013 the global average of the total cost of sending money back home was 8.58%.) So helping migrants move their money as cheaply and easily as possible is an excellent relationship-building opportunity for Canadian financial institutions.

The big C: credit. Suppose you're a fairly affluent migrant whose home country has a strong culture of cash transactions. You used cash there and, upon arriving in Canada, you continue to make most purchases with cash. You figure this is a good thing. Transactions are completed in full without ambiguity or delay. You fulfill your obligations and don't owe anyone anything. You must be a good Canadian, right?

But once you're ready to buy your first home in Canada, despite a sound financial profile, you're denied a mortgage. It turns out that an entity you've never heard of or dealt with, a credit bureau, finds you obscure. In order to get that mortgage, you need to placate the credit bureau by building up a credit history. In other words, in order to get a mortgage, you have to do exactly the opposite of what you might expect: you have to show that you frequently owe people money.

Credit bureaus are nonexistent in many migrant source countries, including the Philippines and many South American and African countries. In India and China, they're just beginning to formalize. Numerous migrants arrive from financial environments where cash transactions remain dominant. They may thus view credit as a tool for only limited and specific use (mortgages only, for instance) or even as a privilege reserved exclusively for the rich.

As recently as a few years ago, then, many new migrants were blindsided by Canadian credit-history expectations. Even after they realized that they needed to build up credit histories, they often had difficulty doing so because of bank rules. Today, newcomers are more likely to be aware of this aspect of Canadian financial life on the day they arrive, and less likely to encounter frustrating roadblocks at their banks.

FIG. 4.5
Initial challenges likely to be credit related

Top 3 banking challenges mentioned

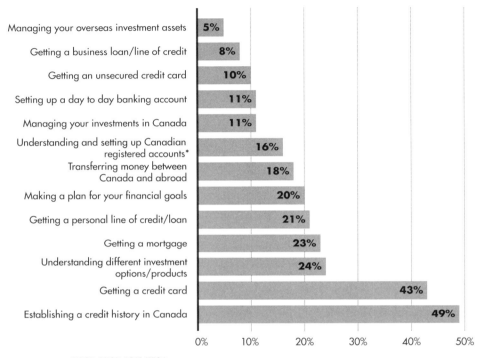

*RRSP, RESP, RRIF, TFSA, etc.

What's changed about newcomers' demand for and access to credit?

- **Online knowledge-sharing among newcomers.** Credit is a common topic in online support groups and communities for migrants. Since many start participating in these forums even before they migrate, they arrive understanding the need to establish credit history early.

- **Orientation programs from financial institutions.** As part of their stepped-up outreach efforts, the banks themselves have gotten better at communicating with newcomers about how to improve their financial lives, including their credit profiles.

- **Credit has gotten easier to come by.** Newcomers' credit situations used to be a Catch-22 very similar to the "Canadian experience" problem they encountered in the job market: they were unable to get credit cards because they had no Canadian credit history, and they were unable to build up Canadian credit history without at least having access to a modest credit card. (Or the banks would issue a credit card only with a deposit equivalent to the very low credit available on the card.) Migrants with upstanding financial histories were galled at being denied credit cards—even secured ones—or at being given credit limits less than that of a typical undergraduate. Today, however, most banks offer an unsecured credit card upon newcomers' arrival or even before arrival. Newcomers can therefore start building their credit history without difficulty right away.

Credit is an excellent case of the imperative for businesses to understand migrants, and the benefits that can flow from doing so. Many migrants to Canada have not just standard household financial needs, but active investing lives. Imagine buying multiple properties at relatively high rates of interest, and later finding out that a secured line of credit or other product could have saved you thousands of dollars—if only your bank had informed you, and treated you as the seasoned professional you are. Scenarios like these early in the settlement process can either cement lifelong loyalty or alienate customers forever. In the last several years, banks have become much smarter about spotting these early relationship- building opportunities and viewing migrants' financial circumstances through the appropriate lenses. Today, credit is a tool that banks use to build trust and engagement with newcomers.

ETHNIC CULTURE

Varied Influence: Big-picture questions (priorities, attitudes to saving) differ across cultures. But for migrants' every-day banking needs, the nitty-gritty of convenience and service matters most.

PRE-MIGRATION INPUTS

Strong influence: Expectations vary significantly depending on role of cash in country of origin, prevalence of credit, trust in banks, and so on.

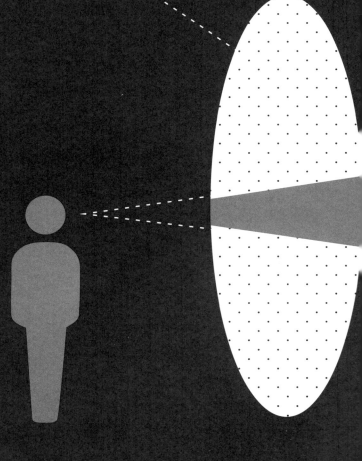

POST-MIGRATION INPUTS

Strong Influence: First-bank relationships are often established during
Disorientation. Banking needs related
to initial settlement (credit, moving
money from home, etc.) are critical.

CULTURAL LENS

Understanding financial needs specific to migration is key. Group-specific
outreach is good but it's more important
that products and services meet migrants'
specific needs (remittances, etc.).

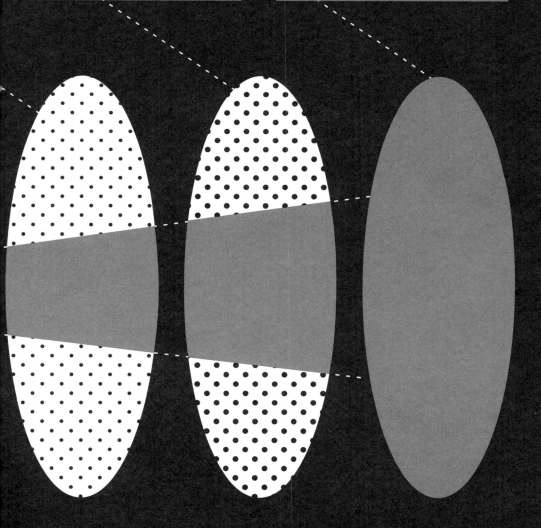

As we mentioned at the outset of this chapter, everyday banking services are a top priority for newcomers. About seven in ten newcomers (71%) report that they opened their first bank account after their arrival in Canada. A smaller proportion—one in five (20%)—say they set up their account during a preparatory visit before their actual migration journey. The vast majority of those who open a bank account after moving to Canada do so within the first month—at the Disorientation stage.

As we described in our general discussion of the Disorientation stage (see Chapter 3), this phase of settlement is overwhelming and confusing. So for newcomers in search of their first Canadian bank relationship, convenience, simplicity, and trust are all important considerations.

First bank—often a quick decision, heavy on convenience and light on research

Given the urgency of setting up a bank account, establishing a first-bank relationship in Canada can be a fairly quick decision. For many, any bank that seems convenient or gets a recommendation from a relative will get their first account.

The tendency to choose a bank quickly and with minimal research doesn't indicate any lack of sophistication about financial institutions on the part of newcomers, or even a lack of complexity in migrants' financial circumstances. Rather, this quick decision is driven by the Disorientation mindset, which temporarily suppresses migrants' diverse needs, circumstances, and financial orientations as they focus on workable short-term solutions. Upon first arriving in Canada, then, it's common for migrants to limit the scope of their first-bank decision by telling themselves, "I just need somewhere to park my money while I get settled."

With their needs stripped down in this way, migrants often make their first-bank choice based on some combination of trust and convenience. Factors influencing the first-bank decision might include

- A recommendation from a friend or relative
- Bank employees who speak the newcomer's language
- The geographic location and/or operating hours of nearest branch
- Confidence in Canada's banking system, and sometimes the reputation of a specific bank

FIG. 4.6

Most migrants open their first bank account during Disorientation—or even pre-arrival

When did you open your first Canadian bank account?

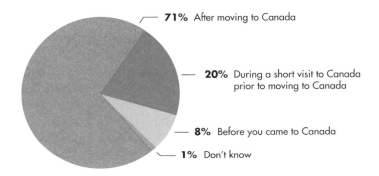

71% After moving to Canada

20% During a short visit to Canada prior to moving to Canada

8% Before you came to Canada

1% Don't know

Although newcomers may intend their quick decision about where to "park their money" to be temporary, the first-bank relationship can become a lasting one. As newcomers become more settled in Canada, their banks can end up holding much more than a small chequing account. Like other Canadians, migrants ultimately seek investment products, save for their children's education, buy property, save for retirement, and so on. For example, earlier we saw that many newcomers come from countries where cash transactions are prevalent, diminishing their familiarity with credit. But in our research, we find evidence of shifting attitudes toward credit as migrants move through the phases of the Settlement Journey in Canada. For instance, among recent Filipino migrants (those who've been in Canada for three years or less), about half (51%) agree with the statement, "Credit is a temptation. I prefer not to have access to it." Among more settled Filipino migrants—those who've been in Canada between four and ten years—agreement with that statement drops to about one in ten (8%).

As their financial lives progress, then, new Canadians become increasingly valuable customers for the banks that "won" their business by once being mentioned by a cousin, or happening to have a branch around the corner from the newcomer's first apartment.

Banks are working hard to establish all-important first-bank relationships

Because the first-bank relationship often ends up being a lasting one, Canadian banks know that major benefits accrue to institutions that can attract newcomers when they first arrive—or even before that. For this reason, the competition to attract newcomers is intense. In the past few years, Canadian banks have moved the battle for migrant customers overseas, attempting to forge relationships with migrants before they migrate by establishing or strengthening their presence in major migrant source countries. For example, in 2010, BMO became the first Canadian bank to incorporate (BMO ChinaCo) in China. Scotiabank leverages its historical presence in areas like Latin America, the Caribbean, and India, while in China it works in partnership with local Chinese banks. (And Canadian banks are by no means alone in courting migrants and recognizing that customers with ties to multiple countries have distinct financial needs. HSBC's branding is heavily international, making appeals to mobile, globalized citizens.)

Whether banks target newcomers before or after their arrival in Canada, success requires focus and resources. Making a bank welcoming to the Disoriented newcomer requires a range of investments. Multilingual staff and written materials, targeted customer service policies, and branch placement can all help. The steps required to reach out to newcomers when they first arrive are significant—but they might well prove less onerous than the work required to woo more settled migrants away from their first-bank relationship. Some migrants, after several years in Canada, actively consider switching financial institutions based on further research or new financial services needs. But many stay put. And as with other Canadians, banks seeking to win customers away from their current financial institutions need to demonstrate concrete benefits in order to entice customers to change their habits and go through the administrative hassles of jumping ship. Better to get newcomers in the door early on, then serve them well to keep them.

Based on what we hear in focus groups, banks are doing a much better job than they did in the past of getting off on the right foot with newcomers across the board. The complaints that were common just five years ago—"I can't get a credit card," "The banks don't take time to help me understand their specialized language," "Any time I'm off work, my bank is closed"—are almost unheard of today. The arrogance that newcomers once spoke of, the sense that banks were rigid and seemed to see migrants' distinct service needs as an inconvenience, is disappearing. Banks have worked hard to become more welcoming and accessible. Most have streamlined account-opening processes and made an unsecured credit card part of their welcome package. Staffing

A NEW FRONTIER FOR BANKS: TEMPORARY RESIDENTS

The number of temporary residents in Canada is on the rise. Temporary residents are people who have permission to be in Canada for a limited time, typically for work or study (and also sometimes for humanitarian reasons) but are not necessarily on track to become citizens. Although people who are here today and gone tomorrow may not seem like a worthwhile target for Canadian banks, there are two reasons why temporary residents warrant some attention. First, a modest proportion (roughly one in ten) are able to get on track to become permanent residents. This proportion is likely to grow in the years ahead, because of a new immigration class called the Canadian Experience Class, designed to keep foreign students and professionals working in Canada after their (initially temporary) stays.

Second, despite the image of temporary foreign workers as predominantly low-wage workers (such as agricultural labourers), most do not fit this description. Many temporary foreign workers are globalized, high-skills professionals who move around the globe in search of opportunity. These people need banking services during their time here, and may be valuable customers for banks that succeed at making their globalized lives more convenient. And some may even wind up in Canada: according to a 2014 Environics survey, although two-thirds (67%) of migrants came to Canada directly from their countries of origin, 22 percent migrated from an intermediate third country where they had spent at least a year, and 11 percent had either worked or studied in Canada prior to becoming landed immigrants.

"Many temporary foreign workers are globalized, high-skills professionals who move around the globe in search of opportunity."

and attitudinal changes also count: banks needed to create organizational cultures that see migrants as prized customers, not as people whose language and service needs take extra time.

Now that banks have gotten the basics down and are no longer alienating newcomers when they first walk through the door, imperatives for the short- and mid-term future revolve around more substantial differentiation on products and services, including credit and investments, to win the hearts of new Canadians.

The future: Seamless global banking

In the short- to mid-term, competitive advantage may go to the bank that best serves newcomers as they embark on their settlement process in Canada. But if permanent migration defined the 19th and 20th centuries, permanent mobility may well define the 21st. For many migrants to Canada, moving back home or to another country is a lingering option—and for those struggling to find their economic footing, that option might win the day. Although not everyone wants to remain in a state of permanent migration, some professionals are quite happy to live in a number of different cities during their prime working years, crossing borders as they climb a multinational corporate ladder or hop from venture to venture. For banks that want to serve these global movers and shakers, the true competitive advantage will go to the institution that can deliver truly seamless global transactions and services.

AHEAD OF THE CURVE: HONG KONG BANKING IN THE 1990s

For almost as long as there's been mass immigration to Canada, banks have tried to attract newcomer customers. In the late 19th and early 20th centuries, the Royal Bank earnestly advised new arrivals that, "it will be in your best interests to visit the nearest branch of this Bank as early as possible and deposit your spare cash."

Competition among banks for newcomer customers began in its contemporary form in the years leading up to the handover of Hong Kong to China in 1997. Between 1984 and 1996, 300,000 people immigrated to Canada from Hong Kong, many out of concern about changes that might come to the city under Chinese rule. As Henry Yu, a UBC history professor, told The Vancouver Sun, these migrants "were really a new kind of Canadian." Yu continued, "They were educated, spoke English and [were] middle class or wealthy. They weren't going to start out as pizza delivery men and working in Chinese laundries. They expected to be first-class citizens, they wanted to live in the best neighbourhoods, wanted the best schools for their kids."

These well-heeled migrants helped make the 1990s the era of Hong Kong banking in Canada. Enter Cantonese bankers, Chinese signage, Chinese New Year celebrations, and such in-branch flourishes as red packets. Many of the Chinese-language written materials found in banks today were first translated in the 1990s. At that time, multicultural banking meant Chinese banking, and Chinese banking meant Cantonese banking—or Hong Kong banking. Some of the Big Five banks appointed Hong Kong executives to oversee their Asian banking divisions, setting the stage for later diversity-in-hiring approaches that are partly about equity and a great deal about connecting with diverse Canadian markets.

Asian banking was also propelled by a number of specialist agencies headed by advertising professionals from Hong Kong. These agencies were at the forefront of a movement that has since gained momentum: mainstream Canadian businesses reaching out to new customers via ethnic-language media (in their case, Cantonese).

Since the days of Hong Kong banking roughly twenty years ago, the banks' relationships with Asian customers have changed dramatically. Not only have banks broadened their focus to include Mandarin Chinese, but they've made considerable strides toward courting South Asians and other groups of significant size.

> "They expected to be first-class citizens, they wanted to live in the best neighbourhoods, wanted the best schools for their kids."

Financial Management

Money touches on some of the most emotionally charged aspects of our lives: our hopes, fears, achievements, relationships, and legacy. As it circulates, money also connects us to people and institutions—from our immediate families to remote banks and governments.

THE CULTURAL LENS

Because money is at once so personal and so social, our attitudes to it tend to be deep-seated and strongly influenced by our culture. The way people see and manage money is tied to both their ethnic culture and the market environment in which they've come of age.

Experiences in Canada do influence migrants' attitudes—over time, the Settlement Journey affects people's tangible needs, the amount they're able to save and invest, and whom they trust for advice and services. But because ethnic culture and pre-migration experiences can be so potent, deep differences tend to persist in people's approaches to financial management even after many years in Canada. Watching your parents lose their savings in an unstable banking system or seeing extended family reflexively act as a social safety net for a struggling relative are experiences that mark people for life. And so while the Settlement Journey may affect the scale of investment or the tools of investment, it tends not to change people's fundamental attitudes toward saving, risk, and other basic concepts associated with financial services.

Money and values

Have you ever had an argument with someone about money and walked away wondering how your views could be so radically different from theirs? The seemingly enormous gulf between what you and another person see as fair and reasonable stems from the fact that our financial behaviours and attitudes are the tip of a huge fundamental-values iceberg. That iceberg is made up of our orientations to things like risk, family and community obligations, deferred versus immediate gratification, desire for legacy, and fatalism versus personal control.

The sociologist Max Weber spent a lifetime studying the interaction between religious and cultural ideas and the economic machinations of different societies. From the Protestant Ethic in Northern Europe to Confucianism and Taoism in China, Weber showed how beliefs that are ostensibly non-economic (ideas about reincarnation, for instance) shaped economies. Nearly everything shapes our economic life, and our economic life shapes nearly everything. As a result, it's not always easy to disentangle the influence of migrants' ethnic culture from the influence of the banking and investment environment they were accustomed to before they migrated.

In the 19th and 20th centuries, English Canada's social attitudes were deeply shaped by the social attitudes of British and Scottish settlers, who were known for fiscal conservatism and frugality. Dictums like "A penny saved is a penny earned" and "Look after the pennies, and the dollars will look after themselves" are emblematic of financial outlooks from that part of the world. A distaste for conspicuous consumption—and the common suggestion that people who engage in it have "more money than brains"—go along with this orientation to money. These attitudes may be the foundation of Canadian economic life, but Scottish-style frugality is no longer the norm.

Today, despite how quickly financial services are being globalized, attitudes toward saving and investment continue to differ strongly by culture. Among migrants to Canada, these distinct attitudes tend to persist long after they've settled in their new society. Migrants' different outlooks reveal themselves on a number of fronts.

Aspirations and emergencies: Goal-oriented versus perpetual saving

In *The Protestant Ethic and the Spirit of Capitalism*, Max Weber characterized the spirit of capitalism as the accumulation of wealth (through labour and trade) for specific goals, often investment. Many of the saving tools available for consumers in the West are designed to cater to precisely this spirit: you save for a home, to start a business, for retirement. The practice of saving money rests on a certain amount of confidence about the future and about the system in which one is saving. This is especially true of retirement planning. We all know we might die early and regret the indulgences we denied ourselves in the name of retirement, but the odds are that saving is a good idea.

What happens without that mindset? What if the future is dramatically more uncertain, and the means of saving and investing are dramatically less reliable? These are some of the realities many migrants to Canada have faced, and we see the results in our research. First, for many migrants, saving is a priority but not a subject of planning and strategizing in the same way it is for many Canadian-born people. Rather, saving is a perpetual task, a duty to oneself and one's family. Instead of accumulating a fund for a specific purchase, migrants are more likely to save for an undefined "rainy day."

Wealth Management

ETHNIC CULTURE

Strong Influence. Culture has a profound influence on people's relationships with money. Major differences in habits and values are evident across groups.

PRE-MIGRATION INPUTS

Strong influence. Many migrants hail from cultures of "perpetual saving," not goal-oriented saving (e.g. for retirement). Experiences of unstable banking systems or corruption affect people deeply.

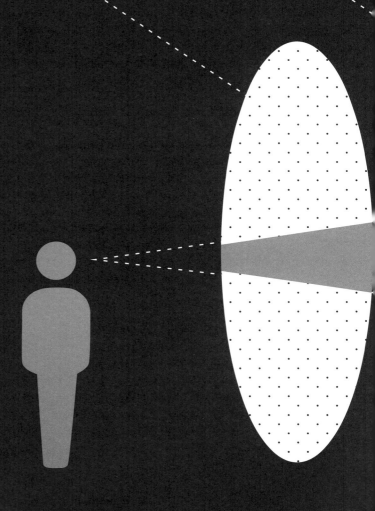

POST-MIGRATION INPUTS

Moderate Influence. Some gradual, partial adoption of traditionally Canadian approaches to saving and investing. Many also pursue investment opportunities across borders, leveraging personal networks.

CULTURAL LENS

Differences among groups are important factors. Needs change as Settlement Journey and life stages unfold, but some differences rooted in ethnic culture are likely to persist.

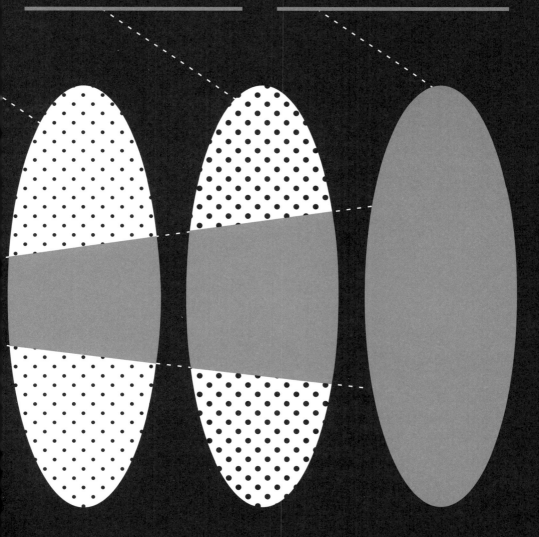

Compared with the Canadian-born, newcomers from Asia and Latin America, for example, are much more likely to cite financial goals that are related to their family responsibilities, including saving for children's education, saving for expenses related to aging parents, saving to send money back to their countries of origin, and saving in case of illness or death in the family. Their financial objectives tend to be multiple and to extend beyond the individual or the immediate family. A common mindset among these populations is that you must save as much as you can all the time because you don't know what the future holds. There's no end to this preparation for possible risk, since many are preparing for a future beyond their own lifespans, a future that continues indefinitely with their descendants. Rainy days are coming—it's just a matter of when.

As Figure 4.7 illustrates, many migrant groups are more likely to see themselves as primarily responsible for elderly family members, whereas the combination of an individualistic culture and a government-provided social safety net makes the Canadian-born less likely to save for this purpose. Latino Canadians are the most likely to cite saving for expenses related to aging parents as a financial goal. This may be because many elderly Hispanics have endured major upheavals in their home societies (such as economic depression in Argentina, coups in Chile and many Central American countries, and extreme inflation). These experiences are likely to affect people's financial behaviours, whether the events have brought actual financial hardship into families or have simply caused them to be extremely careful.

It's not that the Canadian-born don't get sick or don't have expenses associated with aging parents. Most people try to have something set aside for emergencies. But Canadians operate in a different landscape: because Canada's social welfare system is more robust, it doesn't fall exclusively to families to deal with members who can't earn or who run into trouble. Many migrants come from developing countries whose social welfare systems don't exist, are

"[For many migrants] saving is for emergencies, and the amount of money required for dealing with emergencies is unknown. As a result, the more you can save, the better."

FIG. 4.7

Saving to support family networks more prevalent among migrants

Proportion reporting saving for expenses related to aging parents

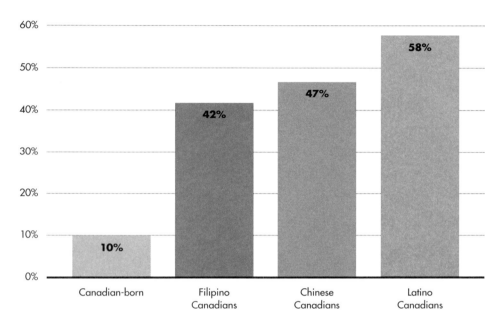

Canadian-born	10%
Filipino Canadians	42%
Chinese Canadians	47%
Latino Canadians	58%

just being established, are being reformed, or in some cases are even being demolished. The idea that the government will take care of you when you're old or sick is almost laughable for some. Financial security comes from careful planning and from strong family bonds—period. Hence perpetual saving. Saving is for emergencies, and the amount of money required for dealing with emergencies is unknown. As a result, the more you can save, the better.

Low trust:
A major difference between the Canadian-born and migrants

Another major difference between migrants and the Canadian-born is migrants' experiences with vehicles for saving. Some newcomers arrive in Canada from societies with unstable banking systems, poorly regulated investment industries, or histories of political and economic instability that have shattered people's trust. Our interviews with Russian migrants to Canada, for example, show that their own or their parents' traumatic experiences with lost savings have substantially reduced their level of trust in *any* financial institution.

In general, our research indicates that the levels of trust migrants express upon arrival in Canada are heavily determined by the levels of trust that prevail in their countries of origin. It is seldom the case that they were trusting back home but are distrustful of people and businesses in Canada. Rather, they tend to carry with them common ideas from their home countries about the trustworthiness of banks, governments, investment advisors, and so on.

Low trust is a very difficult thing to change, since, by definition, it means that people are unlikely to be convinced by assurances about the safety of Canadian banks. This is why we argue that mindsets established prior to migration exert an especially strong influence on the Cultural Lenses migrants bring to financial services. Although it might take just a year or two to get used to Canadian norms around groceries or mobile phones, developing sufficient confidence to entrust your savings to strangers at a big bank (when your parents might see this as madness) is a much taller order. Indeed, lack of trust is often so deeply ingrained that it not only persists through a person's life but is handed down to the next generation.

Implications of perpetual saving

Saving for specific goals may seem dubious. Saving toward a goal demands different tools and approaches from perpetual saving. For instance, those saving for retirement begin by thinking about how much money they'll need to live comfortably in later life. For migrants accustomed to perpetual saving—for inevitable family needs and unforeseen crises—setting a goal may seem unrealistic, or even absurd. Who can predict the future?

Whereas the Canadian-born often find banks' retirement planning tools useful and reassuring, migrants from some regions may see them as self-interested: an attempt on the part of investment salespeople to encourage people to build castles in the sky and then fund them by forking over their savings. Because many migrants already feel low levels of trust toward financial institutions, it will be difficult for these institutions to sell them on both financial products and an entire model of saving that's unfamiliar. So instead of building trust, an invitation from a financial advisor to imagine their retirement may turn them off.

Perpetual saving means you're never too young to start. Many Canadian-born people associate regular saving and investing with retirement planning. As a result, a great number begin to sock money away only when they hit middle age—the point at which old age starts to seem as if it might actually happen to them. But as we've seen, migrants from cultures of perpetual saving are saving up for unknown needs and emergencies across their entire families, not just in their own lives. As a result, they start saving at a much

FIG. 4.8

Saving for personal goals (especially retirement) more prevalent among Canadian-born

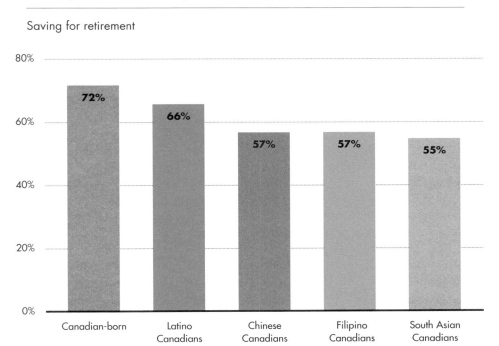

Saving for retirement

younger age than their North American counterparts. Nielsen's 2012 Global Investors study confirmed that investors in the Asia-Pacific region and the Middle East are the youngest worldwide, while North American investors are the oldest. Six in ten North American investors (59%) are over forty, whereas large majorities of investors are *under* the age of forty in Asia-Pacific (78%) and the Middle East (72%). Needless to say, under-forty investors may not be heavily attracted to ads featuring silver-haired lovebirds on a beach. Products, services, and communications, then, must be tailored to meet these young investors' needs and values.

Beyond mutual funds: Diverse investment preferences among migrants

Migrants from a number of different backgrounds, particularly those from Russia, Iran, and Africa who've experienced disruptions and failures of institutions, are broadly similar in their distrust of institutions and the wealth management tools they offer. These migrant groups are alike in the sense that they're unlikely to pursue savings and investment programs that are common in Canada (monthly saving, mutual funds, and so on), but the similarity ends there. Different groups respond to distrust of financial institutions in different ways. Some may simply feel better if they spend the money now. Others will look to safeguard their wealth by making more tangible investments. Gold and silver are common investments in India and among Indo-Canadians, for example. Chinese-Canadian investors often favour real estate, as do investors from some Caribbean countries.

Family-style financial planning: Pooling resources and risk protection

Many recent waves of migrants have arrived from societies in Asia-Pacific, the Middle East, and Africa where relatively collectivist values prevail. In individualistic societies, ties among individuals are loose and all are expected to look after themselves and their immediate families. In collectivist societies, individuals are integrated into stronger, more cohesive groups. Extended families and kinship networks tend to support and protect one another more automatically, and loyalty to family is a strong social imperative.

As a result of these collectivist norms, many migrant families plan their wealth management together. Whereas the average Canadian-born person might plan with a spouse—maybe aided by a little intergenerational advice depending on life stage—many migrants will plan with larger networks involving siblings, cousins, and in-laws. Major purchases often involve the entire extended family. For instance, when a couple or young (nuclear) family is preparing to purchase a home, gifting from an extended-family network toward a down payment is common. Financial planning often involves not just considerations about one's own and one's children's future, but about elderly relatives or others in the kinship group who may need support. These patterns suggest opportunities for products and services that enable extended family members to achieve their collective goals with convenience and efficiency.

Gender dynamics in household financial management

In the model of household finance that prevailed in the land of *Leave It to Beaver*, Dad brought home the bacon, Mom allocated it so that everyone was fed and clothed, and the family stayed on budget. When it came to major purchases like a car, masculine authority asserted itself. Otherwise, Mom held the purse strings. Today, with more women participating in the labour force and fewer women taking sole responsibility for domestic labour, families have a wide range of financial arrangements.

Norms around gender and money vary from culture to culture. For example, in focus groups we've heard that in the Philippines, especially in the suburbs

FIG. 4.9
Use of in-language financial advisors declines but remains high long-term; culture is key

Use of a Chinese-speaking financial advisor among Chinese Canadians
who use financial advisors

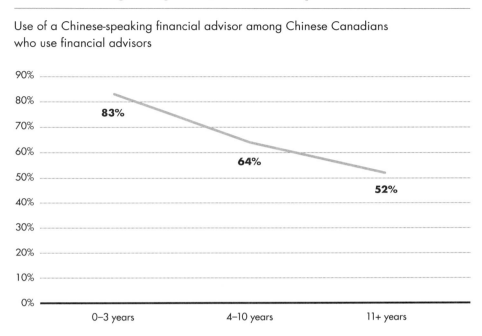

or the provinces, men like to say they let their wives look after their money so that the men won't squander it (although some say it's in fact the women who demand to manage their husbands' salaries). There's even a specific word for the practice of men surreptitiously withholding income from their wives: *kupit*, which can denote either the act of stealing in small quantities or the hidden money itself. In South Asian households it's the men who tend to be primarily responsible for financial decisions, whereas in Chinese families it's typical for women to be responsible for the management of daily household finances while major spending or investment decisions are undertaken jointly between men and women.

Naturally there are variations from family to family in every ethnic group. And just as Canadian norms around gender and money have changed amid the social and economic changes of the past six decades or so, norms among migrants are also likely to show some movement—based on both pre-migration experiences of social change and exposure to Canadian practices.

Seeking advice from someone who speaks "my language"

We argue throughout this book that the settlement process has some typical stages but doesn't always unfold in a simple or automatic way; there's more to the story than people becoming "more Canadian" year after year. And in the world of financial services, it's certainly true that distinct behaviours and preferences persist for many groups long after migration.

Consider, for example, our findings on the use of in-language financial advisors in the Chinese-Canadian community illustrated in Figure 4.9, As one would expect, recent migrants are more likely than settled migrants to report that they receive advice from a financial advisor who speaks Chinese. As migrants become more familiar with the Canadian financial system and confident in their ability to navigate Canadian wealth management tools— and as their language skills improve—they become more open to a non-Chinese-speaking advisor.

Still, even after being in Canada for over a decade, about half (52%) of migrants from China continue to receive financial advice from someone who speaks Chinese. Often these migrants can speak and understand English ex-tremely well, and they receive other services in English. So why seek financial advice in Chinese? It's not a matter of language comprehension, but a matter of culture. When planning what to do with their money and how to prepare for the future, these migrants—even though they're quite advanced in the Settlement Journey—want to speak to someone who understands their values and experiences, as well as the financial expectations of their immediate and extended families.

At what stage of the Settlement Journey does saving and investing begin?

Migrants can begin saving and investing at any stage of the Settlement Journey, since investment tends to be more strongly linked to financial circumstances and overall life stage (age, family status, and so on) than to milestones in the settlement process. The one exception to this rule is the initial Disorientation phase, during which few migrants will have much time or energy to spend on their portfolios.

Nevertheless, as a general rule, longer-tenured migrants tend to have more investment needs. Our research indicates increasing investment activity with time in Canada: migrants become more likely to own investment products and to have more money invested overall. For example, as illustrated in Figure 4.10,

FIG. 4.10
Investment needs increase with tenure

Registered investments ownership by tenure, South Asian Canadians

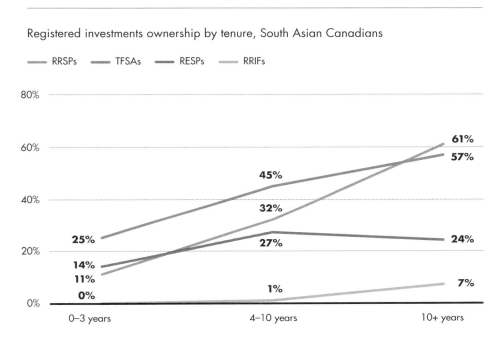

— RRSPs   — TFSAs   — RESPs   — RRIFs

among South Asian migrants the use of registered investment vehicles clearly increases as they spend more time in Canada. The pattern is different for Registered Education Savings Plans (RESPs), since migrants who've been settled in Canada for many years are likely to be old enough that they're no longer saving for their children's education.

Borderless investing

Regardless of where they come from, migrants tend to have experienced at least two commercial environments (their country of origin's and Canada's) and sometimes more along the way. And with today's technology, they need not leave these other contexts entirely behind when they land in Canada: they can take advantage of the best deals, wherever they're found.

Crossing borders to gain commercial advantage is a widespread practice — whether it's Canadians driving into the United States to buy sneakers and jeans at a discount, or corporations or wealthy individuals seeking tax advantages by parking their money abroad. If newcomers arriving from highly dynamic economies know they can get a great return on investment in their countries of origin, why invest in Canada?

Many newcomers arrive from societies—such as the Philippines and various countries in Africa and the Caribbean—where it's difficult to borrow against future income. In these societies, savings rates tend to be relatively high, since purchases that Canadians might finance with credit must instead be paid for with existing savings. So ordinary savings tools similar to GICs are sometimes remarkably rewarding, earning as much as 10% annually. With returns like that, why would migrants move all their money to Canada? Why not leave it back home and let it work harder for them? Migration entails many struggles and challenges, but one of its great advantages is the ability to take advantage of opportunities in more than one place. For many migrants, this means investing across borders. (And just as Canadians who slip across the border for discount jeans must decide whether to reveal their purchases to customs agents, international investors face a choice about whether to be fully transparent with the Canada Revenue Agency about the scope of their portfolios abroad.)

Even if their investment dollars are managed in Canada, many migrants like the idea of investing in international funds or stocks concentrated in their home countries. In fact, their home-country holdings often exceed their North American holdings. Investing back home is a matter of emotional loyalty for some, while others may be driven by genuine informational advantage—knowing the market landscape and the investment opportunities there. In either case, since many migrants to Canada are arriving from societies with rapidly growing economies, investing back home may not be a bad idea.

Borderless investing has a couple of implications for Canadian financial institutions:

1. The share-of-wallet war is not just among Canadian financial institutions, but between Canadian firms and international competitors. A thorough understanding of migrants' investment attitudes and behaviours can empower financial advisors to build long-term relationships of trust with their internationally-minded clients.

2. When migrant investors choose a self-directed investment brokerage, they're likely to see easy-to-use international trading platforms as important features.

Beauty and Personal Care

Evolutionary scientists argue that, regardless of ethnicity, culture, or geography, there are certain physical attributes that attract humans to each other. They claim that when we look at other people, our brains read ancient signals about their fitness as mates—and assess whether they can help us create robust offspring. It's not exactly the stuff of love songs, but when scientists test people's perceptions of others' attractiveness, certain qualities, such as facial symmetry, do seem to hold widespread appeal.

Over and above whatever notions of beauty may be coded into us as human beings, some argue that with globalization the personal care industry has contributed to the homogenization of beauty ideals around the world. With the drastic expansion of media in the 20th century—television, Hollywood movies, increasingly photo-driven fashion magazines, and even the rise of international beauty pageants—beauty imperatives (often originating in Western Europe and North America) have indeed flowed across borders to an unprecedented degree.

THE CULTURAL LENS

Yet societies remain distinct in many of the ways they present beauty, particularly female beauty. As well as defining which physical qualities are beautiful, different cultures affect the ways in which people relate to beauty: how much it matters, what it means, how to achieve it. Add to this the fact that ethnic groups often share certain physiological tendencies (such as hair texture, particularities of perspiration, or skin's vulnerability to sun damage), and we find that even in a globalized world, the way people consume personal care products can be strongly influenced by both cultural preferences and by the market and media environments in the societies where people come of age.

Beauty across cultures: Differences old and new

As with many of the categories we consider in this book, such as wealth management and alcohol consumption, attitudes to grooming and beauty vary by ethnic culture. Ethnic culture can also shape consumer environments. Migrants to Canada not only arrive with culturally transmitted ideas about beauty, hygiene, vanity, and so on; they also come with preferences and expectations that have been shaped by the products and marketing in their countries of origin.

It's impossible to talk about beauty care without considering the role and status of women. Cultures around the world have traditions of female adornment whose subtext is that women are objects to be decorated and displayed, their beauty (hinting at their fertility) being central to their value to society. The adornment of brides is a case of this behaviour in its extreme form—the display of a young woman at her most beautiful at the moment she's transferred (in the patriarchal model of the ritual) from her father to her husband.

Values research finds Canada to be among the least patriarchal countries in the world. Although total equality isn't a done deal, prevailing norms and attitudes in Canada are strongly egalitarian by international standards. Migrants to Canada are therefore often arriving from contexts in which gender inequality is more broadly assumed. This is manifested in beauty products and especially in related marketing.

In Asia and Latin America, one sometimes sees advertising whose explicit message is that if women make themselves beautiful with a specific product, a desirable man will want to marry them. Advertising in Canada certainly plays on the theme of women making themselves attractive, but the "catch a man" angle is typically less explicit. Advertisers must walk a finer line in a society where women want to be attractive but where they're told to value equality and empowerment and where displaying oneself as an object is not always encouraged. Advertisers in Canada therefore tend to foreground the confidence women derive from looking good, making confidence (not superficial physical qualities) the source of their heroine's attractiveness and happiness.

The most talked-about instance of this beauty-from-the-inside-out approach is Dove's "Campaign for Real Beauty," which promotes the idea that all women should see themselves as beautiful in their own way—and that the quest to resemble an "ideal" of beauty is false. These messages align nicely with prevailing Canadian expectations about gender equality, but they may not resonate strongly with migrants.

"Behaviour and spending suggest that women in major source countries of migration to Canada are heavily invested in the beauty and personal care category. "

"Beautiful just the way you are" versus "Beauty is work—but within reach"

According to McCann Truth Central's report, *The Truth About Beauty*, while 35% of women worldwide agree that "everyone is beautiful," only 15% of Chinese women think this is true. Still, Chinese women are more likely (50%) than the global average (30%) to believe that "everyone can be beautiful with a little help." As analyst Emily Tan notes, the Chinese attraction to the idea that beauty is attainable but requires work echoes Coco Chanel's famous dictum that, "There are no ugly women, only lazy ones."

So a Chinese newcomer to Canada may not be attracted by Dove's affirming message that you're beautiful just as you are. She may, however, welcome an aspirational message that beauty is rare and special, but still possible for those who are willing to put in the effort. McCann argues that this link between beauty and effort is an important one in emerging markets, where "beauty equals success." As its report puts it, "Asian women will aggressively chase and acknowledge that being beautiful is a social and career advantage." In this mindset, then, beauty is both an ingredient of success (a leg up in social and professional settings) and a manifestation of success (a sign that you've made the investment in being beautiful).

Whether driven by traditional patriarchal imperatives or by the personal striving common in rapidly changing societies and economies (or some combination of these two influences, old and new), behaviour and spending suggest that women in major source countries of migration to Canada are heavily invested in the beauty and personal care category. McCann finds that "63% of Chinese women and 55% of Brazilian women change their beauty routines every couple of months or more," percentages that are much higher than the global average. (The comparable figure for the U.S. is 33%, the U.K. 29%, and France 25%.)

This high level of involvement in the beauty category is certainly evident in Environics' own research with migrants: we find that key migrant segments in Canada spend heavily on beauty care—certainly more than other Canadians do. One of our recent studies, for instance, found that Filipino Canadians spent on average $42 per month on skin care and cosmetics, which is double the average for the total Canadian population. Moreover, spending was as high among recent newcomers as it was among established migrants.

This behaviour is likely driven partly by the motivators we've already described and partly by the relative youth of migrant populations in Canada compared with the general population. In 2010, for example, Environics' Global Asian

Beauty and Personal Care

ETHNIC CULTURE

Strong Influence. Ideas about how to be beautiful—and how important it is for women specifically to be beautiful—vary across societies.

PRE-MIGRATION INPUTS

Strong influence. Products consumed, favourite brands, and retail habits vary; department store counters are key retail venues in many source countries.

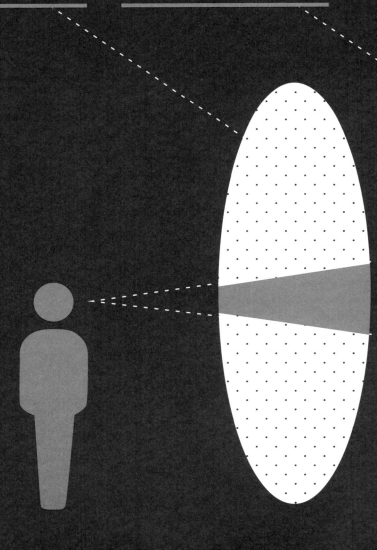

POST-MIGRATION INPUTS

Moderate influence. Migrants' beauty and personal care habits change with time in Canada, but higher overall involvement in the category tends to persist.

CULTURAL LENS

As with food, migrants experiment and explore with personal care products during settlement. Migrants' habits change, but they do not move toward a "Canadian" norm in a linear way.

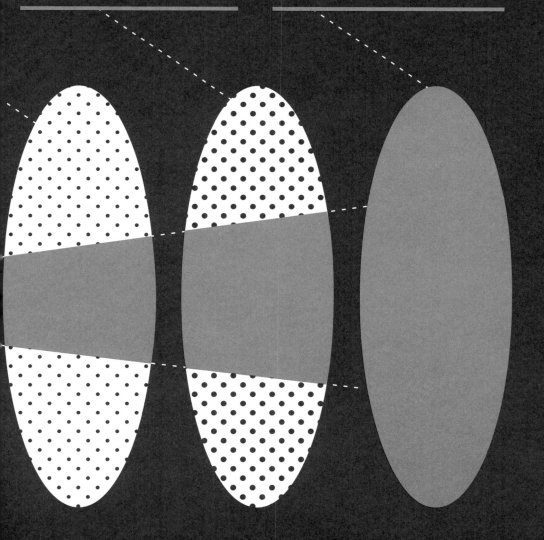

FIG. 4.11

Chinese Canadian habits remain distinct even in second generation

Use of facial cleanser (days per year) among youth aged 15 to 29

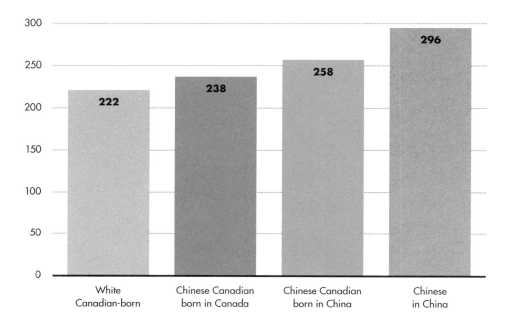

Youth Study found that youth in China used facial cleanser on average 296 days in a year. Among Chinese youth who had migrated to Canada, use declined slightly to 258 days, and among Chinese-Canadian youth born in Canada, usage declined even further to 238. But all these averages are higher than those for Canadian-born white youth, who use facial cleanser 222 days a year.

Figure 4.11 (along with the reverse pattern that we see in deodorant use in Figure 4.12) shows the gulf between the prevailing habits in Canada and in some migrants' pre-migration contexts (in this case China). The patterns also show a process of acculturation—but one that doesn't conclude with either first- or second-generation Chinese Canadians completely matching the habits of their white, Canadian-born compatriots.

Small experiments in the beauty care aisle at a time of big change

Since many newcomers arrive in Canada heavily invested in the beauty category, viewing skin care and cosmetics products as virtual necessities, the beauty category resembles the grocery category in that the decision whether to buy is not a question. The questions are which products and which retailers.

For newcomer consumers, the beauty category is also similar to the grocery category in the sense that it's a safe way to experiment with new experiences — even a new identity — in an unfamiliar environment. Just as an Indian family on a trip to the local No Frills might buy a box of frozen waffles simply to try them out, a Chinese woman filling a prescription at Shoppers Drug Mart might also pick up a Revlon cream — even though in China she only bought Shiseido and only at the department store counter. Trying new personal care products is a low-stakes way of testing the commercial waters in Canada.

Our research finds that recent arrivals from South Asia and China use an above-average number of brands for personal care. That's because they're experimenting with unfamiliar products. Browsing the personal care aisle at Walmart or Shoppers Drug Mart can be an enjoyable distraction and an acceptable bit of "me time" during the stressful Disorientation phase or the more exploratory Orientation phase of the Settlement Journey.

Habits from home:
Chinese Canadians remain distinct — even after many years

Although a certain amount of experimentation is part of the settlement process when it comes to beauty care products, newcomers will also seek out familiar products and gravitate toward familiar sites of purchase. Research that Environics conducted among Chinese and South Asian Canadian women on facial care showed that roughly a third of Chinese Canadians were buying facial care products at department stores, a channel that dominates in Asia. Chinese Canadians also tend to use department store counter brands that are prevalent in Asia, such as Shiseido and Lancôme.

Whereas newcomers tend to gravitate toward department store counters, Chinese-Canadian women who have been in Canada longer are less likely to purchase beauty care products there; their habits in this regard are more similar to the Canadian average. More tenured migrants also stand out from newcomers in the products they buy. In both the cosmetics and the facial care categories, only Chinese Canadians who had been in Canada for over ten years were likely to purchase mass retail brands like Revlon and L'Oréal.

FIG. 4.12

Deodorant use reflects adaptation and distinct Chinese habits

Daily use of deodorant among youth aged 15 to 29

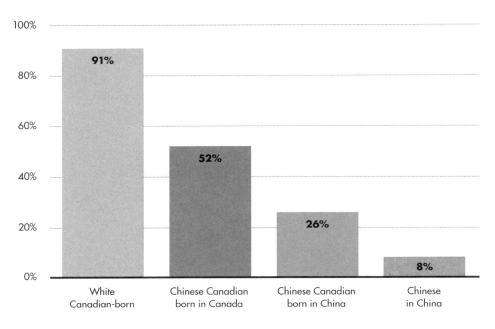

But differences between Chinese Canadians and other Canadians don't disappear entirely with more time spent in Canada: our research found that longer tenured Chinese-Canadian women were buying more specialist spa brands than other Canadians, indicating that the high involvement in the facial care category many of them brought with them from China hasn't abated. Their habits change, but they remain distinct. Another notable preference among longer tenured Chinese Canadians is for Korean brands sold in such Asian retail channels as Chinese grocery stores. Beauty care is yet another category in which acculturation clearly occurs but is not a linear journey toward "mainstream" norms.

South Asian Canadian women in general are closer to Canadian averages in their beauty care purchasing behaviour. They tend toward mass retail brands in both facial care and cosmetics, albeit showing the influence of pre-migration consumer experiences: they favour facial care brands dominant in South Asia, such as Olay and Nivea. Notably, whereas more settled Chinese migrants move away from the department store purchasing that's common in China, the opposite is true among South Asian Canadian women. As they gain their economic footing and become more affluent, these women become more likely to buy counter brands at department stores.

New country, new categories

In the case of skin care and cosmetics, Asian women arrive in Canada with well-established histories of purchasing and use. Migrants arrive, however, with little or no familiarity with some other personal care categories that are common in Canada; the deodorant or anti-perspirant category is one example.

The deodorant and anti-perspirant category is underdeveloped in China. Part of the reason for this is physiological. Typically, people of East Asian descent have fewer apocrine sweat glands (the glands that produce body odour) than other groups. Although marketers are now promoting deodorant in China, use of the category isn't common; our Global Asian Youth Study showed that just over half of Chinese youth living in China never use anti-perspirant or deodorant and only 8% do so daily.

This pre-migration pattern is disrupted by migration to Canada and by the Settlement Journey: we find a clear jump in adoption after migration. Among Chinese youth who have migrated to Canada, only a third never use deodorant and a quarter are using it daily. Among youth of Chinese origin who were born in Canada, just over half use it daily. But while adoption increases with time in Canada and familiarity with Canadian habits, the habits of Chinese youth remain markedly different from those of Canadian-born youth of European descent, 91% of whom use deodorant or anti-perspirant daily. We see the same pattern among South Asian youth.

Adoption is likely triggered by increased awareness of the deodorant category and by word of mouth. Even for those who don't have an obvious need of deodorant, the pressures of adolescence may tend to promote adoption.

Absorbing new norms and conventions around beauty

Sometimes in describing a trip to a foreign city, people will remark on a general enthusiasm—or lack thereof—for fashion and personal care. It's common to hear first-time visitors to Paris, for instance, remark that women of all ages look beautiful and well put together. The general level of engagement with personal appearance varies from place to place.

When they arrive in Canada, migrants are experiencing more than just a change in the brands on the shelf or the retail outlet where they buy their favourite face cream. They're experiencing a change in the whole cultural context in which they present themselves to others. This change of context will have as much or more influence over time as a new assortment of brands and retailers. What's considered attractive? What's considered "too much"? And on a deeper level: How much does it matter? Are women taken seriously regardless of how they look? If men make an effort with their appearance, are they considered dignified or fussy?

Consider the Chinese migrant to Canada who's a heavier user of facial cleanser than her Canadian-born peers, but not as heavy a user as her peers in China. What accounts for the difference? It may be a subtle shift in the migrant's values relating to her personal appearance. In a more pluralistic and less competitive social environment, perhaps the imperative to pursue beauty as an ingredient of success doesn't seem as urgent. Perhaps she's noticed more peers in Canada being perceived as attractive and successful, even though they have relatively relaxed personal care rituals and don't strive for perfection in their appearance. Her deep-seated values may not have changed radically, but her altered sense of what's appropriate and acceptable in her new socio-cultural context is sufficient to have caused a moderate adjustment in behaviour.

Plenty of opportunity during the Settlement Journey— but be careful of assumptions about ethnic culture

In view of the patterns just discussed, those in the beauty, personal care, and grooming business would do well to seek out the opportunities that lie in migrants' above-average involvement in the beauty category.

"When they arrive in Canada, migrants are experiencing more than just a change in the brands on the shelf or the retail outlet where they buy their favourite face cream. They're experiencing a change in the whole cultural context in which they present themselves to others."

Consider where your offering can become part of migrants' Settlement Journey. A good starting point is to understand whether your category is one that your target group was using heavily prior to migration, or whether you're introducing them to something new upon arrival. Retailers and brands can offer enjoyable opportunities for experimentation and exploration during the Orientation stage of the Settlement Journey (see Chapter 3). Conversely, global brands with equity in source countries are well positioned to offer comfort and familiarity for newcomers during the Disorientation stage and beyond.

While pursuing these opportunities, it's vital to remember that the relationship between ethnic culture and beauty is complicated. The range of related issues — gender norms, beauty ideals, vanity, sexuality, and what's "natural" — is huge. These waters are hard to navigate, so it's best to have an experienced guide with considerable knowledge of the specific community.

For instance, there's been much recent media attention on Asian beauty ideals and how they relate to race. Some commentators have suggested that skin whitening products and cosmetic procedures like "double eyelid surgery" (which makes eyes rounder-looking) indicate an aspiration to look more European. Those suggestions are often oversimplifications rooted in a limited Western perspective. As the South Korean writer Euny Hong wrote of her own double-eyelid surgery, "Don't overplay the race issue. It's insulting to those of us who are merely vain."

Skin whitening is popular across East and South Asia. In East Asia in particular it's marketed not as a means of appearing more European but rather as part of a well-established female ideal that includes fair and translucent skin. That beauty ideal of round eyes and a round face for Chinese women long predates Hollywood movies and American fashion magazines. And the roots of South Asian beauty ideals can be traced back to ancient history. The *Kama Sutra* identifies four feminine types, the most desirable of which, the Padmini (Lotus) Woman, has skin that is "fine, tender and fair as the yellow lotus, never dark colored." These centuries-old beauty ideals relate to social status in an Asian context. More recently they've also become entangled with globalized images of beauty, many of which are generated by the Western beauty business. But to characterize the quest for paleness or specific facial qualities as signs of aspiring to a European look is inaccurate — the kind of misunderstanding that good research and expert guidance can help to avoid.

Automotive

Decades ago, newcomers who didn't plan to farm tended to settle in the downtown cores of major cities. Today they often settle in suburban areas as soon they land, driven by the availability and affordability of housing. With many migrants already living in suburbs—and with particular groups often concentrated in so-called "ethnic enclaves"—newcomers can also be drawn to suburbs by the promise of help from their own language groups and ethnocultural communities. (The suburbanization of migrant settlement patterns is discussed in the Introduction.)

This suburbanization means that more migrants need vehicles—and need them very soon after arrival in Canada. Newcomers increasingly arrive well-equipped to navigate their suburban environments: driving experience and international driver's licences have grown markedly more common among new arrivals.

An Environics survey conducted with PrepareforCanada.com found that 42% of newcomers bought a car within the first year after their arrival. Vehicle owner-ship increases to 81% among those who've been in Canada for six to ten years. The survey also included pre-migrants, those who were still in their countries of origin but about to migrate to Canada. Of these, 66% reported that they planned to buy a car within a year of arriving in Canada.

Migrants' automotive needs evolve as they establish themselves in Canada and proceed through the stages of the Settlement Journey. And because so many newcomers buy vehicles soon after arriving, pre-migration experiences of the automotive marketplace are very important part of the Cultural Lens through which they view vehicle offerings in Canada.

THE CULTURAL LENS
Lack of car-buying history

The majority of recent migrants come from countries with markedly lower rates of vehicle ownership than in North America. Indeed, there are relatively few countries that buy and own passenger vehicles at North American rates. In 2009, 608 Canadians per 1,000 owned a vehicle (and in the same year, the U.S. rate was even higher: 803 per 1,000). Compare these numbers with

FIG. 4.13

Where did newcomers seek information before buying their vehicles?

Sources of information about first vehicle purchase in Canada (multiple mentions permitted)

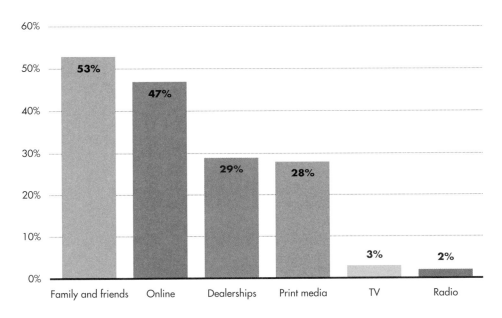

vehicle ownership rates in the top source countries of migrants. In India, 18 people per 1,000 own a vehicle. In the Philippines, it's 29 people per 1,000. And in China, although vehicle ownership has been growing rapidly, it was only in 2013 that the rate of vehicle ownership was expected to crack 10%.

Personal networks trusted over dealerships as information sources

Given such low pre-migration rates, many newcomers to Canada are not only first-time vehicle buyers but also the first generation in their families to own a vehicle. A car or truck is a major investment, and a daunting one for someone with relatively little knowledge of such particulars as features, financing, insurance, and service. Where do newcomers turn for information about what to look for in a new vehicle and how to go about the purchase? Primarily to family and friends.

In our survey of new arrivals who own a vehicle, 53% told us that they turned to their personal networks to gather information and advice about their first purchase of a vehicle in Canada. Online research (47%), an amplified version of word of mouth, was close behind family and friends. Less frequently cited sources of information about vehicle purchase were visits to dealerships (29%), newspapers and magazines (28%), television (3%), and radio (2%).

It's notable that only about a third of newcomers visit dealerships to learn about their products. This is an instance of pre-migration experience shaping people's attitudes and expectations in their new society. Because cars are relatively new—and still quite rare—in many major source countries of immigration to Canada, car culture is less entrenched and expertise about cars is not widespread. As a result, even some dealerships have staff that aren't highly expert in every aspect of their stock, and dealerships don't have the same aura of specialized knowledge that they do in North America.

Automotive marketers trying to reach newcomers through traditional channels may be spinning their wheels

Newcomers' pre-migration experiences help to explain why a substantial majority of them choose not to visit Canadian dealerships to inform their vehicle purchase decisions. And since they're less likely than the Canadian-born to drop by and browse the showroom, the North American marketing strategy of in-dealership promotions—complete with music and balloons—may not succeed in reaching these consumers.

"**The clear implication for Canadian automotive dealers is that special effort is necessary if they hope to keep newcomers' servicing business in-house. Successful initiatives are likely to address newcomers' price sensitivity and to emphasize the importance of appropriate maintenance for the long-term health (and possible resale value) of their vehicles.**"

The other upshot of these findings is that tried-and-true methods of marketing vehicles in North America—including sports sponsorships, billboards, radio or TV ads—may have little traction when it comes to newcomers.

Decoupling of sales and service

In North America, it's common for auto manufacturers to strongly encourage car owners to service their vehicles exclusively at the dealership where they were purchased (or at another of the manufacturer's dealerships). In major source countries of migrants to Canada, however, vehicle sales and vehicle service are more likely to be decoupled. Consumers may be quite brand loyal—loyal to their favourite auto manufacturer and loyal to their favourite auto-servicing business—but loyalty on sales doesn't necessarily mean turning to the sales outfit for service as well.

A related phenomenon is that in emerging markets, consumers often attach greater value to durable goods than to services. For instance, in some societies consumers may be willing to spend thousands of dollars to buy a piece of expensive furniture, but not be willing to pay for the delivery. The furniture itself is something they'll own and see for years to come—and therefore worth the investment—while delivery is a fleeting, one-time service that's more likely to be seen as a waste of money. Given this tendency to value products more than services, some consumers may purchase high-end cars but then demonstrate strong price sensitivity when it comes to maintenance and servicing.

Upon arrival in Canada, among newcomers who purchase vehicles, only about three in ten (29%) seek maintenance at the dealerships where they bought their cars. In our research among newcomers who've been in Canada a year or less, we find that they're more likely to take their car to an independent service centre (40%) and roughly as likely to go to a local garage (28%) as to a dealership. About one in ten do their own maintenance (6%) or forgo regular maintenance altogether (6%). Nevertheless, most are open to persuasion: when asked how likely they'd be to consider an auto service centre other than the one they currently used, 63% said they would consider it.

Dealerships must work hard to keep service in-house

The clear implication for Canadian automotive dealers is that special effort is necessary if they hope to keep newcomers' servicing business in-house. Successful initiatives are likely to address newcomers' price sensitivity and to emphasize the importance of appropriate maintenance for the long-term health (and possible resale value) of their vehicles. Also, because service is more personal than product—since the service provider's skills and judgment are

Automotive

ETHNIC CULTURE

Weak Influence. Ethnic cultures may vary in their interest in ostentatious consumption, for instance, but vehicles have little cultural meaning compared to things like food or money.

PRE-MIGRATION INPUTS

Strong influence. There are huge variations in rates of automobile ownership—and therefore familiarity with the category—across societies.

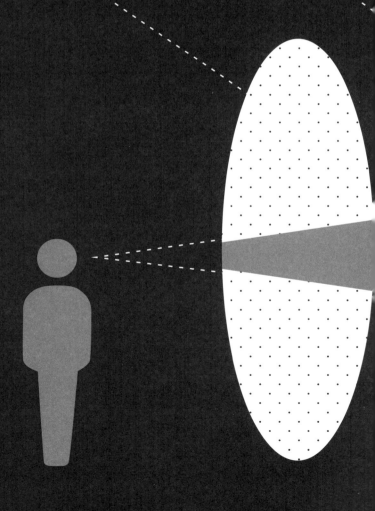

POST-MIGRATION INPUTS

Strong influence. Widespread vehicle ownership in Canada means migrants are more exposed to information about vehicles, features, and financing (via family, colleagues, advertising).

CULTURAL LENS

Culture, climate, and Canadian vehicle-buying norms (e.g. financing from the dealership) all play a role in changing migrants' expectations in the automotive category.

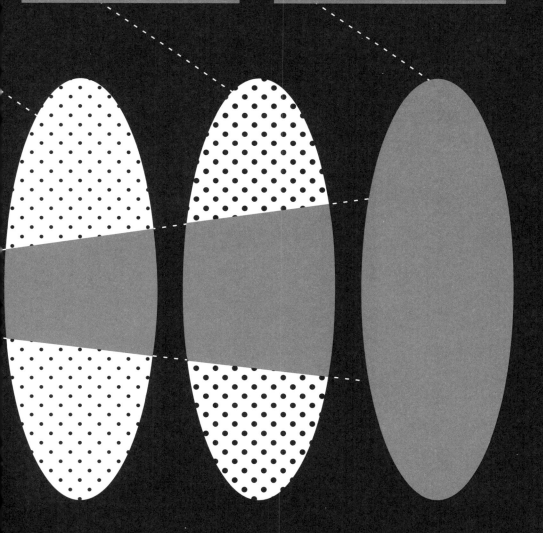

in play—individual relationships and social familiarity may prove more salient in this area. What brands are to vehicle purchase, relationships are to vehicle maintenance.

"Drive now, pay later? Sounds fishy ...":
Skepticism about financing

How often do you hear a TV or radio ad telling you that a car can be yours not for thousands of dollars, but for a remarkably low monthly payment? If you live in North America, this is probably a daily occurrence. Financing is a common and aggressively promoted option for vehicle buyers.

Many newcomers to Canada are baffled by these ads; the experience is similar to being told that a lawnmower or a new suit will cost $5 per month instead of a flat fee. In many major source countries, including the Philippines, India, and China, vehicle financing just isn't on offer—even for the wealthy. In some quickly growing markets, this is beginning to change; for instance, some auto-makers are starting to offer financing in India through non-bank financial companies (NBFCs). In many migrants' experience, however, vehicles are purchases like any other: you take them home once you've paid for them in full.

And it's not only an unfamiliarity with auto financing that's at issue here; the differences across markets go deeper. Because banking systems and credit habits differ around the world, migrants often treat all offers of credit with extreme caution: "What does it mean to 'own' a car for $300 a month? How many months will this go on for? Why is the dealer hiding the total cost? What's the catch?"

For many Canadian-born consumers, financing is an appealing way to take home the wheels one wants, even if one can't afford the full cost today. Newcomers who find their desired model a little out of reach, by contrast, are more likely to simply downgrade their choice. According to our research, 75% of newcomers who bought cars in their first year of living in Canada paid outright, without getting any financing from dealerships or financial institutions.

The upshot for Canadian marketers is that financing may be a red flag rather than an enticement to newcomers. Making offers as concrete and transparent as possible may in fact provide more reassurance and build more trust. More settled migrants are likelier to find financing offers appealing, but especially for newcomers, the lack of pre-migration experiences with credit and deferred payment means that trust and good communication must be important priorities for sellers.

That new-car smell

"Now, mister, the day the lottery I win / I ain't never gonna ride in no used car again." These lines occur in a Bruce Springsteen song about a teenaged boy's shame at his blue-collar family's "new" used car. Migrants to Canada would be more likely than the Canadian-born to understand the boy's embarrassment.

Many rapidly growing markets engender a lust for the new: new cars, new houses, new electronics, new everything. And where rapid growth has drastically changed people's means and lifestyles, what's new is typically seen as high-quality and modern. New possessions also often enjoy some international cachet, acting as signs that their owners have arrived and are participating in a globalized, urban world. What's old suffers by contrast. Older and used items are often seen as cheap, off-brand, out of date. But for many people born in Canada, what's old is charming. People who can afford new purchases poke around looking for vintage treasures, pay a premium for antiques, pop by garage sales to see if something "with character" catches their eye.

These divergent preferences are evident in the automotive market. It's not that most Canadian-born car buyers are looking for the vintage charm of a vehicle with an eight-track player and no seatbelts (most prefer modern fuel efficiency and Bluetooth). But the Canadian-born tend to see used cars as a sensible choice, not an embarrassing one made under duress. In 2001, Environics asked Canadians whether, given $20,000 to spend on a car, they'd rather buy new or a higher-end used vehicle; responses were almost evenly split. Clearly, used vehicles are a socially acceptable choice.

Coming from consumer environments where the preference for new things is pervasive, however, some migrants may be more concerned about loss of face if they buy secondhand, fearing that their choice will be seen not as one of admirable frugality but of desperation.

A preference for new, a budget for used (at first)

In view of this longing for the new, do the 63% of newcomers who buy a car in their first year *all* spring for one that's just rolled off the assembly line? Far from it. Affordability is too strong a consideration. Over three-quarters (78%) of migrants say their first vehicle in Canada was a used one. The difference comes through in more settled migrants, who have a strong preference for new vehicles—a preference that persists after many years in Canada, and that migrants are increasingly able to indulge as they gain ground financially.

Culture matters some; money and roads matter more

Like smartphones, cars are too new to be strongly affected by ethnic culture. Compared with such categories as food and charitable giving, vehicle purchase is only moderately influenced by cultural orientations shared across communities and handed down across generations. Nevertheless, general cultural attitudes on such matters as status, conspicuous consumption, and hedonism can colour people's automotive preferences.

It's by now a cliché to talk about Chinese consumers' love affair with luxury cars. For years, observers have noted that a combination of rapidly growing Chinese wealth and the Chinese cultural tendency toward status and hierarchy has resulted in a great deal of conspicuous consumption in China: people spending new money to demonstrate high social status.

There's no doubt that in the automotive category, Chinese in China have a taste for high-end vehicles. The consultancy McKinsey & Company notes that the luxury car market in China grew at an average rate of 36% annually between 2003 and 2013, faster than the overall auto market, which grew at 26% annually over the same period. McKinsey forecasts that China is likely to surpass the U.S. as the world's top luxury auto market by 2020. Rising wealth over the past decade has obviously played a large role in the expansion of the luxury auto market, but, as in any market, producers still need to connect emotionally in order to convince people to pay a luxury premium. McKinsey developed ten "premium personalities" based on a range of emotional characteristics and found different brands connecting on different personality traits. For instance, one German auto brand "based its appeal on a careful translation to the Chinese market of its global brand DNA of ambition, dynamism, and stylish prosperity," while another "pursued a more understated brand personality marked by attributes consistent with traditional Confucian values, such as reliability, quality, sophistication, and heritage." Both were successful.

"The lesson here may simply be that when it comes to such major purchases as vehicles, infrastructure and other practical considerations can trump culturally rooted preferences."

Enthusiasm for luxury vehicles—indeed, vehicles at large—has been somewhat weaker in India. To the extent that Indians buy cars (which they do at rates lower than people in other emerging markets), they tend to favour modest, fuel-efficient vehicles. Whether this lesser appetite for high-performance vehicles is rooted in aspects of Indian culture or simply Indian roads—which remain extremely uneven in quality—is an open question. It's notable that although India has famously been the source of major technological innovation and expertise, there's also a strain in Indian society that values cheap and ingenious solutions instead of the most obviously sophisticated or powerful ones. There's even a Hindi term, *jugaad*, that refers to such frugal technological innovation. But Indians' appreciation for clever frugality has its limits. The Tata Nano, an Indian creation touted as the world's cheapest car (originally costing about US$2,000) and an exciting *jugaad* breakthrough, sputtered in the Indian market. *The Economist* reports that, in addition to their production problems, the little cars were rejected by the low-income rural Indians who were meant to be their biggest fans; farmers preferred trucks.

The lesson here may simply be that when it comes to such major purchases as vehicles, infrastructure and other practical considerations can trump culturally rooted preferences. This is certainly the case in Canada, where winter weather has frozen the dreams of many a would-be luxury car driver.

A long and slushy road: Settling into Canadian auto pragmatism

When migrants arrive in Canada, they often carry with them a relatively strong inclination toward status and hierarchy, depending on their culture of origin. Environics' Social Values surveys find that overall, the foreign-born tend to score higher than the Canadian-born on values associated with the quest for status through consumption, such as *Need for Status Recognition* and *Ostentatious Consumption*. There may be a variety of reasons for this, from migrants' bringing more status-oriented values with them from their countries of origin to migrants' feeling a stronger pull to display status in order to show that they've made it in their new society. In any case, as they spend time in Canada, migrants run up against two C's that are likely to influence them over time: culture and climate.

Culturally, Canada is a relatively flat society. This is not to say it's without status hierarchies or inequality, but these hierarchies tend not to be as strict or as heavily enforced through etiquette and social norms.

As far as climate goes, Canada is colder and snowier than most migrants' countries of origin. Although almost all understand this prior to migrating, the length and seriousness of Canadian winters is something that tends to sink in fully only with direct experience. Pictures and descriptions of snowy winters can't quite convey the ordeal of digging one's car out of a snowbank or driveway in the pitch-dark at seven a.m. on a Tuesday in February.

Imagine a Chinese migrant who lands in Canada with the goal of buying a high-end car as soon as possible in order to send the right status signals. He buys a basic car (likely a used one) just to get around, but plans to upgrade soon. During his first year in Canada, however, he realizes that his manager at work, who has three kids, drives a basic minivan. He also notices that his own used car has a difficult life: encased in ice, encrusted with salt, struggling to start on frigid mornings. Perhaps a sleek luxury vehicle isn't a pragmatic choice in this environment after all—especially if the social signal it sends matters less.

Not surprisingly, our data show that the proportion of newcomers who end up buying a minivan after arrival in Canada is almost four times higher than the proportion who planned to buy such a vehicle before arriving.

In the case of our Chinese newcomer, his values haven't changed profoundly during his first year in Canada, but the way in which those values translate into a vehicle-buying decision has shifted.

THE SETTLEMENT JOURNEY

As in many product and service categories, it's worth remembering that the Settlement Journey overlaps with one's life journey to a certain degree. Many newcomers will need a car that can accommodate a young family, with room for kids and their belongings as well as safety features that put parents' minds at ease. Later in life, depending on their needs and values, settled migrants may shift toward sedans or something small and sporty that works well for a couple of empty-nesters who visit their grandchildren but don't have to cart their sports equipment around.

As they proceed through the stages of the Settlement Journey, migrants' wariness of financing also abates. They're likely to retain a healthy preference for consuming within their means, but over time they're also likely to observe that auto financing isn't a trick reserved for the most gullible but rather a widespread practice in Canada. They come to understand that, like leasing, it can sometimes—depending on such particulars as the type of car, the payment schedule, and, for small-business people, the possible tax benefits—be a reasonable approach.

5.

Connecting with
Migration Nation

The Cultural Lens provides a strong, strategic foundation for understanding the diverse outlooks and priorities that exist in Migration Nation. The next task is to connect with Migration Nation using marketing and communications strategies rooted in those insights.

When developing any marketing and communication strategy, one of the first priorities is to determine the optimum target based on such factors as demographics, product usage, and budget. Consumer targeting is always challenging, but in Migration Nation it can seem especially daunting given the diversity of the market(s) and the complex ways in which they vary and overlap.

When people begin to tackle "ethnic marketing" or "multicultural marketing," often their first step in paring down this complexity is to ask themselves a simple question: Which cultural group should I target? It's a question that may need to be answered at some point, but we don't think it's the right place to start.

A strategy that begins by defining an "ethnic target" can blind an organization to the full range of opportunities in Migration Nation. It can also obscure the cultural changes Canadian companies and organizations need to make in order to succeed in Migration Nation. And by "cultural changes" we don't simply mean attracting a diverse leadership team. That may help, but we're talking about a profound shift in thinking.

There's a lot of talk in business and marketing circles about the "new main-stream," the "new majority," and the "minority-majority" ("visible minorities" constituting demographic majorities) in Canadian cities. True, the numbers are impressive. But for us the key point isn't the ascendancy or even the dominance of "minorities"; it's the cultural cross-pollination between groups formerly understood as "ethnic" and "mainstream." Canada's cultural diversity is reshaping *all* Canadians' expectations about culture and affecting the kinds of messages they find appealing. This multi-directional exchange is what really defines the new mainstream—and it's the cultural shift that Canadian companies and organizations need to monitor and mirror. Paying attention to this interplay is the foundation of a total-market approach.

There's still much debate over what it means to adopt this "total market" strategy. One feature seems to cut across most definitions, however: a total-market approach brings culture into the centre of strategic planning. In Migration Nation (as in other diverse societies), "culture" encompasses both specific ethnic cultures and the interplay of ethnic cultures. That interplay—as manifested in the work of comedians like Russell Peters and Margaret Cho, and in movies like *Bend It Like Beckham* and *My Big Fat Greek Wedding*—is a central cultural dynamic and preoccupation of our times. Organizations' communications don't have to be *about* this dynamic, but nor can they completely ignore or exclude it without seeming out of touch. A total-market strategy is rooted in an awareness of—and ideally an ability to go with the flow of—this dynamic. It looks at a diverse population as a landscape in which widespread or universal needs (for food, leisure, services, and so on) are filtered through ethnic cultures that overlap and influence each other.

"WE LEAD WITH ETHNIC INSIGHTS"
This striking statement comes from Neil Golden, the CMO of McDonald's. What does it mean to "lead with ethnic insights"? Sometimes when we conduct research focused on one ethnic group, our client realizes that the insights emerging from the research are actually relevant across their entire market—they'd just never thought about it before. We think this happens because culture itself can be invisible; people can be blind to the habits and preferences that shape their daily lives. But sometimes looking through the Cultural Lens of a specific group can bring wider cultural insights into view. This is how "ethnic insights" can actually drive a whole strategy—and not just enable the targeting of a narrow segment.

As a team of Millward Brown researchers has argued in their book *Marketing to the New Majority*, communications developed on the basis of "ethnic insights" can have widespread appeal. People belonging to an ethnocultural community depicted in and targeted by an ad are likely to embrace that ad. Notably, however, people outside that group don't necessarily view the ad as *not* for them unless there are explicit cues to that effect—for instance, that the ads are in a language they don't understand. "Mainstream" consumers in a given market are generally open to ads featuring people who don't look like them. They may even find that such ads appeal to their sense of living in a modern, interesting society. At a minimum, they usually won't be offended by them. In fact, many "mainstream" Canadian consumers, especially youth and urban dwellers who tend to celebrate and brag about cultural diversity, expect advertising to reflect the culturally diverse world they live in. Such advertising is often perceived to be more authentic, aware, and engaging. Appeals to this generalized sense of ease with diversity have been evident in, for example, Heineken's recent "Open Your World" global campaign and Coca-Cola's 2014 "America the Beautiful" Super Bowl commercial.

In a sense, the total-market approach to multicultural marketing is the application of the best global-marketing practices at a domestic level. In global marketing, one of the biggest challenges marketers face is to find the right balance between standardization of products and offers and customization for local markets. Efficiency is compromised with too much localization, while without adequate customization, the effectiveness of offers and messages in local or national markets can suffer. Finding a balance between efficiency and effectiveness in the world of "borderless marketing," then, is a variation on the total-market challenge that multicultural marketers experience in places like Canada.

When companies reach out to global markets, the goal is to reach growth markets worldwide. When companies reach out to multicultural markets in Canada, the goal is to reach growth pockets within the country that haven't yet been fully tapped with existing ("mainstream") marketing activities. The importance of global or overseas markets doesn't diminish the importance of home markets, just as the importance of "ethnic" markets doesn't diminish the importance of the "mainstream" market. Keeping all these balls in the air is the objective of both global and multicultural marketers. In Migration Nation, effective total-market strategies will transcend the borders or boundaries between ethnicities and between ethnic markets and the mainstream. Transcending the boundaries doesn't mean pretending they don't exist. Rather, it means understanding that they're porous and flexible; ideas and tastes move across groups.

So what exactly does a total-market approach look like?

A colleague of ours once told us that a good way to pique people's interest in multicultural marketing is to begin presentations with "There's an ancient Asian saying …" Although it may seem a little gimmicky, people do tend to be intrigued by intellectual traditions that are not their own. Perhaps we all have a secret hope that insights from another time and place will help us crack the stubborn or confusing problems right in front of us.

Certainly the recent surge in popularity of the Chinese military strategist Sun Tzu (also rendered as Sun Zi) and his text *The Art of War* seems to owe something to business leaders' longing for durable wisdom from an ancient source. So you want to know how to build a total-market approach? We have some age-old Asian insights to guide you! But first, it's worth acknowledging that total-market initiatives are in their early stages in North America, and that so far there's no consensus on the best single approach. Many clients and agencies like the idea of achieving efficiency but are concerned about how to properly implement total market, as well as how to measure its impact. We think that at a strategic level, total market can be defined with some general principles; tactics and execution, however, are still likely to vary widely.

"There's an ancient Asian saying ..." (Part 1)

Sun Tzu said, "Strategy without tactics is the slowest road to victory; tactics without strategy is the noise before defeat." To be successful in Migration Nation, businesses and organizations need to have a fully integrated cross-cultural strategy, with specific tactics for individual segments aligned under one overarching approach.

To connect with Migration Nation, it's important to start macro and then go micro—ensuring that any group-specific targeting isn't an "ethnic afterthought" but rather connected to a larger vision. In other words, strategy planning should begin with a big, inclusive vision that takes diverse segments into account as elements of and influences on the total market—and then let the overall vision guide the development of specific tactics for specific segments. This in itself represents a reversal for many multicultural marketers, who often begin with an ethnic target and then work back to the "macro" vision (the very practice we referred to earlier when we cautioned that starting a strategy by defining the "ethnic target" risks blinding organizations to the full range of opportunities).

Connecting with Migration Nation, then, requires an initial understanding of both the total market and of specific segments—a foundation of "human" insights that cuts across groups as well as the nuances and preferences of groups within the wider society. Not every marketer or even every team can know everything, so getting a good picture of the total market—complete with cultural nuances—will require not only collaboration across organizations and agencies but also plenty of communication and coordination, from the inception of the strategy right through to its execution.

"There's an ancient Asian saying ..." (Part 2)

Sun Tzu said, "If you know the enemy and know yourself, you win every battle you fight." This bit of wisdom has many applications in Migration Nation. It might mean, for instance, that in order to reach out across cultures effectively, you have to understand your own Cultural Lens. You must learn to see your own assumptions and expectations not as "normal" but as one way among many to relate to the world around you, including products, services, and messages.

For the purposes of connecting with Migration Nation, we think the most important take-away from Sun Tzu's aphorism is a kind of organizational self-awareness. Multicultural marketers can spend a great deal of time thinking about the desires and habits of multicultural consumers—the "externals" of

CONDENSED MILK: A TOTAL-MARKET OPPORTUNITY

If you're selling sweetened condensed milk in Canada, your traditional customer base consists primarily of home bakers (mainly of European origin) who use it in desserts. The bad news is that that customer base is aging, and the jury is still out on whether the large millennial cohort that's starting to build families and households is going to bake with the same enthusiasm. The good news is that there may be plenty of opportunities for growth in Migration Nation. Chinese and Southeast Asian Canadians are heavy users of sweetened condensed milk; they use it not so much in baking but as an addition to hot beverages or as a dip.

Here's what an "ethnic marketing" strategy from twenty years ago would say: keep doing what you're doing with your "mainstream" European-origin bakers, and develop narrowly targeted campaigns to promote your product among Asians who use the same product in other ways.

But is there a total-market campaign that's more than the sum of these parts? Can one carefully crafted appeal reach a wider swath of Migration Nation, speaking to both mainstream and "ethnic" segments, leveraging cultural diversity, and celebrating the pleasure and comfort that sweetened condensed milk brings into Canadian homes regardless of how it's used? In the best-case scenario, you hit the trifecta: winning over older European-origin bakers and Asian-origin Canadians, and inspiring millennials to use the product in both ways—the way Mom uses it in baking and the way their Asian friends use it in drinks.

"In the best-case scenario, you hit the trifecta: winning over older European-origin bakers and Asian-origin Canadians, and inspiring millennials to use the product in both ways—the way Mom uses it in baking and the way their Asian friends use it in drinks."

their challenge. Something we often find receives too little attention, however, is the issue of organizational readiness—the "internals." Is your team well prepared to succeed in Migration Nation?

Today, multicultural marketing is often seen as an add-on. It might be the responsibility of a small team that's called on to roll out a pre-existing campaign in ethnic media. It might be allocated to someone who wears multiple hats and does "multicultural" on the side. It might be treated as a stand-alone project, the responsibility of the multicultural person or division within the company. It might be carefully planned or it might be somewhat arbitrary—a matter of translating existing materials and learning which ones "happen to work" with multicultural consumers. Many companies have a "mainstream" agency and a "multicultural" agency, the former setting the strategy without effectively integrating multicultural segments from the beginning of the planning process.

A successful total-market approach asks you to reconsider whether these approaches are really the best way to reach Migration Nation. "Knowing yourself" in order to gain competitive advantage, growth, and efficiency may require you to step back and take a more inclusive view—of both your process and your target market.

Use the full Cultural Lens (not just ethnic culture)

While total-market approaches point to different opportunities for different organizations, the Cultural Lens provides a framework that we see as useful across categories. A successful total-market approach demands a sense of the

"A successful total-market approach demands a sense of the traditional, dominant, or mainstream market for a given product as well as a sense of the emerging perspectives and expectations that exist in a newly diverse landscape."

traditional, dominant, or mainstream market for a given product as well as a sense of the emerging perspectives and expectations that exist in a newly diverse landscape. Developing a sound strategy also requires an understanding of how these new and old frameworks overlap and interact. The Cultural Lens can provide the building blocks for this total-market understanding.

As we've argued elsewhere, "which ethnic target?" isn't the best question to start with, partly because it forecloses other opportunities, and partly because ethnic culture is just one element of the Cultural Lens. So even if a specific ethnocultural segment is likely to be a fruitful target for your organization, overemphasizing ethnic culture at the expense of pre- or post-migration inputs (including the Settlement Journey) can steer you off course. Before developing any ethnic strategy (whether it's an isolated one or a component of a total-market approach), it's important to ask whether ethnic culture matters in the category at hand—and if so, why and how much.

Other questions also matter. What is the role and reputation of your brand or category globally? How have foreign-born Canadians of all ethnicities experienced your brand or category before arriving in Canada? How have these experiences shaped their expectations? And how much are people's motivations around your offering likely to change as they move through the stages of the Settlement Journey?

If the Settlement Journey is a key component of people's needs and motivations around your offering—for example banking and credit needs determined by their pre-arrival and early stages of life in Canada—then your next step is to find and connect with these newcomers. Ethnic culture is a secondary consideration.

Even if you can't answer each of these questions in great depth right away, thinking through them is a good way to begin disentangling the relevant considerations. Once you've arrived at a solid picture of the relevance (or irrelevance) of the different elements of the Cultural Lens, you can begin to define target groups based on those factors and develop targeted advertising and communications.

CREATIVE IMPLICATIONS OF THE CULTURAL LENS

Once the total-market strategy is developed, it's time for targeting—ensuring that the overarching strategy is effectively "translated" (whether literally or figuratively) into the various markets. Now is the time to determine the most effective languages and media, and to work in whatever nuances and special appeals might be most effective with specific segments.

FIG. 5.1
Targeted ads and messages are typically welcome

Agree strongly or somewhat on a 5-point scale

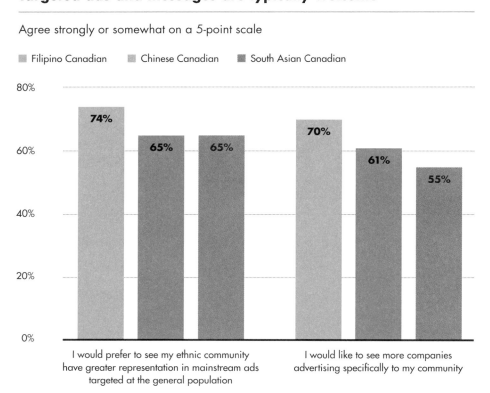

FIG. 5.1
Targeted ads and messages are typically welcome

Agree strongly or somewhat on a 5-point scale

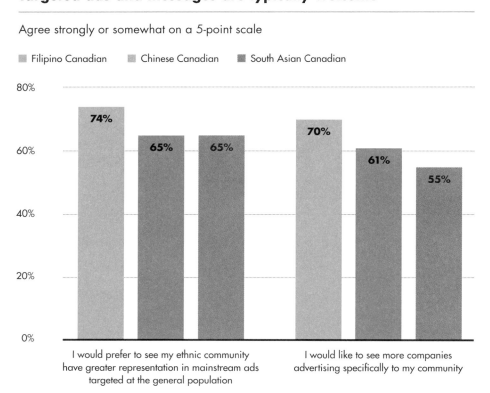

Legend: Filipino Canadian · Chinese Canadian · South Asian Canadian

Chart values:
- I would prefer to see my ethnic community have greater representation in mainstream ads targeted at the general population: 74%, 65%, 65%
- I would like to see more companies advertising specifically to my community: 70%, 61%, 55%

Pre-migration experiences are increasingly high-quality— so beware of cutting corners

The quality of advertising creative in major source countries of migrants to Canada has improved significantly in recent years. Especially in newer channels like social media, some advertising has in fact leapfrogged Canada's in its quality and sophistication. And with advertising budgets in markets like India and China dwarfing those in Canada, migrants arriving from these markets are used to strong creative that's well executed and has high production values. So although people arriving from these markets appreciate advertising that's targeted at them, such advertising can backfire if the execution or production is of poor quality. Of course, no one sets out to make bad advertising—but compromises in quality can and do occur when the budget for "multicultural" is an afterthought. In short, a shoddy targeted campaign can be worse than no community-specific outreach at all.

The Settlement Journey shapes not just needs but also attention and communication priorities

In Chapter 3 we describe the stages of a newcomer's Settlement Journey in detail. For each stage of the journey—Disorientation, Orientation, Belonging, and Independence—migrants not only have different concrete needs for products and services, but also different levels of openness and attention to advertising. Aligning message and tone with the Settlement Journey, then, is a powerful means of relating to foreign-born Canadians.

At the Disorientation stage, for instance, when stress and uncertainty are high, newcomers are looking for simplicity, reassurance, and familiarity. Complex messages or offers that require too much thought will be dismissed if they're noticed at all. Connecting with people at this stage of the Settlement Journey— and establishing the trust necessary to begin a relationship—is a difficult task that requires focus and investment. So it's worth asking yourself whether it's vital to connect immediately during Disorientation, whether it's worth the investment required to overcome newcomers' heightened skepticism at this difficult time of life. (For banks and mobile providers, the answer is usually yes. For a cosmetics company, it's probably no.)

As newcomers move through the stages of their Settlement Journeys, different messages, media, and offers will find openings. Those who would have reflex- ively avoided an in-store sample offer during Disorientation might happily stop and try the same product just a few months later once they've moved into the Orientation phase.

Ethnic culture: To target or not to target?

One question we often get asked about multicultural advertising is whether the various ethnic communities in Canada actually want it. Do they want to be singled out according to their ethnic culture? Generally speaking, yes. Culture and ethnicity are important parts of many people's identities, and although no one wants to be singled out in a negative way, typically people would rather be visible than invisible. According to our research, well over half of Chinese, South Asian, and Filipino Canadians would like to see more advertising targeted specifically at them (see Figure 5.1). Most people also say they feel closer to companies that advertise specifically to their community.

But it's important to remember that wanting to be addressed specifically as a member of an ethnocultural community isn't the same as wanting to be segre- gated. It's noteworthy that members of minority ethnocultural communities also want to see greater representation of their groups in mainstream advertising.

In fact, the proportion who'd like to see more representation in mainstream ads is greater than the proportion who want to see more communications targeted specifically at their communities.

Representation isn't the core of multicultural marketing— but in some cases it can go a long way

As Figure 5.1 shows, Filipino Canadians stand out from other groups in wanting to see more advertising specifically aimed at their community *and* greater representation of Filipinos in mainstream Canadian advertising. Why would Filipino Canaidans score especially high on these questions? (It's safe to assume that their desire for Filipino-targeted advertising isn't driven by difficulty understanding mainstream advertising; Filipino Canadians are on average highly proficient in English.)

Based on qualitative discussions with many Filipino Canadians, it appears that their desire for more targeted ads and more Filipino representation stems simply from the fact that there isn't much of either happening now.

When we show Filipino-targeted communication to our respondents, we often see greater appreciation than we do among other communities. Chinese Canadians are quite used to seeing Chinese-language communication in established Chinese media channels; they may like it, but it's too familiar to be impressive. For Filipino Canadians, however, there's still a novelty to being recognized and addressed as a significant community in Canada. Mass migration from the Philippines is somewhat more recent than mass migration from India and China. The Philippines has recently overtaken China and India as the top source country of migrants to Canada on an annual basis, but the Indian- and Chinese-Canadian communities remain larger in absolute terms. The Filipino-Canadian community is 454,000 strong—and growing—but in the media environment it remains something of a new kid in town, so Filipino Canadians are often particularly happy to be addressed as such in advertising.

A similar dynamic is at work in the representation of Filipinos in mainstream advertising. As we've noted elsewhere, everyone (not just migrant communities, but older people, same-sex couples, people who aren't model-skinny, and so on) tends to like seeing themselves represented in the advertising that is such a ubiquitous part of our environments. While for some groups (such as Chinese and South Asian Canadians) this experience is by now more familiar, for Filipino Canadians there's still a bit more of the "Hey, that's us!" excitement.

There's one more reason why representation feels especially significant to many Filipino Canadians as compared with South Asian or Chinese Canadians.

APPEALING TO GOAL-ORIENTED AND PERPETUAL SAVERS ALIKE: A TOTAL MARKET FOR FINANCIAL SERVICES

As we saw in the Financial Management section, people of different cultural backgrounds have different attitudes to and habits of saving money. Financial service providers, therefore, will inevitably face the challenge of finding efficiency in reaching out to the various segments of Migration Nation.

For example, telling people how much they'd have in their retirement if they set aside only $50 a month may be persuasive to mainstream clients, but it's probably irrelevant to clients from perpetual-saving cultures. Perpetual savers don't need to be convinced to save—they're already putting aside as much as they can—but they may need to be persuaded about which tools and institutions can be most helpful to them.

As in the case of sweetened condensed milk (page 177), financial service providers could develop a specific campaign for perpetual savers. But is that the most efficient and effective approach? Are there ways to be more inclusive, to save time and money by developing messages that resonate with people who save in different ways and for different reasons? What's the human side of saving that cuts across Migration Nation?

"Are there ways to be more inclusive, to save time and money by developing messages that resonate with people who save in different ways and for different reasons?"

These communities are not only unequal in size (the Chinese-Canadian community is about 20% larger than the Filipino-Canadian community, for instance) but also in the social capital they have in Canada. Currently, Filipino Canadians are on average less affluent, and the community is less politically influential than some other ethnocultural communities. These dynamics also drive a desire for recognition.

In the past we saw a similar trend among South Asian Canadians, who felt less widely recognized as a vibrant, contributing ethnocultural group than Chinese Canadians. Most if not all communities want to be recognized for their successes and contributions to Canadian society. The sense of urgency about being recognized can diminish as groups achieve numbers, success, and cultural confidence in Canada—this has been the case with the Chinese community—but we're all human beings with social needs, so the desire to be viewed positively never goes away entirely. (For instance, although men are economically and socially dominant in myriad measurable ways, many men still feel stung and offended by the smart-wife-stupid-husband clichés that are so common in advertising.)

In-language or in English?

Any discussion of ethnic culture that doesn't touch on language is incomplete. One of the most frequent objectives of the research we conduct on multicultural advertising is to determine the importance of language for the target group. About three-quarters (77%) of those who've arrived in Canada since 2001 list a non-official language as their mother tongue, and over half (55%) use a non-official language most often at home. For some groups—notably Chinese Canadians—attachment to and use of their mother tongue remains stronger

"The sense of urgency about being recognized can diminish as groups achieve numbers, success, and cultural confidence in Canada ... but we're all human beings with social needs, so the desire to be viewed positively never goes away entirely."

than the average among migrants. So even if it isn't essential for comprehension, in-language communication can be an important way of generating a sense of closeness and relevance—of making migrants feel seen and spoken to.

It's worth considering each of these reasons for in-language communication: improved comprehension and improved relevance.

Comprehension. This is obviously fundamental: if your audience doesn't understand your message, all is lost. Overall, just 10% of first-generation migrants in Canada don't understand English and French, and yet for certain target audiences, only in-language communication can ensure complete understanding. For instance, although 90% of first-generation South Asian immigrants whose mother tongue isn't English can speak English, among those who are over sixty-five, English comprehension drops from 90% to 61%. Among Punjabi-speaking Canadians in the sixty-five-plus age group, less than half speak English. These older audiences may be a small proportion of the total South Asian population, but they can have a big influence on marketers' decisions about such channels as ethnic TV. And of course, even those who speak some English may not be fully proficient; many younger migrants who speak—and even work in—English or French may still be more at ease in their mother tongue.

As is the case with South Asian migrants, among migrants whose mother tongue is Spanish or Portuguese, about nine in ten (92%) have at least some proficiency in one of Canada's official languages.

People who live in major Canadian cities might find that they see Chinese-language advertising more often than advertising in other languages. This is no coincidence. Knowledge of English is moderately lower among Chinese Canadians, partly because English isn't very prevalent in most people's pre-migration experiences in China and Hong Kong. Although the majority of Chinese Canadians have some proficiency in English (79% of migrants who list Chinese as their mother tongue have knowledge of English), English comprehension in this group tends to be relatively weaker upon arrival than it is among those from countries where English is more widely used.

Lower levels of English comprehension occur among both Mandarin-speaking newcomers and established Cantonese-speaking immigrants. For this reason, some argue that Chinese Canadians are the one large migrant community that really needs in-language communications, and marketers are indeed more likely to make it their default mode for this community. And because Chinese-language media are so well established in Canada, it is easier (and arguably more imperative) for marketers to develop Chinese-language communications.

It's worth remembering that not all communication is alike. Picture yourself sitting on a bus trying to read an ad in a language you understand moderately well. You'd probably get it: just a bit of copy, and plenty of time to think it through. But if your phone rang and someone started speaking to you in that same language, you might be completely lost. In other words, we find that in-language communication can be more important for spoken than for written messages. In-language can be especially critical when interaction is required.

Relevance. Simple comprehension isn't everything. Nuances of language—colloquialisms, accents, and so on—can help people feel close to the message and the messenger. For example, we've seen that Filipino Canadians are on average highly proficient in English. Nevertheless, this group appreciates communication in Tagalog—and that appreciation doesn't stem from a need for comprehension, but rather a desire to be addressed.

As the Filipino case illustrates, when it comes to in-language communication, one rule does not fit all. And since comprehension isn't the only consideration, decisions about what language to use become part of the discussion on communication strategy. What's the strategy to build relevance for the audience? What role will language play in that strategy? What other elements of communication will connect with the audience's ethnocultural identity? How strong are the other non-language-related brand cues?

This discussion becomes especially complex in the case of South Asian languages. For instance, Punjabi is the mother tongue of 433,280 Canadians. But given that many Punjabi speakers are highly proficient in English, when is the use of Punjabi appropriate? Meanwhile, Hindi is spoken across India—and so will arguably cast a wider net—but it's less closely associated with ethnocultural identity, so may not resonate as strongly as Punjabi does with its audience. Finally, there's the question of Hinglish—the colloquial mixture of English and Hindi familiar to many Canadians of Indian origin. If you were to use Hinglish, would it sound savvy or silly?

Answering these questions isn't easy, but here are a few helpful questions to consider with your team:

- *Who is speaking?* Consider not just the character or voice of the ad, but the brand or organization itself. South Asian Canadians may expect a South Asian entertainment company to speak to them in Hinglish. But they may not expect it or want it from a Canadian financial services or health care provider.

- *What is the objective of the communication?* Is it intended to increase an emotional connection with the audience? Or is it more tactical and intended to communicate information about the product or the service?

- *What is the medium?* For example, many Chinese Canadians who prefer spoken communication in Chinese are happy to switch to English online, especially if they feel that English may provide more clarity. Industries where complexity and specialized language are factors—such as financial services—should bear this in mind.

One final point on language: it's better to have good English- or French-language communication than poor in-language communication. We cautioned earlier that foreign-born Canadians react negatively to advertising that's in their language but lower-budget or otherwise less impressive than mainstream advertising (whether mainstream in Canada or mainstream in migrants' countries of origin). A similar principle can be applied to customer service delivered through call centres. For instance, if Chinese-language call centre agents aren't as knowledgeable as their English-language counterparts and need to transfer the call, customers can come away frustrated.

MEDIA IN MIGRATION NATION

Targeted communication isn't complete without targeted media. Messages crafted for specific segments need to be communicated through the most relevant and effective channels. While the media landscape will continue to evolve over time, ethnic specialty media are likely to remain a useful venue for targeted messages, owing to their availability and size. They'll often—though not always—be part of a sound total-market strategy.

Measurement of the use of ethnic-specialty media is a challenge in Canada. The main sources of media measurement, such as BBM (originally the Bureau of Broadcast Measurement) and PMB (the Print Measurement Bureau), don't include ethnic media properties. They don't engage in in-language data collection, nor do they capture sufficient samples of minority-language communities to enable analysis.

One source of information on ethnic-specialty media is the comprehensive 2012 survey of Chinese and South Asian media use conducted by Environics on behalf of Mediabrands. (Mediabrands Research is a research division of IPG that provides consumer and media research for many of the top media organizations and advertisers in Canada.) The Multicultural Media Study, the largest and most recent multicultural media study in Canada, examined the use of ethnic media among first-generation Chinese Canadians and South Asian Canadians in Toronto and Vancouver. Data and insights from MacLaren Cultura the multicultural marketing arm of MacLaren McCann, have also helped us in the development of this section.

Media targeting Chinese Canadians

Multicultural media has significant reach among Chinese-Canadian residents of Toronto and Vancouver. Among those who use a Chinese dialect most often at home, 86% consume in-language TV, radio, or print in an average week. These in-language media users are typically devoting fifteen hours each week to Chinese-language media. Although 91% of this group also consumes English-language media, in-language media is perceived as more relevant and engaging. In fact, 69% of Chinese agree that they pay more attention to TV, radio, and print communications that are in Chinese dialects.

In-language TV is the most consumed media among Chinese Canadians in Toronto and Vancouver. Among Chinese Canadians who consume in-language media, 76% watched Chinese-language TV in the past week. Two Canadian stations dominate Chinese-language TV: Fairchild TV, which broadcasts in both Cantonese and Mandarin, and Talentvision, which broadcasts primarily in Mandarin.

Fairchild Media Group also dominates the Chinese radio market, with owner-ship of Fairchild Radio (the top station) as well as a 50% share in the runner-up A1 Chinese Radio, broadcasting in both Cantonese and Mandarin.

The Chinese community in Canada has published newspapers for over a hundred years, beginning with the *China Reform Gazette*, which launched in Vancouver in 1903. Today, 64% of Chinese Canadians have read a Chinese-language print publication in the past week. *Sing Tao Daily* and *Ming Pao Daily* are the two most dominant publications in the community. Established to serve the wave of Cantonese-speaking immigrants that came from Hong Kong at the end of the 20th century, both *Sing Tao Daily* and *Ming Pao Daily* are printed in Traditional Chinese. Demand for Simplified Chinese newspapers is increasing as more migrants from mainland China, who read that script, arrive in Canada. For now, however, Simplified Chinese newspapers are mostly weeklies with smaller circulation.

Of course, new media is playing an increasingly important role in communication, with a range of Chinese-language websites, community forums, and blogs targeting Chinese communities living in Canada. One pioneer, a local Chinese portal called YorkBBS, started in 2002 and targeted primarily international students; it has since grown to over 550,000 registered members and attracts 15 million views monthly.

As for social media, Chinese Canadians favour Weibo, a microblogging platform that's popular in China and that might be described as a hybrid of Twitter and Facebook. Sina Weibo is in fact the most popular Chinese social media platform among the Chinese diaspora, with over 500 million registered users worldwide and over 300,000 active users in Canada. Although Chinese Canadians naturally have access to Twitter, Facebook, and all other social media sites in use in Western countries, the Chinese government restricts the use of these sites in China (blocking them with "The Great Firewall of China"). As a result, many Chinese migrants in Canada opt to use Weibo in order to stay connected with their friends and family back home. (After all, a social networking platform isn't much use if important members of your social network can't access it.) Local Chinese-Canadian influencers in Toronto have strong presences on Weibo; YorkBBS has well over 30,000 followers.

And Chinese Canadians aren't the only Canadians using Weibo—people who want to be relevant to Chinese Canadians also have a presence there. The mayor of Vancouver, Gregor Robertson, has a following of over 75,000 on Weibo. Brenda Halloran, the mayor of Waterloo, Ontario, is a user. So is Chinese-Canadian politician Olivia Chow.

Naturally, these outreach efforts aren't limited to politicians. With support from Chinese specialist communications agency Sensu Communications, Canadian fashion retailer Holt Renfrew has been using Weibo to build relationships with current and potential Chinese customers. Holt Renfrew's Weibo presence is thriving, with thousands of followers, and Sensu is also helping the high-end retailer increase its presence on WeChat, a mobile text and voice-messaging service that's extremely popular in China and among Chinese Canadians. WeChat provides location-based services and allows users to accept push notifications from brands that are of interest to them; Holt Renfrew is connecting with thousands of Chinese Canadians using these tools.

Media targeting South Asian Canadians

Among South Asian Canadians in Vancouver and Toronto, 83% have consumed some English-language media in the past week, excluding digital media. But that doesn't mean they're not engaged in South Asian media. About a quarter (27%) of South Asian Canadians prefer in-language communication, and 85% have consumed South Asian media in the past week.

As with Chinese Canadians, TV is the most commonly used ethnic specialty media among South Asian Canadians. The Canadian offering is dominated by two companies, Asian Television Network (ATN) and The Ethnic Channels Group (ECG). Although each carries a wide variety of channels (not just South

Asian), the top six channels are in Hindi/Hinglish, which allows for a broad reach, since it's most likely to be understood across the many South Asian cultural groups in Canada. Most of the content for these channels comes from a global South Asian entertainment culture that's obviously very well developed. Drama is the most popular content, followed by Bollywood movies, news, and of course the beloved cricket.

The term "South Asian" incorporates a diverse range of cultures and nationalities; South Asian media is equally diverse. Regional channels (especially in Punjabi, such as Alpha TV Punjabi) are popular. Tamil-language channels like Star Vijay also have large followings. Geo TV is favoured by many Pakistani Canadians.

When it comes to print media, 50% of South Asians have read an ethnic print publication in the past week (compared with 64% of Chinese). A wide array of weekly print publications is available to South Asian readers; for example, in Ontario, Mississauga alone boasts over thirty publications serving South Asian Canadian communities. Most of these publications are free, and have attracted wide audiences. Some of the most popular South Asian Canadian publications are English language; these include *Weekly Voice* and *South Asian Focus* (part of the *Brampton Guardian*). Still, although South Asian Canadian media is an active landscape in terms of content, it's relatively inactive in advertising. These many small publications are currently hindered by the fact that they have trouble presenting a measurable, unified media-buying option; as a result, they tend to feature mainly local ads. But publishers are aware of this issue, and South Asian print media offerings are likely on the cusp of some significant changes.

"Targeted offers, approaches, and messages can be important tactics within an overall total-market strategy crafted to reach all Canadians; the important thing is to view targeted approaches in the wider context of Migration Nation and not to treat them as siloed efforts aimed at communities that are cut off from the mainstream."

Radio is a popular medium among South Asian Canadians; just over half of South Asians in Toronto and Vancouver have listened to a South Asian ethnic specialty station in the past week. To some extent, listening to the radio is a media consumption habit carried over by South Asian migrants who hail from rural areas in their countries of origin. Punjabi radio shows are extremely popular with the Punjabi community, and Tamil programs featuring local community news and call-in shows are also popular among the Sri Lankan community.

Like Chinese Canadians, South Asian Canadians use digital media more than other Canadians do. English-language sites from South Asia, such as timesofindia.com, are popular. And just as it does for other migrant communities, social media represents a way for foreign-born South Asian Canadians to stay in touch with family and friends back home at either minimal cost or no cost at all. And because South Asians living in Asia aren't restricted in their internet access to the same extent as Chinese living in China, Facebook represents a key platform for communication between South Asian diasporas and their homelands. Skype is also popular.

Ethnic specialty platforms and total market can go hand in hand

Understanding and using these ethnic specialty media channels isn't necessarily at odds with taking a total-market approach to Migration Nation. Marketers need to bear three things in mind. First, culture matters—and the Cultural Lens can help illuminate cultural differences and perspectives. Second, communities don't exist in isolation; minority and mainstream interact and overlap. Third, achieving optimum growth means understanding and tapping the various currents that flow into the Canadian mainstream. Targeted offers, approaches, and messages can be important tactics within an overall total-market strategy crafted to reach all Canadians; the important thing is to view targeted approaches in the wider context of Migration Nation and not to treat them as siloed efforts aimed at communities that are cut off from the mainstream. Navigating these currents requires cultural dexterity. But for those who can weave different cultural threads together into an effective total-market strategy, the potential rewards are substantial.

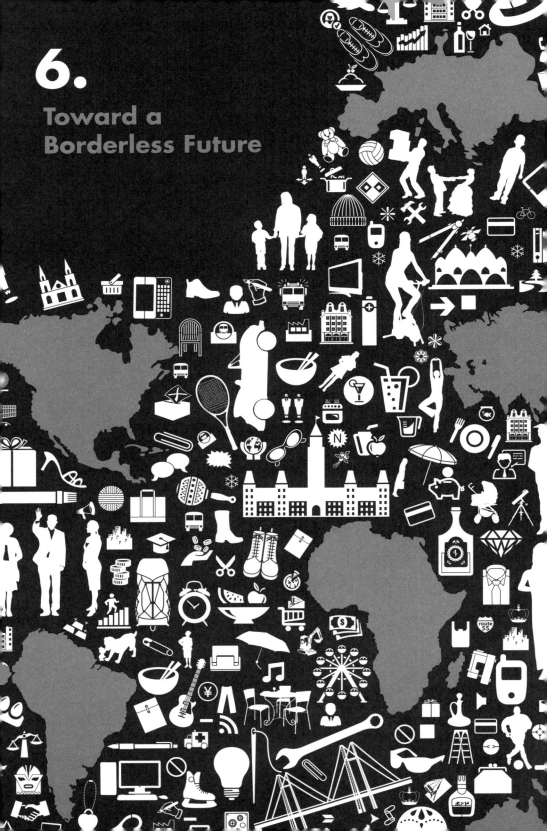

6.

Toward a
Borderless Future

Throughout this book we've discussed the implications for marketers of a world in which people, products, brands, attitudes, messages, expectations, and ideas flow across borders—all with less and less friction. This raises the question: in a world where national borders are less meaningful, what will become of Migration Nation?

We see international marketing and multicultural marketing as essentially the same discipline: one that targets consumers of diverse cultural backgrounds, whether they live in different regions or in different units of the same apartment building. Despite some obvious logistical and administrative distinctions, we see the kind of marketing multinational corporations do (with country-level brand management, for instance) and the work of top multicultural marketers in Canada as variations on the same theme.

In short, we believe that the future of marketing is borderless—especially in Migration Nation. This may seem paradoxical: How can marketing within a set of national borders (Canada's) be described as borderless? But in our view multicultural Canada is a microcosm of a globalized world. In particular, we think Canada's hyperdiverse cities are at the leading edge of an emerging globalism that is at once worldwide and strongly local.

Global meets local in hyperdiverse cities

Cities around the world are both sites of and engines for globalization. According to a UN report, "Globally, the level of urbanization is expected to rise from 52 per cent in 2011 to 67 per cent in 2050." By that time, the world's urban population is projected to be the same size as the world's *total* 2002 population. And Canada is well ahead of the global norm in this regard, with 81% of its population living in urban areas.

Urbanization, then, is a necessary context for Migration Nation. And although Canada's cities are unusual in their hyperdiversity, they certainly don't exist in isolation; they're strongly connected to global trends and offer some hints about the future.

For one thing, we find that the line between domestic and international markets is blurring. Are young South Asians living in the Toronto suburbs of Brampton and Mississauga, for instance, more influenced by local "mainstream" English-language media or by their scores of online connections with peers living in Asia—and in turn by the media and cultural influences those peers are taking in?

In the past, marketers might have simply waited for young people with distinctly Asian cultural tastes to acculturate—to become "more Canadian." Today, smart marketers won't be holding their breath awaiting that outcome. Tastes and expectations in Canada's large diasporas will evolve, but they'll continue to feature mixes and hybrids. And these hybrids will in turn become increasingly mainstream, embraced by other diasporas and by the Canadian-born of all backgrounds. Here again, the flow of cultural influence isn't one-way, with migrants and their children absorbing Anglo- or Franco-European norms and adapting; it's multi-directional, with globalized cities taking in and sending out influences that will connect Canada to the world and change the flavour of Canadian society.

Just as influence doesn't simply flow from Canada to migrant, it no longer flows primarily from West to East. As globalization gained speed in the 1990s, many people expressed anxiety about the Westernization—or even Americanization—of the world, with U.S. brands like Coca-Cola and McDonald's steamrolling the planet. But today, as global economic power shifts away from North America and especially to China, such concerns seem increasingly irrelevant.

We're unlikely to see one unified global culture (let alone one defined by a single world power); rather, we see global cultures, each with multiple hubs. The McKinsey report *Urban World: Mapping the Economic Power of Cities* found that six hundred urban centres generate approximately 60% of the world's GDP, and that more than 20% of global GDP in 2007 came from 190 North American cities. But McKinsey predicts a significant shift: "By 2025, 136 new cities are expected to enter the top 600, all of them from the developing world" —with many of these in Asia.

What happens when global culture no longer emanates primarily from North America but from multiple regions? Clearly the worldwide spread of K-pop from Korea and its merging with multi-ethnic influences doesn't fit neatly into the notion of American cultural hegemony. Nor does the growing influence of Bollywood alongside Hollywood. Starbucks may have replaced McDonald's as a symbol of American cultural hegemony—but it's significant that Starbucks' recent product innovations derive from Asian tastes. Oprah—that most American of cultural icons—has announced her partnership with Starbucks featuring a co-branded product with roots in South Asia: Teavana Oprah Chai Tea.

It's a very uncertain but exciting time to be in the marketing business—globally and also in Canada. Diversity, diasporas, globalized cities, globalized cultures—for the time being, Canada *is* the world, only more so. It's an excellent place from which to think forward to a borderless future. In this final chapter, we explore two important facets of this emerging world: the incredible growth and power of diasporas that connect far-flung people with shared threads of identity, and the global rise of Asian youth culture.

THE AGE OF DIASPORAS

Human beings are living in the age of diasporas: mass migration has created large populations of people who share ethnic cultures but are geographically dispersed. Today, about 40 million Chinese and 25 million Indians live overseas, and in each case about 20% are living in the Americas. As Robert Guest, business editor of *The Economist*, notes, there are more Chinese people living outside China than there are French people in France. The Indian economist Bibek Debroy has written that in England, more people are employed by Indian restaurants than by iron, steel, coal, and shipbuilding combined.

In Chapter 1 we described what's new about Canadian diversity today:

- Hyperdiversity—the sheer number of migrants and the numerous countries from which they arrive

- Technological connectivity—migrants' ability to remain in close touch with their countries of origin, promoting cultural and economic exchange

- New attitudes toward difference—minority identities seen not as problems to be suppressed or overcome, but marks of positive distinction

- New economic dynamism in source countries—the rising fortunes of such major source countries as India and China

The combined result of these trends is that the spread of diasporas represents an exceptionally powerful force in Canada. They're a major reason why, according to the KOF Index of Globalization, Canada ranks among the fifteen most globalized nations in the world.

Canada's largest diasporic populations hail from Asia, and although China and India constitute big slices of the diasporic pie, they're by no means the whole story. In 2009, 215 million people were living outside the country in which they were born. This represents 3% of the world's population, and an increase of 40% since 1990. Of these global migrants, 7.2 million are living in Canada.

And there's every sign that the trend toward migration will continue. Sixteen percent of the world's adults say they'd like to move to another country permanently if they had the chance. This translates to about 700 million people worldwide.

Diasporas' effects flow both ways

In the past, when long-distance travel and communication were both more difficult, the effects of migration were felt mainly in the destination country. But Robert Guest argues that today's diasporic networks have a number of important effects on both migrants' source countries and destination countries. They spread information—not least about business opportunities and economic trends—across borders. They foster the trust that underpins business relationships: family and friends may take each other's word for the honesty or good work of a prospective partner or supplier far away. And they build relationships that help people living in different contexts collaborate on a range of initiatives—from business to science. One study, by William Kerr and Fritz Foley of Harvard Business School, found that U.S. firms that have large numbers of Chinese-American employees had an easier time setting up operations in China even in the absence of formal partnerships with Chinese firms.

It's not just commercial activity that makes money flow across diasporic networks: individuals are sending huge amounts of money to family and friends in their countries of origin. According to the World Bank, of the $529 billion in remittances that flowed around the world in 2012, $23.9 billion flowed out of Canada. On a per capita basis, Canadian migrants are among the largest senders of remittances, whose top destinations were China ($3.9 billion), India ($3.5 billion), and the Philippines ($2 billion).

Links of personal and professional familiarity combine with a global media environment that is prolific and itself increasingly social network-driven to create a world in which everything spreads faster and more extensively—business offerings, ideas, trends, even communicable diseases.

"**Diasporas are one more way in which Canadian diversity today feels different and functions differently than it did in the past. They're one more reason why Canada isn't just a country with a lot of immigrants, but a place called Migration Nation.** "

Diasporas are one more way in which Canadian diversity today feels different and functions differently than it did in the past.

THE RISE OF ASIAN YOUTH CULTURE:
BOB AND DOUG, MEET HAROLD AND KUMAR

Thirty years ago, Canadian teenagers and young adults laughed at the beer-soaked antics of homegrown hosers Bob and Doug McKenzie, played by Rick Moranis and Dave Thomas. Stoner icons Cheech and Chong, who emerged just a few years before Bob and Doug, also had a devoted constituency who enjoyed watching the pair trip through their adventures in a haze of marijuana smoke.

Over the past decade, those who appreciate a good bromance between lovably confused young men have been offered a new duo: Harold and Kumar. The sophistication of the humour hasn't changed much since the 1970s, but what's notable about Harold and Kumar is that they're not of Scottish stock like Bob and Doug or Latino like Cheech, but Korean American (Harold Lee) and Indo-American (Kumar Patel). Harold and Kumar may not be the proudest achievement of North America's Asian-heritage population, but their existence certainly mirrors a dramatic demographic shift among the continent's young population.

This shift is especially strong in Canada, and especially in cities. Currently, 35% of Toronto's under-twenty-five population is of either South Asian or East Asian descent. In Vancouver that figure is 39%. And by 2031, those proportions are expected to reach 46% and 52%, respectively. In both of Canada's largest urban areas, the time when Asian-origin youth outnumber European-origin youth is not far off.

Harold and Kumar's ethnicities are significant for the way they reflect demographic change in North America. But they're perhaps even more significant in another way: how little they matter. Their Asian heritage may drive some of the humour and storylines (Kumar is dispatched to Guantanamo Bay at one point), but in these movies racism is treated as a minor annoyance, trivial and mundane compared with the great struggles of Harold and Kumar's lives, such as getting to a fast-food place for a burger when they're high and have the munchies.

For urban Canadians of all ages, even those who grew up in a whiter, more monocultural Canada (Bob and Doug's Canada), ethnocultural diversity is simply part of the background of daily life. And for younger people, who've been immersed in the hyperdiversity of Canadian schools since kindergarten, ethnocultural diversity is even more unremarkable.

Young people are the heart of Migration Nation

One can't talk about migration and diasporas without talking about the young. This is true for three main reasons.

First, migrants are generally younger than other Canadians. The median age of a newcomer to Canada in 2011 was 31.7, almost six years younger than the median age for the general population (37.3).

Second, many families migrate with young children. Among migrant households, 53% have young children at home, while the same is true of just 40% of households headed by the Canadian-born. Among migrants who've been in Canada for less than a decade, the numbers are even higher: 64% of those who've been here for four years or less have young children at home, as do 72% of households whose heads have been in Canada for between five and nine years.

People who migrate as children with their parents are generally referred to as the "1.5 generation." Although they're first-generation migrants because they were born elsewhere, they differ from those who arrive as adults because they grow up in Canadian neighbourhoods and are educated in Canadian schools alongside Canadian-born peers. Culturally, then, their experiences are somewhere between those of their migrant parents (first generation), and of Canadian-born children of migrants (second generation)—hence "1.5 generation."

Third, many people first become migrants when they go abroad to study. As of 2009 there were 3.7 million international students worldwide, and the OECD has estimated that by the year 2025, 7.2 million students will travel to another country for post-secondary education. In 2012, there were over 265,000 foreign students pursuing education at Canadian institutions, a number that had increased by 94% since 2001. In early 2014, the federal government announced its intention to double the number again; it released the International Education Strategy, whose goal is to attract 450,000 foreign students by 2022. As of 2010, just under a third of the foreign students in Canada were from China and a further 10% were from India. Significant numbers also came from other Asian countries including Korea and Japan. These overseas students, combined with young, Asian-Canadian residents and citizens, contribute to a booming Asian student population—and not all of them will go home when they complete their degrees. The recent introduction of the Canadian Experience Class in Canadian immigration policy allows many foreign students who've graduated from Canadian institutions to apply to stay permanently in the country, adding more young, educated, diasporic stock to Canada's cities.

The implication of these trends for anyone communicating to youth in Canadian urban centres is that they're targeting a demographic that's not only heavily Asian in demographic terms, but strongly influenced by Asian socio-cultural currents.

Speaking to youth means speaking to Asian youth

How big are the implications of a much more Asian youth population? For some industries that are already highly globalized, the implications might be fairly minor. When it comes to fashion and electronics, for instance, kids in most major cities tend to want more or less the same clothes and the same devices. Automotive is another industry that may not feel the influence of Asian youth culture as heavily as some.

In other categories, however, an increasingly Asian and Asian-influenced youth population will make a big difference. Recall, for instance, Bob and Doug McKenzie and their fondness for brews. The people who were once Bob and Doug's biggest fans have traditionally been crucial for beer sales in Canada; brewers have relied on young males for a large proportion of the volume of beer they sell. But, as we discussed in Chapter 4, Asian-Canadian youth drink less and drink differently than the Bob and Doug demographic. The silver lining is that young Asian men in North America do show some of the preference for high-end spirits that exists in East Asian and South Asian countries: a few years ago, club owners in Los Angeles started taking notice when the dollars from drink sales were markedly higher at events organized by Climax Global Entertainment. It turned out that Climax courted a heavily Asian-American demographic who were buying premium liquor to a much greater extent than the predominantly non-Asian youth who attended the clubs on other nights.

But while beer marketers face a real possibility of declining consumption, other categories will get a boost from an increasingly Asian-Canadian youth demo-graphic. For example, those in the telecom business can rely on the fact that young Asian Canadians show the same strong enthusiasm for new technology that exists in Asian markets. And young Asian-Canadian women resemble their peers in Asia in their enthusiasm for high-end skin care brands.

It's important to note that ethnic culture doesn't always play a straightforward or predictable role in the tastes of young (especially 1.5-generation) Asian Canadians. But when it comes to food and beverages, categories strongly influenced by ethnic culture, there's no doubt that the tastes of Asian youth are distinct. We know that young Chinese Canadians consume some carbonated soft drinks but not in a way that completely resembles their Canadian-born age peers: rather, like their peers in Asia, they gravitate to tea-based drinks like bubble tea or iced tea. It's also true that young, second-generation and 1.5-generation Canadians will favour flavours that are predominant in the diets of their parents. Canada is thus seeing an increase in the popularity of mango-flavoured desserts and Asian flavours like teriyaki and wasabi, for example.

In some categories, it's too early to tell what the influence of this large, young Asian-Canadian population will be. For instance, it's not clear whether second-generation and 1.5-generation Canadians will share their parents' distinct values and preferences when it comes to financial services, saving, and investing.

What role does ethnic culture play for young, globalized people immersed in hyperdiversity?

To be successful in the emerging Canadian youth market, businesses need to look closely at Asian Canadians with a view to understanding how their ethnic culture and their participation—and growing dominance—in young, Canadian urban life shape their tastes, habits, and outlooks. Understanding the role of ethnic culture among youth is more complex than understanding it among older people who've migrated as adults. Although adult migrants adapt to a new life in Canada in diverse ways (arriving at their own unique definitions of Belonging and Independence in the Settlement Journey), their youthful counterparts are participating in a young, urban, Can-Asian culture that's developing its own distinct character.

We've seen how different elements of the Cultural Lens vary in importance from category to category. Still, among first-generation migrants who've emerged from the Disorientation phase of the Settlement Journey, it's safe to

"Although young people may be extremely comfortable with ethno-cultural difference—perhaps more comfortable than any previous generation—living in an environment of hyperdiversity doesn't necessarily diminish the salience or significance of ethnic culture."

assume that their ethnic cultures and pre-migration experiences have made their preferences, habits, and attitudes somewhat distinct from those of other Canadians. Marketers have some frame of reference from which to build offerings and communications for these people. But what about these migrants' children who were either born in Canada or raised here from the age of six or ten or thirteen?

We know that, although they're living in Canada, parents will to some degree transmit their ethnic culture (as is the case for most humans) in the food they cook, family relationships, the values they model, and so on. We know that these young people are strongly connected digitally both with peers in Canada and with global diasporas. We know that through such networks they're exposed to cultural and consumer offerings from around the world. And we know that they're experiencing and developing their ethnocultural identities in an environment charged with diversity and teeming with cross-cultural exchange.

Although young people may be extremely comfortable with ethnocultural difference—perhaps more comfortable than any previous generation—living in an environment of hyperdiversity doesn't necessarily diminish the salience or significance of ethnic culture. Rather, ethnicity still matters as a building block of identity and as a point of curiosity and conversation. The popularity of the Indo-Canadian comedian Russell Peters, who delivers cheeky humour on ethnic themes, is a sign of hyperdiversity stoking—not erasing—interest in ethnocultural difference. Peters's shows have set attendance records (he was the first stand-up comedian to fill Toronto's Air Canada Centre), and his audiences tend to be diverse groups who gather to hear him riff on the foibles of different cultural groups, including his own. Although Peters does things that in a normal context would be seen as racist (he liberally impersonates other groups' accents, for instance), there's an all-in-the-family spirit about his shows that tends to make people feel they're in a laughing-with, not laughing-at sort of crowd.

Young people have also begun to reclaim expressions that used to be mean-spirited epithets, such as FOB (meaning "fresh off the boat"). Teresa Wu, an Asian American who started a blog-turned-book called My Mom Is a FOB with her friend Serena Wu (unrelated), described their use of the term on America's NPR: "FOB used to be a derogatory term that people used to make fun of immigrants. But in my generation at least, growing up, it was never used as a derogatory term. It was kind of a friendly, joking way of describing people who are half-Asian, half-American." The Wus' book features an introduction from Margaret Cho, a Korean-American comedian whose loving but no-holds-barred impressions of her own "FOB" mother have been the heart of her act for many years.

In short, for young North Americans of Asian origin, ethnic culture can be a point of pride, amusement, pleasure, and occasional embarrassment (in the way that our parents can always embarrass us). It doesn't define them or their tastes, but it does influence them—and shows no sign of disappearing. The complexities of the emerging Asian-influenced youth culture can be daunting for those seeking to communicate effectively with young people in Canada. But for those seeking relevance among youth, the task is critical. It's not only the sheer numbers of Asian-heritage youth that make this group significant, but their strong and growing cultural influence over other young people of all backgrounds. In other words, Asian influence is not only on the rise in Canada; Asian youth culture is increasingly influential around the world. More and more, Asian pop culture is global pop culture.

Asian pop culture: South Asia goes viral

To understand how the rise of diasporas spreads the influence of Asian youth culture across borders—and has been doing so for decades already—it's interesting to map the cultural and geographical journey that the song "Beware the Boys (Mundian To Bach Ke)" took to reach the top of the global music charts. The song was originally performed by Indian-based Punjabi artist Labh Janjua. It travelled to the U.K., where it was remixed by British Indian hip-hop artist Punjabi MC, who incorporated the bass line from the theme song of the 1980s American television show *Knight Rider*. Now infused with this winking bit of U.S. pop culture from the past, the song then travelled across the Atlantic, where it was picked up by a superstar of contemporary U.S. pop culture, Jay-Z. Combining the song's existing bhangra beat and Punjabi vocals with his own rap, Jay-Z launched the song into the pop-culture stratosphere. It hit the top of the charts in numerous countries, including Canada—back in 2003.

This is just one drop in the growing flood of influence that South Asian pop culture has had on global popular culture in the last ten years. And its complex global journey isn't unusual. The young South Asian diaspora in Canada's cities acts as a receiver and amplifier for South Asian pop culture. It was significant that the major awards event for the Indian film industry, the International Indian Film Academy Awards, was held in Toronto in 2011. The festival event drew an estimated 50,000 people; the 22,000 tickets for the awards show itself sold out within ten minutes of going on sale. The fact that Ontario's then premier, Dalton McGuinty, worked so hard to ensure that the event was held in Toronto—and that he was personally associated with it—is evidence of the Indian diaspora's political strength in Canada. But the screaming young South Asian Canadian girls who attended the awards and accompanying festival didn't come to see Mr. McGuinty. They came to see Shahrukh Khan and the other heartthrobs who light up the big screens at Bollywood movie nights in Toronto's suburbs.

Many of those screaming Indo-Canadian fans would have been aware of Khan's role as Coca-Cola brand ambassador, not to mention Coca-Cola's promotional tie-in to his popular *Ra.One* movie. And that awareness likely came via the digitally connected South Asian diaspora, through which flows a continual, massive volume of information. Foreign-born youth in Canada have an average of just over 350 friends of various social networking sites, many of them abroad—with entertainment being one of the topics most likely to animate these cross-border digital conversations. So it follows that South Asian entertainment culture is a common platform for youth to connect across the South Asian diaspora. And this dynamic network of communication is a potentially rich territory for marketers. With one in five Toronto residents aged under twenty-five identified as South Asian, brand communication emanating from South Asia, like Khan's work for Coca-Cola, surges into the city gigabyte by gigabyte on a daily basis.

The Chinese youth diaspora isn't as culturally cohesive

South Asian pop culture has been developing and spreading globally for at least thirty years. Its role as a massive communication platform for South Asian youth is helped by the fact that much of that communication is in English. And yet, although young Chinese Canadians are just as digitally connected, the same sense of shared pop culture doesn't exist among overseas Chinese youth. According to our Global Asian Youth survey, Canadian-born Chinese are much less likely to enjoy Chinese pop music and movies. More significantly, the survey also found that Canadian-born Chinese youth feel they're more likely to share values and interests with non-Chinese young people in Canada than with their peers in China. One reason for this is that Chinese youth culture itself is undeveloped. The recent economic growth of China has generated an affluent and independent young generation, but they haven't had the time to develop a distinct transnational culture to inspire the Chinese youth diaspora. For example, according to the survey, Chinese-Canadian youth enjoy Korean movies as much as Chinese ones. Young Chinese in Canada, then, are more likely to look to other Asian markets than to China for pop culture.

BORDERLESS MARKETING
The trends we've sketched in this chapter present opportunities for companies and brands to thrive in the territory where "ethnic" and "mainstream" intersect, and even where domestic markets meet global ones. But of course, this is easier said than done.

We wrote this book to make it a little easier for Canadian businesses and organizations to engage today's Canada. We know this is more difficult than it used to be. Not only are there seismic changes in the way people communicate and consume, but businesses and organizations in the past simply didn't need to work as hard to understand their customers, consumers, donors, members, and employees. In a more homogeneous, less mobile, less connected society, understanding your market was easier. Leaders didn't need to stretch their imaginations to speculate about the tastes and desires of the Canadian population; most could see a microcosm of middle-class Canada in their own families, friends, and neighbourhoods. Today, even people with mixed families and diverse groups of friends are unlikely to get a complete picture of Canada's demographic and cultural realities.

The diversity of the Canadian population clearly creates big challenges—and meeting these challenges is essential for achieving growth. Businesses must become as global in their thinking as their customers are. Fortunately, even for organizations that aren't global in scope, insights into global cultures are near at hand: no plane ticket required. Hop onto a local transit system and check out a neighbourhood you've never visited before—whether it's a hyperdiverse inner suburb full of newcomers or a more homogeneous "ethnic enclave" full of tenured migrants. Look over your kid's shoulder and see what he or she is doing online. Whatever your background, go to a mall whose main customer base is people who are outside your group.

Companies and organizations that already operate internationally should start to see their global presence not simply as an organizational reality, but also as a means of gathering insight into modern, globalized Canada. Can a call or an email to colleagues in India, China, or the Philippines help you develop an understanding of Canadians in the next province or on the next block?

Migration Nation isn't always a comfortable place. It may be fun to navigate as a city dweller or a foodie, but for organizations seeking to fulfill business objectives it can be an intimidating landscape. Communication can be awkward, and failures can not only fall flat but even offend. The good news is that Migration Nation is also a landscape full of opportunity. For businesses and organizations that wish to thrive in a globalized world, now is the time to gather the tools and develop the skills to navigate successfully in globalized Canada.

ACKNOWLEDGMENTS

We could not have completed this book without the support and encouragement of many friends, colleagues, clients, and collaborators.

For a pair of researchers interested in diversity, migration, and multiculturalism, it's hard to imagine a better home than Environics Research Group. Environics' history of working in the multicultural field stretches back to the 1980s, when the company conducted a series of studies on ethnic media consumption for then-trailblazing CHIN Radio/TV International, Canada's first multilingual broadcast outlet.

In the creation of this book we have benefited from not only the research and expertise of our Environics colleagues, but from the conversations, presentations, "in case you missed this" emails, and all the exchanges large and small that happen in a curious, engaged workplace like the one we are fortunate to operate in. The research and thinking behind this book—and indeed the Cultural Markets practice through which we serve our clients—are simply the most recent and most public additions to an Environics tradition of diversity research that is not only long-standing but increasingly active and multi-faceted.

Another Environics tradition in which we are participating with this book is a strong publishing tradition; this is the seventh book produced under the banner of Environics Research Group. Founding president Michael Adams's books have been important contributions to public discourse about Canadian public opinion, social values, and national identity. His 2007 book *Unlikely Utopia: The Surprising Triumph of Canadian Multiculturalism* was an important milestone in Environics' multicultural work and has done a great deal to shape our thinking. We are grateful for Michael's thoughtful foreword to *Migration Nation*. Although *Migration Nation* is meant to offer practical advice more than pure analysis, we hope readers will find it in keeping with the Environics tradition of insightful reflection on research data.

In addition to much support and encouragement from our colleagues at Environics Research, we have received invaluable help from others in the Environics Group of Companies.

- Environics Analytics supplied not only a wealth of smart data but also important insights on the changing Canadian population. We appreciate their specific contributions to this work as well as their general thought leadership in the field of multicultural marketing. We are especially grateful to Doug Norris for his Introduction to the book.

- Environics Communications helped to inform us on the practical realities of communication strategies in Migration Nation, and have also offered important guidance and help in the promotion of this project.
- The Environics Institute shared data from Focus Canada, one of the longest-running omnibus studies in Canada and therefore a valuable source of historical perspective on public attitudes and experiences.

Our friends in the Canadian marketing and communication industry engaged us with generosity and insight as we worked on this book.
In particular we would like to thank:

- David Frattini, Managing Partner, Destination Canada Information Inc.
- Stanley Furtado, President, Represent Communications
- Bruce MacLellan, President of Environics Communications
- Jacob Moshinsky
- Lana Novikova, IntegralMR.com
- Rupen Seoni, Vice President, Environics Analytics
- Dolly Shao & Roxanne Tsui, Managing Partners, Sensu Communications
- Meghna Srinivas, Director of Client Service, Maclaren Cultura
- Donald Williams
- Marvi Yap, Partner, AV Communications Inc
- Albert Yue, President & CEO of Dyversity Communications Inc.

Finally, we are pleased to be able to share and continue the work contained between these covers with online audiences. We invite readers to check for news and updates about the fast-changing world of Canadian multicultural marketing at migrationnation.ca.

GLOSSARY

Ethnic culture refers to the values and habits that tend to predominate among specific groups of people who have traditionally shared language, food, religion, and so on. Everyone is shaped by an ethnic culture in some form, and sometimes by more than one. It is important to note that we never mean "ethnic" as a catch-all category that refers to Canadians who are not of French or British heritage. (Those Canadians have ethnicities and ethnic cultures as well, of course.)

Ethnic marketing refers to the practice of targeting specific ethnic segments using communications designed with their ethnic culture or identity in mind. Although this term is sometimes used interchangeably with "multicultural marketing," it is more accurate to think of ethnic marketing as the practice of targeting a specific segment. "Multicultural marketing" implies multiple ethnocultural segments. (See entry on Multicultural Marketing.)

Generation status refers to the number of generations a person or their family have spent in Canada.

> **First generation** refers to people who were born outside Canada: they are the first generation of their families to live here. (Colloquially, there is a bit of confusion about this term since some people who were born in Canada consider themselves "first generation"—meaning the first generation of their families *born* here.) The 2011 NHS data showed there were about 7.2-million people in the first generation in 2011, or 22.0% of the total population. This is a diverse group, hailing from about 200 countries of origin. The vast majority (93.9%) are individuals who are, or have been, immigrants to Canada. In addition, 4.9% are temporary residents (see entry below), defined as people from another country who, at the time of the survey, have a work or study permit or who are refugee claimants.

> A subset of first-generation Canadians is the **1.5 generation**. These are first-generation Canadians who arrived as children or adolescents. Depending on a number of factors (such as their age upon arrival, where they live, where they have come from, and other influences) their relationship with Canada and their ethnic culture can vary a great deal. The roles they play in immigrant diasporas also vary. Some are confident bridge-builders and cultural interpreters, relating easily with Canadians of other backgrounds and helping parents and grandparents navigate Canada. Some 1.5s, however, feel unmoored and disconnected from both Canada and "back home."

> **Second generation** includes individuals who were born in Canada and had at least one parent born outside Canada. In 2011, this group consisted of just over 5,702,700 people, representing 17.4% of the total population. For just over half (54.8%) of them, both parents were born outside Canada.

> **Third generation** or more refers to people who are born in Canada with both parents born in Canada. In 2011, this group comprised 19,932,300 individuals, accounting for 60.7% of the total population. They may have several generations of ancestors born in Canada, or their grandparents may have been born abroad.

Immigration class. In Canada there are four categories of immigrants: **economic class** (such as skilled workers and entrepreneurs; 160,819 of these applicants were accepted in 2012), **family class** (people closely related to people who have settled in Canada; 65,008 were accepted in 2012), **refugee** (people who are escaping or face the risk of persecution, torture, or cruel and unusual punishment in their home countries; 23,094 were accepted in 2012) and

other (people who are not technically refugees but are accepted for humanitarian or compassionate reasons; 8,961 were accepted in 2012).

The economic class is a diverse one. It includes:

skilled workers (91,469 accepted in 2012): those who are accepted as permanent residents mainly based on their education, work experience, knowledge of English and/or French

provincial/territorial nominees (40,899 accepted in 2012): those who are nominated for immigration to Canada by a provincial or territorial government. Nominees have the skills, education and work experience needed to make an immediate economic contribution to the province or territory that nominates them

Canadian experience class (9,359 accepted in 2012): an immigration category that allows temporary foreign workers or recently graduated international students working in Canada to apply for permanent residence

live-in caregivers (9,012 accepted in 2012) People qualified to provide care for children, elderly people, or people with disabilities in private homes without supervision. A live-in caregiver must live in the private home of their employer while they work in Canada.

investors, entrepreneurs and self-employed (10,080 accepted in 2012). People who have specific business experience and/or meet requirements on net worth, investment capacity, or ability to employ Canadians. The self-employment class accepts those who intend and are able to become self-employed in Canada in fields such as athletics, farm management, or the arts.

The size of each of these categories changes with Canada's immigration policies.

Multicultural marketing is often used interchangeably with "ethnic marketing," denoting the practice of targeting groups who might not be effectively reached with "mainstream" marketing activities. Multicultural marketing, however, is more inclusive than ethnic marketing. In Migration Nation, everyone belongs to a cultural group and the multicultural landscape is everyone's business. (See entry on **Ethnic marketing**.)

Permanent residents are those who have legally immigrated to Canada but are not yet Canadian citizens. In the world of marketing, whether people are Canadian citizens or not is not very relevant; people can live in Canada for many years without applying for citizenship (although about nine in ten foreign-born Canadians are citizens). When marketers refer to permanent residents as a target, they usually include both citizens and non-citizens. The group against which permanent residents can be most usefully contrasted is not citizens (a group that includes foreign-born and Canadian-born) but temporary residents.

Source country refers to a migrant's country of residence prior to moving to Canada. Source country is not always an indication of a migrant's cultural background. For example, a self-identified South Asian may have worked and lived in Dubai or the United Kingdom for a number of years before immigrating to Canada, an immigrant from the United States may very well be someone originally from South America, the Philippines, China, or literally any part of the world. However, source country is highly relevant for categories where pre-migration experiences or the frames or reference are most important such as banking and telecommunications, while ethnicity is more relevant when marketers need to understand ethnocultural characteristics for categories such as food and beauty care.

Temporary residents are foreign nationals who are in Canada legally for a limited period. Temporary residents include international visa students, temporary foreign workers, and visitors, such as tourists. Although the vast majority of the work to date in multicultural marketing has focused on permanent residents, it is worthwhile for some businesses (notably banks and telecoms companies) to make efforts to understand temporary residents. There are a couple of reasons for this. First, they are a sizeable and growing group. According to Citizenship and Immigration Canada, as of December 2012 there were about three quarters of a million temporary residents in Canada. (See page 20 for a chart showing growth in stocks of temporary residents over time.) These people have unique needs due to their temporary status. Second, some temporary residents apply for immigration and eventually become permanent residents and long-term consumers in Canada.

Visible minority is a term unique to Canada. In Canada, anyone who considers him/herself neither white nor aboriginal is classified by the government as a visible minority. The term has been put to a number of uses, including the promotion of labour market fairness since visible minorities are one of four groups covered by the federal Employment Equity Act. Increasingly, the term "visible minority" is considered arbitrary and obsolete. This is true partly because the way Canadians talk about ethnicity has evolved; it is more useful to talk about specific ethnicities (for instance, their labour market outcomes) than to lump together everyone who does not self-identify as white. Also significant is the fact that as Canadian demographics change, "minorities" are no longer in the minority in some jurisdictions. Whether the term will be retired in the social economics scene is unknown, but it is largely irrelevant in the world of marketing (except when referring to Statistics Canada's demographic information). We use "visible minority" in this book when we are referring to Statistics Canada data and on a few occasions when it is useful as a proxy for growing demographic diversity.

INDEX

everyday banking. see banking, everyday
extended family
and financial management, 144
and meal preparation, 70, 76
and young South Asian men, 101

GSM network, 117
Guinness, 99

of cars, 168
and charitable giving, 86–7
of everyday banking, 124
of food, 67–70, 71
of grocery retail, 102, 105
quality of advertising campaigns, 180
with telecoms, 116
of vehicle ownership, 160–1
of vehicle service and maintenance, 163
prepared food, 102–3
price sensitivity
grocery shopping behaviour, 109
vehicle service and maintenance, 163
Punjabi-language
advertising, 186
media, 190, 191

R
radio stations
targeting Chinese, 188
targeting South Asians, 191
ready-to-eat food, 102–3
real estate, investing in, 144
Reckitt Benckiser, 72
refugees, 19
registered investment vehicles, 146–7, 147f
religion and charitable giving, 84–5
remittances to family back home, 62, 125, 196
retail experiences, 37. See also grocery retail
retirement planning, 137, 143f, 144
Royal Bank, 135
Royal Commission on Bilingualism and
    Biculturalism, 9
Royal Ontario Museum, 91

S
Sabzi Mandi Supermarket, 108
Sax, David, 27
sayings. see ancient sayings
Scotch whisky, 94, 99
Scotiabank, 132
Search for Roots, 47
Sensu Communications, 189
service style and conventions, 37
Settlement Journey, 38
and alcohol beverage, 98–101

and automotive needs, 170
and beauty and personal care products, 155–9
Belonging, 56–9
and charitable giving, 87–92
Disorientation, 54–5
and everyday banking, 130–4
and financial management, 146–8
and food and CPG, 70–82
and grocery retail, 108, 110–14
Independence, 59–62
and openness to advertising, 181
Orientation, 55–6
stages of, 40–1, 53
settlement patterns, 14f, 20f, 21, 23
Sharia-compliant banks, 37
Simplified Chinese newspapers, 188
Sina Weibo (social media platform), 189
skin whitening products, 159
smartphones, 116
snacks, 82
social diversity, 11
Social Learning, 47
social media and networking
and Chinese Canadians, 189
and keeping in touch with back home, 50–1,
    189, 191
outreach to Chinese Canadians, 189
quality of advertising campaigns, 180
and South Asian Canadians, 191
use by foreign-born youth, 203
social values
and alcohol beverage, 100
changing, 47
and charitable giving, 85
and money, 136–7
social welfare systems, 140–1
soft drinks, 199
source countries, investing in, 147–8
South Asian Canadians. See also Indian
    Canadians
in Belonging phase, 57
comprehension of English, 185
financial responsibility by gender, 145
grocery shopping behaviour, 104f, 105, 108
instant coffee brands, 71
and Kraft Dinner, 83
media targeting, 189–91
recognition in Canadian society, 184

NOTES & REFERENCES

General notes
- Some of the data mentioned in *Migration Nation* is drawn from Environics Research Group or Environics Analytics research that is not in the public domain. Readers seeking further information about these studies are invited to contact the authors.
- Due to rounding, percentages in some charts may not total to 100.

Foreword
p. 5: In one widely cited 2006 estimate...
Statistics Canada. (2010). *Projections of the Diversity of the Canadian Population, 2006 to 2031.* (Statistics Canada Catalogue no. 91-551-X) Retrieved from http://www.statcan.gc.ca/pub/91-551-x/91-551-x2010001-eng.pdf

p. 6: Fig 0.1
Environics Analytics. (2013). HouseholdSpend.

Introduction
Unless otherwise noted, all numbers in this introduction are from Statistics Canada. Current data are drawn from the 2011 National Household Survey. Historical data are drawn from past waves of the Census.

National Household Survey: Statistics Canada. (2011). *2011 National Household Survey: Analytical products, 2011, Immigration and Ethnocultural Diversity in Canada.* (Statistics Canada Catalogue no. 99-010-X). Retrieved from http://www12.statcan.gc.ca/nhs-enm/2011/as-sa/99-010-x/99-010-x2011001-eng.cfm

p. 17: In 1966, 87 percent of Canada's immigrants had been of European origin...
Government of Canada. (2006). Chapter 6: Trail-Blazing Initiatives, Canada abolishes its racist immigration policy. *ARCHIVED – Forging Our Legacy: Canadian Citizenship and Immigration, 1900-1977.* Retrieved from http://www.cic.gc.ca/english/resources/publications/legacy/chap-6.asp#chap6-3

p. 19: In 2012, Canada accepted 160,819 Economic Class immigrants...
Government of Canada. (2012). *Facts and figures 2012 – Immigration overview: Permanent and temporary residents.* Retrieved from http://www.cic.gc.ca/english/resources/statistics/facts2012/permanent/02.asp

p. 23: As of 2006, only about 4% of Canadian couples (3.9%, representing 289,400 couples) were mixed unions....
Milan, A., Maheu, H. and Chui, T. (2010). A portrait of couples in mixed unions. *Statistics Canada, ARCHIVED – PDF document.* (Catalogue no. 11-008-X). Retrieved from http://www.statcan.gc.ca/pub/11-008-x/2010001/article/11143-eng.pdf

p. 25: ...over two hundred languages being spoken most often in Canadian homes. Of these, twenty-two languages are spoken by a hundred thousand people or more.
Statistics Canada. (2011). *2011 National Household Survey: Analytical products, 2011, Immigrant Languages in Canada.* (Statistics Canada Catalogue no. 98-314-X-2011003). Retrieved from: http://www12.statcan.gc.ca/census-recensement/2011/as-sa/98-314-x/98-314-x2011003_2-eng.cfm

Chapter 1
p. 27: A Toronto journalist named David Sax...

Sax, D. (2012, June 20). Fixing Fusion Confusion. *The Grid*. Retrieved from http://www.thegridto.com/life/food-drink/fixing-fusion-confusion/

p. 31: ...the 39% of the population made up of migrants and their children...
Statistics Canada. (2011). 2011 National Household Survey: Analytical products, 2011, Immigration and Ethnocultural Diversity in Canada. (Catalogue no. 99-010-X). Retrieved from http://www12.statcan.gc.ca/nhs-enm/2011/as-sa/99-010-x/99-010-x2011001-eng.cfm

p. 31: ...1.77 million Canadians of South Asian origin or the 1.56 million Canadians of Chinese origin...
Environics Analytics. (2013). Projections from DemoStat based on Statistics Canada data.

p. 34: In 1854, an English-born settler in Canada...and habit has reconciled them to the flavour.
Parr Traill, C. (1854). *The Female Emigrant's Guide, and Hints on Canadian Housekeeping*. Toronto: Maclear. Retrieved from https://archive.org/details/cihm_41417

p. 35: ...a 2011 Nielsen report...
Nielsen Global Private Label Report. (2011, April 3). The Rise of the Value-Conscious Shopper. Retrieved from http://www.nielsen.com/us/en/reports/2011/rise-of-the-value-conscious-shopper.html

p. 36: ... A telling vignette appeared in the New Yorker...
Osnos, E. (2011, April 18). The Grand Tour: Europe on Fifteen Hundred Yuan a Day. *The New Yorker*. Retrieved from http://www.newyorker.com/reporting/2011/04/18/110418fa_fact_osnos?currentPage=all

Chapter 2
p. 43: But Greater Toronto, for instance...accounted for only two-thirds of the foreign-born population.
Statistics Canada. (2011). *2011 National Household Survey: Analytical products, 2011, Immigration and Ethnocultural Diversity in Canada*. (Catalogue no. 99-010-X). Retrieved from http://www12.statcan.gc.ca/nhs-enm/2011/as-sa/99-010-x/99-010-x2011001-eng.cfm

p. 44: Figure 2.1
Statistics Canada. (2011). *NHS Profile, Toronto, CMA, Ontario, 2011*. (Catalogue no. 99-004-XWE). Retrieved from http://www12.statcan.gc.ca/nhs-enm/2011/dp-pd/prof/details/page.cfm?Lang=E&Geo1=CMA&Code1=535&Data=Count&SearchText=toronto&SearchType=Begins&SearchPR=01&A1=All&B1=All&Custom=&TABID=1

p. 45: First, Canada has proportionally more immigrants than the U.S. (20.6% of the Canadian population is foreign-born, as compared with 12.9% south of the border).
Statistics Canada. (2013, May 8). The Daily, Wednesday May 8. 2013. *2011 National Household Survey: Immigration, place of birth, citizenship, ethnic origin, visible minorities, language and religion*. (Survey no. 5178). Retrieved from http://www.statcan.gc.ca/daily-quotidien/130508/dq130508b-eng.htm

p. 47: In Environics' 2011 Social Values survey, 83% of Canadians...who come from all kinds of backgrounds."
Environics Research Group. (2011). *Social Values Survey*.

p. 47: Canadians of all backgrounds are mixing more.
The Environics Institute. (2011). *Focus Canada 2011*. Retrieved from http://www.environicsinstitute.org/institute-projects/current-projects/focus-canada

p. 48: A Canadian prime minister has said, "Our multicultural nature...
Canada, Prime Minister's Office. (1986). *Notes for an Address by the Right Honourable Brian Mulroney, P.C., M.P., Prime Minister of Canada, to the "Multiculturalism Means Business" Conference, Toronto, Ontario, April 12, 1986.*

p. 49: When asked whether immigrants "take away jobs from other Canadians," the public rejects this idea...
The Environics Institute. (2010). *Focus Canada 2010.* Retrieved from http://www.environicsinstitute.org/institute-projects/current-projects/focus-canada

p. 49: For instance, China and India—whose rapid economic growth needs no summary here—were the top source countries for migrants to Canada for many years before the Philippines overtook them both in 2010. Together, people born in these two countries account for more than a million Canadians...
Statistics Canada. (2011). NHS Data. *National Household Survey Profile, Canada, 2011.* Retrieved from https://www12.statcan.gc.ca/nhs-enm/2011/dp-pd/prof/details/page.cfm?Lang=E&Geo1=PR&Code1=01&Data=Count&SearchText=01&SearchType=Begins&Search-PR=01&A1=All&B1=All&Custom=&TABID=3

p. 49: ... and people who claim "Chinese" or "East Indian" as part of their ethnic heritage account for more than 2.6 million Canadians.
Statistics Canada. (2011). *2011 National Household Survey: Data Tables.* Retrieved from http://www12.statcan.gc.ca/nhs-enm/2011/dp-pd/dt-td/Rp-eng.cfm?LANG=E&APATH=3&-DETAIL=0&DIM=0&FL=A&FREE=0&GC=0&GID=0&GK=0&GRP=1&PID=105396&PRID=0&PTY-PE=105277&S=0&SHOWALL=0&SUB=0&Temporal=2013&THEME=95&VID=0&VNAMEE&VNAMEF

p. 49: ... desire to immigrate to the West is significantly more prevalent among the richest top 20% of people living in countries with relatively low GDP...
Ray, J and Esipova, N. (2011, July 5). World's Potential Migrants Are Often Young, Educated, Well-Off. *Gallup World.* Retrieved from http://www.gallup.com/poll/148376/world-potential-migrants-often-young-educated-off.aspx

p. 50: "while immigrants make up an eighth of America's population, they founded a quarter of the country's technology and engineering firms."
The magic of diasporas. (2011, November 19). *The Economist.* Retrieved from http://www.economist.com/node/21538742

p. 51: Our survey of migrant youth in Canada...
Environics Research Group. (2012). *Global Asian Youth Survey*

Chapter 4
Food & Consumer Packaged Goods
p. 66: "Our objective is to be the No. 1 ethnic player in Canada."
Strauss, M. (2011, February 24). Ethnic consumer the goal for new Loblaw president. *The Globe and Mail.* Retrieved from http://www.theglobeandmail.com/globe-investor/ethnic-consumer-the-goal-for-new-loblaw-president/article578346/

p. 66: ...the NPD Group's 2011 *Eating Patterns in Canada* report.
NPD GROUP. (2011, October 18). *Canada's Asian Population Influencing Shift in National Eating Patterns.* Retrieved from https://www.npd.com/wps/portal/npd/us/news/press-releases/pr_111018/

p. 71: ...there were 1,165,000 people classified as having "East Indian" ethnicity...
Statistics Canada. (2011). *2011 National Household Survey: Data Tables.* Retrieved from

http://www12.statcan.gc.ca/nhs-enm/2011/dp-pd/dt-td/Rp-eng.cfm?LANG=E&APATH=3&-DETAIL=0&DIM=0&FL=A&FREE=0&GC=0&GID=0&GK=0&GRP=1&PID=105396&PRID=0&PTY-PE=105277&S=0&SHOWALL=0&SUB=0&Temporal=2013&THEME=95&VID=0&VNAMEE&VNAMEF

Charitable Giving
p. 84: ...Canada is tied for the second most giving society...
Charities Aid Foundation. (2013). *The World Giving Index 2013.* Retrieved from https://www.cafon-line.org/publications/2013-publications/world-giving-index-2013.aspx

p. 84: While three-quarters of the Canadian-born population have some religion affili-ation, among migrants the proportion is slightly higher: 80%.
Statistics Canada. (2011). *2011 National Household Survey: Analytical products, 2011, Immigration and Ethnocultural Diversity in Canada.* (Catalogue no. 99-010-X). Retrieved from http://www12.statcan.gc.ca/nhs-enm/2011/as-sa/99-010-x/99-010-x2011001-eng.cfm

p. 84: According to Statistics Canada, the average amount donated annually by migrants who've been in Canada for under ten years...
Statistics Canada. (2007, 2010). *Donor rate and average and median annual donations, by im-migrant status and time immigrants spent in Canada, population aged 15 and over, 2007 and 2010* [Table]. (Catalogue no. 11-008-X). Retrieved from http://www.statcan.gc.ca/pub/11-008-x/2012001/t/11669/tbl01-eng.htm

Alcohol Beverage
p. 93: ...the average Canadian aged fifteen and over consumed 8.1 litres of pure alcohol per capita in 2012. Canadians derive about half of their total alcohol intake from beer.
World Health Organization. (2013). Patterns of Consumption: Alcohol consumers, past 12 months, Data by country. *Global Health Observatory Data Repository.* Retrieved from http://apps.who.int/gho/data/node.main.A1044?lang=en

p. 93: Over three-quarters of Canadians (78%) have had an alcoholic drink...say they'd bent an elbow.
Health Canada. (2011). Alcohol: Prevalence of Alcohol Use, Low-risk Alcohol Use. *Canadian Alcohol and Drug Use Monitoring Survey, Summary of Results for 2011.* Retrieved from http://www.hc-sc.gc.ca/hc-ps/drugs-drogues/stat/_2011/summary-sommaire-eng.php#a7

p. 94: The picture in major source countries of immigration to Canada is different...
World Health Organization. (2013). Levels of Consumption: Recorded alcohol per capita consumption, from 1990, Data by country. *Global Health Observatory Data Repository.* Retrieved from http://apps.who.int/gho/data/node.main.A1025?lang=en

p. 94: The gender difference in consumption is markedly greater there...
World Health Organization, (2013, April). Alcohol and alcohol-related harm in China: policy changes needed. *Bulletin of the World Health Organization* 91 (4), 327-312. Retrieved from http://www.who.int/bulletin/volumes/91/4/12-107318/en/

p. 94: Indian consumption is lower than either Canada or China, at 2.46 litres per capita (in 2010).
World Health Organization. (2013). Levels of Consumption: Recorded alcohol per capita consumption, from 1990, Data by country. *Global Health Observatory Data Repository.* Retrieved from http://apps.who.int/gho/data/node.main.A1025?lang=en

p. 94: According to the Indian Centre for Alcohol Studies, only a minority of Indians have at least one drink a year....

Aravindan, A. and Bose, N. (2013, March 18). India's female drinkers brave public censure. *The Globe and Mail.* Retrieved from http://www.theglobeandmail.com/report-on-business/international-business/asian-pacific-business/indias-female-drinkers-brave-public-censure/article9887197/

p. 94: Chinese interest in high-end spirits extends well beyond cognac; purchases of Scotch whisky in China increased roughly tenfold between 2001 and 2011.
Lynch, R. (2013, April 20). Whisky galore as Chinese get the taste for Scotch. *The Independent.* Retrieved from http://www.independent.co.uk/news/business/analysis-and-features/whisky-galore-as-chinese-get-the-taste-for-scotch-8581134.html

p. 94: India is the largest whisky market in the world...
Madonna, A. (2013, November 5). Slowdown in global spirits market trickles into India. *Business Standard.* Retrieved from http://www.business-standard.com/article/companies/slowdown-in-global-spirits-market-trickles-into-india-113110500228_1.html.

p. 95: ...in Iran, non-alcoholic beer sales quadrupled between 2007 and 2012.
Brewers in the Middle East: Sin-free ale. (2013, August 1). *The Economist.* Retrieved from http://www.economist.com/news/business/21582531-non-alcoholic-beer-taking-among-muslim-consumers-sin-free-ale

p. 95: "As a statement of a globalised lifestyle beer, even if non-alcoholic, may be more potent than Coca-Cola."
The Economist Explains: Why are sales of non-alcoholic beer booming? (2013, April 11). *The Economist.* Retrieved from http://www.economist.com/blogs/economist-explains/2013/08/economist-explains-3

Grocery Retail
Unless otherwise noted, numbers reported in this section come from Environics Research Group's Chinese and South Asian Grocery Survey, 2014.

p. 105: According to *The Economist*, less than 10% of grocery sales take place in "organized" shops...
Indian retail: The supermarket's last frontier. (2011, December 3). *The Economist.* Retrieved from http://www.economist.com/node/21541017

p. 108: ... in research we conducted in 2013, we found that in 56% of South Asian households in Canada, men bear either primary or partial responsibility for grocery shopping.
Environics Research Group. (2014). Chinese and South Asian Grocery Survey.

p. 109: About four in ten Chinese and South Asian immigrants (41% in a combined sample) say that their day-to-day living expenses in Canada are higher...
Newcomers find managing finances in Canada more difficult than expected: RBC poll. (2010, September 27). *RBC.* Retrieved from http://www.rbc.com/newsroom/news/2010/20100927-welcome.html

p. 109: The average Canadian household has 2.5 people...
Statistics Canada. (2011). Census of Population. (Catalogue no. 98-313-XCB). Retrieved from http://www.statcan.gc.ca/tables-tableaux/sum-som/l01/cst01/famil53a-eng.htm

p. 112: Environics' research has found that most households take two kinds of grocery trips: quick trips and stock-up trips...packaged goods.
Environics Research Group. (2010). World of the Shopper.

p. 112: ...research conducted in 2008 by Solutions Research Group Consultants, which

found that the average Chinese-Canadian grocery spend was about $136.
Androich, A. (2010, November 23). How to reach ethnic consumers. *Canadian Grocer*. Retrieved from http://www.canadiangrocer.com/top-stories/reach-and-retain-649

Telecoms
p. 117: The Philippines is known as "Text Capital of the World"...
Research and Markets: Philippines – Mobile Communications – Market Overview. (2010, November 18). *Business Wire*. Retrieved from http://www.businesswire.com/news/home/20101118006329/en/Research-Markets-Philippines—Mobile-Communications-#.U1WW9qlnV9A

p. 117: ...research conducted by Environics in 2012 showed that Filipino Canadians are spending an average of $91 per month on wireless services...
Environics Analytics data based on Statistics Canada's Survey of Household Spending, 2009.

Everyday Banking
Unless otherwise noted, findings in this section come from Environics Research Group's 2013 survey on financial service use among new Canadians.

p. 125: ...the World Bank estimates that in 2012 migrants were responsible for the movement of $529 billion...
Pew Research. (2014, February 20). Remittance Flows Worldwide in 2012: U.S. top sending country; India top receiving country [World Bank 2012 Bilateral Remittance Matrix]. *Social & Demographic Trends*. Retrieved from http://www.pewsocialtrends.org/2014/02/20/remittance-map/

p. 125: at the close of 2013 the global average of the total cost of sending money back home was 8.58%
The World Bank. (2013, December). An Analysis of Trends in the Average Total Cost of Migrant Remittance Services. *Remittance Prices Worldwide* 8. Retrieved from https://remittanceprices.worldbank.org/sites/default/files/RPW_Report_Dec2013.pdf

p. 133: ...although two-thirds (67%) of migrants came to Canada directly from their countries of origin...
Environics Research Group. (2014). New Canadian Financial Services Omnibus Survey.

p. 135: Between 1984 and 1996, 300,000 people immigrated to Canada from Hong Kong...
Statistics Canada. (2011). *2011 Analytical products: Immigrant languages in Canada*. (Catalogue no. 98-314-X-2011003). Retrieved from http://www12.statcan.gc.ca/census-recensement/2011/as-sa/98-314-x/98-314-x2011003_2-eng.cfm

p. 135: ...these migrants "were really a new kind of Canadian."
The Vancouver Sun. (2007, June 30). Chinese Vancouver: A decade of change. *Canada.com classic edition*. Retrieved from http://www.canada.com/vancouversun/story.html?id=011b7438-172c-4126-ba42-2c85828bd6ce&k=44011

Financial Management
Unless otherwise noted, findings in this section come from Environics Research Group's 2013 survey on financial service use among new Canadians.

p. 143: Nielsen's 2012 Global Investors study confirmed that investors in the Asia-Pacific region and the Middle East are the youngest worldwide, while North American investors are the oldest.
Nielsen Global Survey. (2012, July). *Decoding Global Investment Attitudes*. Retrieved from http://www.nielsen.com/us/en/reports/2012/decoding-global-investment-attitudes.html

Beauty and Personal Care
Unless otherwise noted, findings in this section, including charts, come from Environics Research Group's 2010 Global Asian Youth Survey.

p. 151: According to McCann Truth Central's report, *The Truth About Beauty...*
McCann Truth Central. Introduction, Truth 4. In *The Truth About Asian Women*. Retrieved from http://issuu.com/mccanntruthcentral/docs/truthaboutasianwomen/7

p. 151: "There are no ugly women, only lazy ones."
Tan, E. (2012, September 11). Treat women as individuals, not as a category: McCann. *Collectible Ads: Gadget, Technology and Business News Portal*. Retrieved from http://collectibleads.blogspot.ca/2012/09/treat-women-as-individuals-not-as.html#

p. 151: "63% of Chinese women and 55% of Brazilian women change their beauty routines every couple of months or more,"
McCann Truth Central. (2012). *The Truth About Beauty*. Retrieved from http://mccann.com/wp-content/uploads/2012/06/McCann_Truth_About_Beauty.pdf

p. 159: Euny Hong wrote of her own double-eyelid surgery...
Hong, E. (2013, September 18). I Got Eyelid Surgery, but Not to Look White. *The Wall Street Journal*. Retrieved from http://online.wsj.com/news/articles/SB10001424127887323352700457908124308 7841758

Automotive
Unless otherwise noted, all survey results in this section are from Environics Research Group's 2013 Newcomer Automotive Survey, conducted with PrepareforCanada.com.

p. 160: In 2009, 608 Canadians per 1,000 owned a vehicle...
The World Bank. Motor vehicles (per 1,000 people). Retrieved from http://data.worldbank.org/indicator/IS.VEH.NVEH.P3

p. 168: The consultancy McKinsey & Company notes that the luxury car market in China grew...
Sha Sha, Huang, T. and Gabardi, E. (2013, March). *Upward Mobility: The Future of China's Premium Car Market*. McKinsey & Company.

p. 169: ...the little cars were rejected by the low-income rural Indians...
Tata's Nano: Stuck in low gear. (2011, August 18). *The Economist*. Retrieved from http://www.economist.com/node/21526374

Chapter 5
As a team of Millward Brown researchers has argued in their book *Marketing to the New Majority...*
Burgos, D. and Mobolade, O. (2011). *Marketing to the New Majority: Strategies for a Diverse World*. New York: Palgrave Macmillan. p. 174

Chapter 6
Unless otherwise noted, findings in this chapter come from Environics Research Group's 2010 Global Asian Youth Survey.

p. 193: "Globally, the level of urbanization is expected to rise from 52 per cent in 2011...

United Nations. (2011, March). World Urbanization Prospects: The 2011 Revision, Highlights. (ESA/P/WP/224). *Department of Economic and Social Affairs, Population Division.* Retrieved from http://esa.un.org/unup/pdf/WUP2011_Highlights.pdf

p. 193: ...with 81% of its population living in urban areas.
Statistics Canada. (2011). Population, urban and rural, by province and territory. *Summary Tables, 2011 Census.* Retrieved from http://www.statcan.gc.ca/tables-tableaux/sum-som/l01/cst01/demo62a-eng.htm

p. 194: The McKinsey report *Urban World: Mapping the Economic Power of Cities* found that six hundred urban centres...
Dobbs, R., Smit, S., Remes, J, Manyika, J. Roxburgh, C. and Restrepo, A. (2011, March). Urban World: Mapping the economic power of cities. *Report: McKinsey Global Institute.* Retrieved from http://www.mckinsey.com/insights/urbanization/urban_world

p. 195: Today, about 40 million Chinese and 25 million Indians live overseas...
Guest, R. (2011). *Borderless Economics: Chinese Sea Turtles, Indian Fridges and the New Fruits of Global Capitalism.* New York: Palgrave Macmillan.

p. 195: there are more Chinese people living outside China than there are French people in France
The World Economy: The magic of diasporas (2011, November 19). *The Economist.* Retrieved from http://www.economist.com/node/21538742

p. 195: ...in England, more people are employed by Indian restaurants...
Debroy, B. (2008, November 24). India's Soft Power and Cultural Influence. *Challenges of Economic Growth, Inequality and Conflict in South Asia: Proceedings of the 4th International Conference on South Asia.* [Google Books]. Singapore: World Scientific.

p. 195: ...Canada ranks among the fifteen most globalized nations in the world.
ETH (Swiss Federal Institute of Technology Zurich). (2010). *KOF Index of Globalization.* Retrieved from http://globalization.kof.ethz.ch/

p. 195: In 2009, 215 million people were living outside the country in which they were born. This represents 3% of the world's population, and an increase of 40% since 1990.
The World Economy: The magic of diasporas (2011, November 19). *The Economist.* Retrieved from http://www.economist.com/node/21538742

p. 195: Of these global migrants, about 7-million are living in Canada.
Statistics Canada. (2011). *2011 National Household Survey: Analytical products, 2011, Immigration and Ethnocultural Diversity in Canada.* (Catalogue no. 99-010-X). Retrieved from http://www12.statcan.gc.ca/nhs-enm/2011/as-sa/99-010-x/99-010-x2011001-eng.cfm

p. 195: Sixteen percent of the world's adults say they'd like to move to another country permanently if they had the chance. This translates to about 700 million people worldwide.
Migration and business: Weaving the world together. (2011, November 16). *The Economist.* Retrieved from http://www.economist.com/node/21538700

p. 196: One study, by William Kerr and Fritz Foley of Harvard Business School...
Ibid.

p. 196: According to the World Bank, of the $529 billion in remittances that flowed

around the world...

Pew Research. (2014, February 20). Remittance Flows Worldwide in 2012: U.S. top sending country; India top receiving country [World Bank 2012 Bilateral Remittance Matrix]. *Social & Demographic Trends*. Retrieved from http://www.pewsocialtrends.org/2014/02/20/remittance-map/

p. 197: Currently, 26% of Toronto's under-twenty-five population ...the time when Asian-origin youth outnumber European-origin youth is not far off.

Statistics Canada. (2011). *2011 National Household Survey: Analytical products, 2011, Immigration and Ethnocultural Diversity in Canada*. (Catalogue no. 99-010-X). Retrieved from http://www12.statcan.gc.ca/nhs-enm/2011/as-sa/99-010-x/99-010-x2011001-eng.cfm

p. 198: The median age of a newcomer to Canada in 2011 was 31.7...

Statistics Canada. (2011). *2011 National Household Survey: Analytical products, 2011, Immigration and Ethnocultural Diversity in Canada*. (Catalogue no. 99-010-X). Retrieved from http://www12.statcan.gc.ca/nhs-enm/2011/as-sa/99-010-x/99-010-x2011001-eng.cfm

p. 198: As of 2009, there were 3.7 million international students worldwide...

Canadian Bureau for International Education. Canada's performance in international education, 2012, *Facts and Figures*. Retrieved from http://www.cbie-bcei.ca/about-ie/facts-and-figures/

p. 198: In early 2014, the federal government announced...

Bradshaw, J. (2014, January 15). Ottawa aims to boost international students from six priority regions. *The Globe and Mail*. Retrieved from http://www.theglobeandmail.com/news/politics/ottawa-aims-to-boost-international-students-from-six-key-countries/article16344061/

p. 201: FOB used to be a derogatory term that people used to make fun of immigrants. But in my generation...

NPR. (2011, February 3). My Mom: 'Fresh Off The Boat.' [Transcript]. *Arts & Life: Books*. Retrieved from http://www.npr.org/2011/02/03/133467033/My-Mom-Fresh-Off-The-Boat

BIOGRAPHIES

Robin Brown, Environics' Senior Vice President of Consumer Insights and Cultural Markets, is a living embodiment of *Migration Nation*. He has over twenty years of experience in research agencies based in the UK, Asia and Canada providing marketing research and consultancy to some of the world's leading companies. He moved to Canada in 2003 after spending ten years working in Asia, providing consumer insights to guide both local and multinational companies on marketing strategies. Although he is a native of the UK, throughout his life he has lived in five different countries and worked in many more. Along the way he has developed a unique "Third Culture" perspective.

Kathy Cheng, Environics' Vice President of Cultural Markets, is a leading researcher in Canada's multicultural and newcomer markets. She has 16 years of global marketing research and consultancy experience, working with ACNielsen and Ipsos Reid prior to joining Environics. Kathy has helped clients in the financial services, consumer packaged goods, telecommunications, retail, media, and nonprofit sectors understand Canada's rapidly changing multicultural markets. In 2001, Kathy moved to Canada from Shanghai. While based in China, she travelled extensively, conducting qualitative research to help multinational companies understand the Chinese context and grow their presence in that dynamic emerging market.

33 Bloor Street East, Suite 900
Toronto, Ontario
Canada M4W 3H1

robin.brown@environics.ca
kathy.cheng@environics.ca

Editorial Support: Amy Langstaff
Copy Editor: Karen Alliston
Design: Studio:Blackwell, Kelsey Blackwell with Meredith Holigroski
Illustration: Flavia Lopez

ISBN 978-0-9866104-1-7

Environics Research Group is global company based in Canada, Environics offers a full range of quantitative and qualitative research services, as well as a unique social values methodology and unrivaled advanced analytics capabilities.

The Environics Cultural Markets Practice leads the research field in understanding the values and attitudes of migrants and their children. Our knowledge of this dynamic segment of the Canadian population comes from our robust syndicated studies, our team's extensive global experience, and nearly a decade of custom research work with clients in industries ranging from banking and automotive to beauty care and consumer packaged goods.

www.migrationnation.ca
www.environics.ca

Printed and bound in Canada
Cataloguing data available from Library and Archives Canada.

ENVIRONICS
P U B L I S H I N G